SINS OF OMISSION

Shaping the News at CBC TV

BARRY COOPER

SINS OF OMISSION

Shaping the News at CBC TV

UNIVERSITY OF TORONTO PRESS
Toronto Buffalo London

© University of Toronto Press Incorporated 1994
Toronto Buffalo London
Printed in Canada

ISBN 0-8020-0597-7

Printed on acid-free paper

Canadian Cataloguing in Publication Data

Cooper, Barry, 1943–
    Sins of omission : shaping the news at CBC TV

    Includes bibliographical references and index.
    ISBN 0-8020-0597-7

    1. Television broadcasting of news – Canada.
    2. Canadian Broadcasting Corporation. I. Title.

    PN4914.T4C66 1994   070.1'95   C93-095003-8

This book has been published with assistance from
the Canada Council and the Ontario Arts Council
under their block grant programs.

This study is dedicated to the taxpayers of Canada, who, for several years, have involuntarily paid for public broadcasting in this country and who know, very clearly, the value they have received.

Owen would never have claimed that he 'knew' what God wanted; he always hated the sermon part of the service – of any service. He hated anyone who claimed to 'know' God's opinion of current events.

– John Irving, *A Prayer for Owen Meany*

Reading the newspaper is the modern man's morning benediction.

– Hegel

Contents

x   Contents

Preface

Several years ago I supervised a pilot study of CBC AM network radio shows. It employed several students over the summer and brought to light perceptions of imbalance in the perspective conventionally assumed by the CBC with respect to politics generally, particularly in reference to western Canada. In broad terms, the students saw the CBC as preoccupied with central Canada, with what Westerners, with pardonable simplification, call the East; they found that the CBC had an uncongenial view of the West, and that it, on the whole, adopted a left-wing rather than right-wing critical stance. Since this perception was widely shared by the students, who themselves had divergent political allegiances, the interesting question centred on determining the significance of these facts. Most of the paper that reported these findings (to an academic audience) was concerned with accounting for why the CBC might be imbalanced in this way, not whether it was.

In the event, press reports diffused this radio study to a wider audience, including important persons in the CBC. Controversy followed. At one point I was threatened with a lawsuit, apparently on the grounds of faulty methodology.

Such events do not come every day to the life of a university teacher, and I found it all very curious. Naturally, I followed the instinct of scholars and investigated further the attitudes and procedures typical of journalists. Through a series of fortuitous circumstances, I was able to accumulate additional research money to undertake the necessary collection of materials on which the analysis presented here is based. The original study included analysis of TV news coverage of the West, but it is omitted here for reasons of space. I can say, however, that CBC television differs not a whit from CBC AM radio in its visualization of politics and society in western Canada.

Readers of an earlier version of this book, who, by conventions of academic review, hide themselves in anonymity, thought that I had intended to attack the Corporation. That is not my intention. These anonymous reviewers could hardly know my intentions with respect to the CBC apart from the evidence and analysis of it that I have offered. I readily admit that the evidence and my analysis do not indicate that the CBC should be unreservedly praised, and I expect that many academics who – let us be frank – have been beneficiaries of CBC benevolence might not like what the evidence and the analysis show, but that, surely, is another question. To them, and to others who find this evidence and analysis uncongenial, I say: show me where I have erred; show me where my analysis is arbitrary and unsupported; above all, show me how the CBC (and CTV, for that matter) has changed its tune. That is how science, including political science, progresses, and we would all be grateful for the correction. Otherwise, keep your peace and meditate upon the wisdom of Owen Meany.

Several people have assisted me financially and through discussion. The University of Calgary, the Department of External Affairs, and the Canadian Institute for International Peace and Security provided much-needed financial support. Jim Keeley and Keith Archer, of the Department of Political Science, and Irving Hexam, of the Department of Religious Studies, at the University of Calgary, and Ken Reshaur, of the Department of Political Science at the University of Manitoba, have read and corrected various chapters. Keith Archer was very helpful in assisting me with the quantitative analysis undertaken at an earlier stage in this project. I have also benefited from conversations with several elected political leaders, whom, because they could be harmed by unfavourable media coverage, I will not name. Special thanks as well must go to Lydia Miljan, who took part in the radio study and now manages the National Media Archive in Vancouver, and to John von Heyking, who did splendid duty as an uncomplaining research assistant. Bart Testa read and improved an earlier version and was always encouraging; for that I am very grateful.

SINS OF OMISSION

Shaping the News at CBC TV

CHAPTER ONE

Observing Television News

1 CONTENT ANALYSIS AND SECONDARY ORALITY

Most of the studies of television that have been undertaken in North America have concentrated on describing and analysing the message content of TV broadcasts.[1] There are several reasons for this focus. Historically, following the First World War, the effects that propaganda diffused through the mass media might have on a population were a matter of concern. Interest in this subject continued throughout the interwar period and intensified in the years leading up to the Second World War. During that war, propaganda was used extensively as a weapon by the victorious Allies, as well as by their adversaries.

The scientific study of propaganda, based on a comparatively crude stimulus–response model, assumed that social behaviour (the response) might be the direct effect of media content (the stimulus). Since the Second World War, a series of additional or 'intervening' variables (age, sex, education, the role of primary groups, and so on) has been postulated. These intervening variables, according to the argument, alter the effects of messages.[2] However, the assumption remains the same: *what* is transmitted matters more than the means by which the transmission is accomplished. Accordingly, our first task is to justify the use of content analysis, which was initially developed to study printed messages, to study television news.

Harold Innis, and then Marshall McLuhan, challenged the doctrine that what counted in media studies was the meaning of the message. In a series of well-known books and aphorisms, Innis and McLuhan questioned the primacy of content and considered instead the importance of form. Innis argued that different media lead to different kinds of social control: for example, manuscripts, which require considerable skill to encode and decode their messages, have most often been used by a small group, hierarchically positioned to gain access to the required skills. In contrast, a readily accessible medium will tend to be highly democratic in its cultural consequences. Innis also argued that communications media express a 'bias' either towards time and cultural stability or towards space and cultural change. For example, whereas carving messages on stone is an example of the former bias because stone lasts a long time and is difficult to move through space, papyrus is an example of a 'space biased' medium as it allowed the Romans to communicate widely and administer an extensive empire. Compared with the Mesopotamian or Egyptian Empire, however, that of the Romans was comparatively unstable: papyrus disintegrated rapidly as compared with stone-inscribed and usually monumental messages.

A focus on the content of media transmissions is usually accompanied by a neglect of the impact of the form; that is, the medium of delivery is usually treated as neutral with respect to the message being delivered. Content analysis of comics and newspapers and television is carried on, by and large, as if the medium involved would not influence the meaning of the message transmitted. But, if there is one thing that is well known in contemporary media studies, it is that the medium *does* influence the message.

To Innis's teaching, McLuhan added the notion or image of 'sensory balance.' Communications media were to be understood as extensions of human senses, and the dominance of successive media reflected shifting balances among the several senses. Specifically, oral cultures have been succeeded by cultures whose literacy allowed them to substitute, in McLuhan's phrase, 'an eye for an ear.' Literacy allowed for introspection and abstraction; round huts and round villages gave way to urban grids. Finally, according to McLuhan, electronic media are akin to an extended nervous system, which somewhat breaks the analogy of sensory balance.[3] Walter J. Ong proposed a revision of McLuhan's notion of understanding electronic media in terms of the human nervous system, and has spoken of 'secondary orality.'[4] This concept is central to the approach to television news taken in this study.

By applying the term, 'secondary orality' to television, Ong indicated that TV and, more broadly, electronic media share certain characteristics with orally based thought. These characteristics appear to literates as surprising, and often as defects, which is one reason why scholars, who are invariably literate, so often disapprove of television and pretensions made on its behalf by persons who work in television and who are also – or once were – literate.

Whereas literate discourse relies chiefly on grammatical structures of subordination, oral discourse is additive and relies on gestures and intonation to convey meaning. Oral style is aggregative, redundant, and formular rather than analytic, linear, and discrete. Oral knowledge is conservative or traditional, and innovation appears on the occasion of the performance of the story, not from speculation or new information. The secondary orality of television news shares these characteristics in a slightly transformed mode: gestures and intonation convey information, but often the speech of an anchor or correspondent has previously been written out; the formulas tend to be visual or musical rather than verbal: the House of Commons, a logo or musical theme that introduces a program, a warship or tank, a cheering crowd. Moreover, visuals are redundant in the sense that they have been chosen to reinforce the discourse of the anchor or correspondent.[5] The introduction or opening remarks and the conclusion or wrap-up by the anchor often restate the main theme of the story presented by the correspondent.

To summarize all these familiar attributes is to say that television is theatre. The events of the world are not accompanied by music, but the events of the operatic stage are. The anchor is more than a reader; he or she welcomes us, the audience, into the theatrical space of the newscast and then guides us to the various locales where filmed sequences and local correspondents show us around. The anchor then welcomes us back when the correspondent is finished. Such a role is aptly named: an anchor is the solid centre of control in the chaotic seas of the external world, much of which is simply seen as catastrophe.

Television journalism also tends to be traditional or conservative in the sense that, once a story line or angle is established, there is little likelihood that it will be changed. The reason is not that new information is unavailable, but that such changes are believed to reduce 'credibility.' Credibility is central to television, just as it is to the familiar oral cultures of childhood fairy tales and the remote oral cultures of antiquity. The reason is obvious enough: since it is harder to fake an expression than to make up 'facts,' the inherent appeal of television is that it can be believed. Truth, for TV, is therefore indistinguishable from belief. Credibility, as Neil Postman said, 'does not refer to the past record of the teller for making statements that have survived the rigors of reality-testing. It refers only to the impression of sincerity, authenticity, vulnerability or attractiveness (choose one or more) conveyed by the actor/reporter.'[6] One study found, for example, that about 90 per cent of sources in news outlets offered no evidence to support their assertions or claims.[7] For TV news, credibility is all. More generally, trustworthiness is important in oral and secondary oral cultures as an index of the validity of the information transmitted. This is one reason why television news is presented without ambiguity or uncertainty. As Weaver has argued, 'there is hardly an aspect of the scripting, casting, and staging of a television news program that is not designed to convey an impression of authority and omniscience.'[8] The mantle of authority is worn most conspicuously by the anchor, but the correspondent speaks with equal authority and self-confidence about everything he or she encounters: the meaning of events is clear to such people, as are people's motives and intentions; trends are obvious, problems and solutions perfectly understood. Anything that challenges this pose, such as altering the perspective on a story, is bound to be resisted.

Most Canadians and Americans are incapable of challenging this authoritative pretence. That, in part, explains why so many people persistently indicate that television is their main source of news, despite the fact that network news transmits only a small amount of information as compared with all but the most popular or vulgar newspaper. Moreover, television is believed (by a wide margin) to provide the most intelligent, complete, and objective news.[9] This style of presentation is, of course, deliberate on the part of the news producers: television 'speaks to the audience as a provider of authoritative information. It solicits nothing beyond their attention, solicits of them no active role vis-à-vis the political material reported; indeed, the authoritative and detached style of the report and the finality of the sign-off leave the impression that the matters discussed are essentially closed, at least until the next broadcast.'[10] But, even if news producers did not aim at establishing themselves as 'authorized knowers,'[11] the structure or the grammar of the medium would ensure that such an effect would result.

Other characteristics shared by oral cultures and television are more obvious. Both conceptualize and verbalize all their knowledge in terms of what is already familiar and concrete: put negatively, neither oral cultures nor television has much use for abstractions, such as statistics, or for complex discussion. Conflict and struggle are central to both because they can provide a meaningful and dramatic context. The name-calling of children's oral communication is recapitulated in the television sound-bite. The description of physical violence is enthusiastic in oral poetry and is achieved on television by the equally enthusiastic use of visuals. Knowledge for both television and oral culture is intimate and participatory, not objective or separated. Just as oral societies live in the present and quickly forget irrelevant memories, so too, nothing is as stale as yesterday's news. There are dictionaries neither for television nor for oral cultures, with the result that words acquire much of their meaning from the repertoire of human expressiveness. Neither oral cultures nor television is particularly concerned with logical relations: there is no problem discussing the 'Reagan revolution,' which was 'conservative,' right after a discussion of 'conservatives' in the Politburo who are hard-line communists but opposed the 'reforms' of Gorbachev. And what is he? A soft-line communist perhaps?

Given the affinities of television to oral culture and theatre, the application of content-analysis techniques must seem highly questionable. To begin with, content analysis presumes that words are things. For an oral culture, words are not things but rather performances, events that are present only in passing out of existence.[12] Thus, for example, by the time you hear the syllable -*ence* in the word *existence*, *exist* is gone. Alphabetization presents sound as a thing. Moreover, writing is, in principle, correct. An oral bard does not correct his performance because stopping and starting over again would detract from his persuasiveness: he would lose his audience. With writing, corrections are productive because they are invisible.

But it is just here that we must notice the importance of the adjective in Ong's concept. Television is an instance of *secondary* orality. Unlike oral cultures, televised orality is in no way spontaneous. With less than 5 per cent of the film footage shot being broadcast, and then only after being heavily edited, television is much more like a book that has been invisibly corrected through several drafts.[13] With the exception of live sports, where the requirements of orality are still obvious (in the performance of Don Cherry, for instance), television production may go through several 'drafts.' The correspondent's submission may be cut, spliced and edited; the anchor's words are scripted; several takes or 'fakes' of visuals can be made; file visuals may be used, along with soundtracks and special effects. For these reasons, no producer can ever excuse her own work by saying that the news dictated her treatment of the story. We will consider some of the details of news production below, in section 2: it is sufficient to notice here what has become a commonplace in media studies – that TV news is the deliberate production of a new reality.

The deliberateness of secondary orality makes it suitable for content analysis. Indeed, one can go farther: electronic transformation of the word has increased the spatial bias of communication, and so continued the bias of writing and print. But it has also transformed consciousness into a novel mode of orality, and so eroded the importance of writing and print – or, in general, of literacy. This apparent paradox can be dissolved by a distinction. On the *production* side, the electronic transformation of literacy means that drafts are even more disposable: archivists and scholars will have *no* early versions of a poem or a book composed on a word-processor. However, on the *consumption* side, electronically transformed expression is akin to that of the preliterate age of orality. This study is concerned chiefly with what is consumed, i.e., the product – specifically, TV news – and not with the means by which it has been produced.

Televised oral messages are not formular units spontaneously stitched together by a rhapsode. They are deliberate and contrived word mosaics, in which each piece has been carefully shaped to fit the overall picture. It may be that television producers are Machiavellian manipulators, with their own purposes. There is no reason to doubt that such people, like political leaders, union leaders, business leaders, church leaders, corner grocers, and anyone else, may be interested in managing, directing, or deflecting public opinion. But the reason why television news is necessarily contrived has nothing to do with the noble or base intentions, or even more obscure motives, of news producers. The reason is that television news is resolutely based on print and on literate consciousness. This characteristic also makes content analysis of television legitimate.

The notion of 'the media' would not exist in an oral culture, or in a purely literate culture either. The observation was made earlier that content analysis of 'the media' grew out of a concern for the effects of propaganda diffused through both print and radio; that is, the phenomenon of secondary orality is coeval with both the notion of 'the media' and the procedures of content analysis. The elective affinities may well be artefacts of a triumphant stimulus–response model, but, if so, we are then faced with accounting for the introduction and success of such a model. Let us resist the temptation of such expansive speculation and focus instead on the obvious implication that the notion of a medium of communication brings with it – namely, that it is a kind of pipeline transferring units, called information, between places. Most obviously information is moved from the television studio into the presence of an audience. It is less clear whether information moves from the outside world into the television studio. However that may be, the model is that of a unit of information that is encoded, transmitted, and decoded. The media model is a sufficiently accurate representation of the reality of television transmission and reception to make content analysis of those transmissions a legitimate undertaking.

One may see the significance of secondary orality in another way as well. Unmediated human communication, especially oral communication, anticipates a response. Senders are receivers. In common-sense language, if you speak, you speak to somebody. Human communication is reciprocally intersubjective. This is not a model but an everyday experienced reality.

Normal people do not talk to nobody, or to themselves, unless they conduct that interior dialogue 'between me and myself' we call 'thinking.' Moreover, because of the response you anticipate, you speak differently when addressing a child, a game warden, a friend, or the Queen. But what if you do not know to whom you are speaking? Or worse, what if you are talking to, or projecting into, a camera that is transmitting your speech to an unseen and inaudible audience? Whatever else such communication may be, it is not intersubjective. The audience of a television show is not, therefore, an oral community. We will indicate what it is below.

The point of the previous paragraph was that the media model may not be misleading; that is, the undoubted orality of television is also capable of treating speech as information, just as do writing and print. Like oral cultures, the secondary orality of the media is a performance, a way of doing something to someone, but, like print, it is a one-way information street, so the authors of a television production must always imagine their audience, just as do the authors of books such as this one.

The political significance of television depends on the difference between oral and written communication. Speech is politically more important than writing because, paradoxically, it is closer to silence. When speakers converse, they know when to be silent; they know silence can be meaningful. Writers do not know this. Considered from the perspective of oral communication, writing cannot stop talking. Because writing is detached from the speaker and from the guidance of speech, it has no idea where it is or where it is going. Speech is the living presence of the speaker, whereas writing is the trace, not of a presence, but of an absence, an absent speaker.

These somewhat Platonic remarks may suggest the political significance of the difference between writing and speech, and thereby the importance of television. Because conversation is intersubjective, we can adjust it in light of the nature of our interlocutor, just as the equity of a judge may temper the strict written law to the circumstances of the individual case. Writing cannot adjust itself; it is like a code that must be applied in the same way to all cases. Television combines aspects of both speech and writing, but to the disadvantage of both. Like speech, it appeals to the ear and enters the mind through an open door; unlike speech, it admits of no discussion and it is not, properly speaking, a conversation. Like writing, it is detached from the guidance of conversation and so must act on assumptions about its audience; unlike writing, it does stop talking. Indeed, it must stop talking, because the monologue of television takes real time: unlike a book you put down and come back to, TV is watched as a performative presence (this is true even with VCRs). One may say, therefore, that television combines the disadvantages of orality – namely, real-time immediacy – with the disadvantages of literacy – namely, no conversational guidance. Politically, television demands an extreme separation of agent and patient, of active and passive, of production and consumption. In plain language, it is inherently manipulative, even when it is not deliberately so. This aspect is apparent as well from studies of news production.

2   PRODUCING NEWS

'Journalists,' wrote Herbert Gans, 'almost always have more available information than they can use.'[14] Moreover, news could not exist without technology to diffuse it and to enable audiences to attend to it. The events would take place, of course, but they would not be news. An unreported famine in Ethiopia, for example, has no meaning for us. News, therefore, is not merely produced, but is an event that happens nowhere on earth except through the intervention of media technologies. Those technologies make it possible to move information out of one context, where it actually takes place (for example, Ethiopia), across vast distances and into another quite different context (for example, a bar in Prince Rupert). In other words, television creates the form within which the 'news of the day' exists.[15] Controversy surrounds, not its ontological status as an artefact, but the factors that condition the creation of news.

Several 'theories' of news selection or news creation have been advanced over the last few years as scholars have turned their attention to the media, and journalists have responded to that attention. Probably the simplest is the 'mirror theory,' according to which events determine story selection and emphasis, and journalists merely report what happens. This image appealed to network executives in the United States, particularly during the late 1960s. The CBC, in turn, followed the U.S. lead, treating the CRTC to the opinion that 'the very purpose of news broadcasts ... is to report on events, to hold up a mirror to the reality of the day.'[16] In 1969, and with characteristic good humour, U.S. vice-president Spiro Agnew contended that television news was produced by a 'tiny and closed fraternity of privileged men.' By implication, the mirror image was inadequate. More cautious than Mr Agnew, scholars pointed to two general reasons why the image of a mirror was inappropriate. First, as has already been suggested, events are transformed into news; second, not all events count as news.[17]

When confronted with the obvious distortions in the mirror, journalists have responded with the assertion that they are 'professionals' and so 'expert knowers' or 'knowledge producers.'[18] Such 'professionalism' implies that, even if they did not mirror reality in their reports, their professional skills ensured that they did not distort the reality they reported. Moreover, this same professional skill ensured that what was reported really was most worth knowing.

But, as Epstein pointed out, if journalists are professionals, they are unlike other professionals, such as lawyers, doctors, or professors of political science, because their activities are in no way autonomous or independent of the organization that employs them. Nor are they certified on the basis of formal criteria. A social science dean does not assign research topics to his administrative subordinates; a hospital administrator does not direct his surgical staff to operate or not to operate. In so far as journalists are individual members of an organization, their alleged 'professionalism' simply does not hold. Gans, however, seemed to think it does.[19] One reason for this opinion was that journalists, considered as an organization or as a configuration of power, *do* have autonomy. As individuals, anchors and correspondents may be directed by editors and producers, but, taken together, 'news teams' have an 'autonomy unparalleled in other ... institutional spheres.'[20] Even when misleading, inaccurate, and harmful information is broadcast, there is little that offended parties may do to seek recourse. Considered from the perspective of a news source, journalistic professionalism means learning 'to handle the fact that the news accounts themselves will be routinely experienced as "bad": inaccurate, distorted, unfair, biased, and wrong.'[21] If this qualification is admitted, it would seem that journalists are professionals only in the sense that their organizational purposes are their own.

Nevertheless, it is not self-evident that events transfigured into news are the most important or the most worth knowing. Before one could make such a judgment it would be necessary to establish criteria by which the importance of an event could be evaluated. In order to do so, however, even more fundamental questions must be considered. Two such questions are: What is worth knowing? Can it be formulated as news? These two matters alone can generate many more questions than answers.[22] Raising them, however, is likely to generate a certain degree of impatience from journalists.

The reason for their impatience has nothing to do with the goodwill or thoughtfulness of journalists. Quite properly, they are not concerned with the grounds of their own practice. Nor are corporate lawyers particularly concerned with jurisprudence. One may understand the diverse concerns of journalists and lawyers, on the one hand, and professors of political science or of law, on the other, as a splendid example of intellectual division of labour; that is, there is no more reason to expect journalists to be able to account coherently for what they do than there is to expect a bicycle rider to account for his ability to keep his balance by providing details on how he adjusts the curvature of the path of the bicycle in proportion to the ratio of imbalance divided by the square of the bicycle's velocity. He knows how to ride his bike and that is enough. Can the same argument be applied to journalists and the practice of journalism?

We have already drawn attention to the question of secondary orality, a term seldom (if ever) used on television. The concept of secondary orality has already introduced the question of 'media as epistemology,' to borrow Postman's term.[23] The implication of Postman's notion may be stated boldly: 'As a culture moves from orality to writing to printing to televising [or secondary orality], its ideas of truth move with it.'[24] If this is so, a question immediately arises: What is the 'idea of truth' associated with secondary orality? The legitimacy of raising this question is what distinguishes TV journalists from bicycle riders.

Postman himself has argued with considerable persuasiveness that the epistemology of television not only is hostile to literacy but promotes incoherent and trivial discourse: 'the phrase "serious television" is a contradiction in terms [because] television speaks in only one persistent voice – the voice of entertainment.'[25] The 'idea of truth' associated with secondary orality cannot consist of logical coherence, which properly belongs to literacy. The meaning Postman conveyed by the phrase 'idea of truth' was broader than logical coherence. One might indicate it approximately by such terms as 'truth of existence' or 'meaning of life' or 'purpose of human being.' Such questions do not admit of answers in the form 'the meaning of life is ... X.' On the contrary, such answers as may be given take the form of stories. Using the conceptual language of political philosophy, these stories are the symbolic expressions of experienced realities.

When we consider television in this context, an immediate difficulty is encountered: television mediates reality in such a way that one's experience is always of television and not of reality that transcends the medium. Conceptually, one might say that the medium is opaque with respect to reality that transcends it. Accordingly, television cuts off experience from anything transcendent to itself. In other words, television can be a universal mediator of the world to itself. In common-sense language (as distinct from the language of political philosophy), it is part of our way of experiencing reality and part of the reality we experience. That is the reason why it is so much easier to discuss what is *on* television than to discuss the impact of television as such. More simply still, we are adjusted to it.

Examples are often more persuasive than abstruse argument. Postman reported that he watched forty-two hours of tele-evangelical shows before writing the chapter in his book dealing with religion on TV. Five hours, he said, would have been sufficient to draw two important and general conclusions. First, religion on television is as entertaining as a game show or a football game. 'Everything that makes religion an historic, profound and sacred human activity is stripped away; there is no ritual, no dogma, no tradition, no theology and above all, no sense of spiritual transcendence.' Second, what makes religion so entertaining is not the intentions or the motives of the preachers, which doubtless are varied, but the demands of the medium. Christianity, at least as it is practised in churches, is an experientially demanding and serious religion, not Sunday entertainment. The threat posed by television to religious practice, therefore, 'is not that religion has become the content of television shows but that television shows may become the content of religion.'[26]

We must, therefore, make a second sailing and attempt to understand the epistemology of television news from the practice of TV journalism. Granted that the 'mirror theory' and the fall-back position, 'professionalism,' are inadequate, it does not yet necessarily follow that the truth of existence expressed by TV news is that life can be fulfilled in continuous amusement. What makes Postman's argument at least party persuasive, however, is the epistemological indecisiveness of competing accounts of news production.

Epstein has argued that organizational imperatives, chiefly political and economic ones, establish the 'operating rules' of news production. Such 'rules' do not predetermine any particular story, but they do define the general characteristics of all stories: time, ease of transmission, the 'on-the-one-hand/on-the-other-hand' or point/counterpoint format, definitions of context by trends and not individual reportorial choices or 'events,' – all give consistency to television news.[27] Gans has likewise provided an analysis of a series of 'considerations' that influence news judgments.[28] The indecisiveness of such accounts is indicated by the observation that such 'considerations' make it highly inappropriate to question whether the news tells what happened. Such questions, to repeat, belong in a literate culture, not one characterized by secondary orality.

A recent study of the CBC outlet in Toronto and of *The Globe and Mail* approached this problem by asking a different question: What is the method of contemporary journalism? The authors' answer was that 'visualization – making something visible to the mind even if it is not visible to the eye – is the essence of journalism as a method.'[29] This is a promising insight. Visualization is an appropriate method for the study of secondary orality. It is, to begin with, distinct from argument, reporting, or conversation. In practising his method, a journalist offers an account of reality that, in his view, allows, enables, or prompts his audience to visualize adequately the meaning of events. Other scholarly accounts support this approach.

'News,' declared Susan R. Brooker-Gross, 'eludes definition.'[30] Perhaps; but what makes one visualization of events newsworthy and another not may be described with a certain degree of clarity. Specifically, 'deviance is *the* defining characteristic of what journalists regard as newsworthy.'[31] By the term deviance, the authors mean non-normal behaviour. The range of non-normal behaviour can extend from serious criminality to trivial violations of common opinions and expected order. The social, and often the political, response to deviance is control; journalism, therefore, contributes to social consensus, and thereby to social order, by highlighting what is odd.

The argument is subtle but not complex. First, news means news of deviance. Such news is often dramatic. In the widely quoted words of Reuven Frank, every news story 'should, without any sacrifice of probity or responsibility, display the attributes of fiction, of drama.' It should follow the venerable Aristotelian form of beginning, middle, and end. Aristotle, however, was concerned with dramatic form, not with reporting events. In Frank's view, this is a distinction without a difference because, like all television producers, he was concerned with what he called 'symbolic truth.' Indeed, Frank said, 'the picture is not a fact but a symbol.'[32] The language is not, perhaps, the best. After all, symbols must be symbols of something. In the more adequate but less pungent language of social science: 'While the reporter may be several steps removed from the symbolically constructed reality she reports on,' Ericson, Baranek, and Chan observed, 'senior administrators ... are in the same position of being at the nth level of knowledge production regarding work on individual occurrences or internal practices and politics.'[33] The 'truth' involved may be symbolic, but it is also abstract and constructed, not immediate.[34] Even so, this 'dramatic' or 'symbolic' structure confirms Postman's point (not to say everyday experience) that news must be entertaining. News of deviance almost invariably is.

But deviance is also the story of the failure of social control. For this reason, Gans argued that 'the news is not so much conservative or liberal as it is reformist.'[35] So far as it goes, this is true enough; but it is important to push the dialectic of failure and reform somewhat farther. The experience of failure is essential to the creation of visions of what might be improved. Accordingly, discussions of failure or of deviance are essential constituent elements of discussions of improvement or, to use the contemporary symbol, of discussions of progress.[36] The logic of the argument is straightforward: news, which is ostensibly news of deviance or of failure, is essential to a belief in progress. More boldly: since there can be no vision of progress without a vision of failure, news that emphasizes failure (because it is more dramatic, entertaining, and so on – that is, because it makes for good TV) reinforces success and so fosters the imaginative purposes of 'progress.' Good TV necessarily enhances the ideological commitment of mass technological societies to a belief in 'progress,' especially when TV news reports deviance.

Implicit in this first attribute of news as a progressive or reformist visualization of deviance is the role of the journalist as storyteller. In order to 'tell' a good story, journalists regularly use 'fakes' (unrelated visuals) and 'staging' (actors, rehearsed interviews, and so on). What counts in a story is not factual accuracy – in the sense that factual accuracy is not central to 'Little Red Riding Hood' – but transmitting a meaningful message. A 'good' journalist, therefore, is not necessarily a good reporter, but a good interpreter or visualizer of reality as news, that is, as deviance. The consequence of these visualizations, a topic to which we return below, is that, by incorporating important and emotionally engaging natural social and political dramas, the news helps 'to create their communities within the mythical configurations employed by authorized knowers. The myths become deeply embedded in consciousness, so that they do indeed direct our ways of knowing, as well as our knowledge of the world.'[37] In other words, a central element in the ideological reproduction of progress is visualization of deviance by the media.[38]

A final consideration along these lines is that journalists are disposed to tell the stories they do, not merely because they sell or because they meet other organizational demands, but because such visualizations of reality fulfil journalists' own inner needs. In *The Media Elite*, the authors report on the results of Thematic Apperception Tests (TATs) administered to a sample of élite U.S. journalists.[39] The assumption governing such tests, like those of the Rorschach ink-blot test, is that, by explaining what is expressed in an ambiguous picture, subjects will reveal their own personalities, including the emotional depths that sustain their explicit preferences. The conclusion reached by independent professional analysts of the TAT stories was that the subjects – namely, the élite journalists – have, as a group, a heightened but ambivalent concern for power, strong narcissistic needs, and relatively low needs for personal achievement or personal intimacy.

On the surface, such individuals are concerned with power and competi-

16 Sins of Omission

tion, and with an adversarial style of living. Now, many of the scholars who have asked journalists how they decide what's news have been given metaphorical or vague answers that mention a nose for news or an instinct or an otherwise inexplicable capacity of 'just knowing' what news is. But no scholar is likely to be satisfied when a journalist tells her he just knows news when he sees it, or that he is blessed with an extraordinary olfactory organ and can simply sniff it out. No doubt it was partly in response to such replies that media scholars postulated and emphasized organizational and other considerations. However, Lichter and colleagues have indicated that the internal psychological disposition of journalists reinforces external organizational considerations.

There are more subtle psychodynamics involved as well. Let us grant, at least provisionally, that the news product expresses the inner needs of those who produce it. There remains, however, the question of ambivalence towards power. According to the TAT profiles, journalists tend to want power *and* to be afraid of it. One way of dealing with such feelings is to attack those who are perceived to be powerful and to rationalize the attack, not by reference to one's own power needs, but in terms of the public good. This strategy allows one to experience power and aggression (and the satisfaction of personal needs) while calling it something else (and so satisfying other and antithetical needs). There is nothing sinister in such rationalizations; indeed, they are a kind of psychological commonplace. The president of General Motors was once ridiculed for identifying the interests of his country with those of his corporation. The premier of Ontario, whoever may hold the office, (and perhaps also the citizens of that province) commonly identifies the interests of that province with those of Canada. It should hardly be a surprise if journalists also identify their own activity with the public good.

One final observation of the Lichter study worth noting concerns narcissism and relatively low needs for achievement and intimacy. Certainly the last two personality attributes must be counted as journalistic assets. When your task is to treat human suffering and tragedy as an occasion to visualize a story rather than to provide assistance or relief, people with greater needs for intimacy would find it extremely difficult to maintain a cool head. A lack of concern for achievement is also useful for visualizing deviance. Not that journalists are unambitious or unconcerned with success, but that success is not defined in terms of a job well done. Satisfaction comes from the experience of the process of production rather than from the beauty and truth of the product. Of course, deadlines do not make it easy to reflect on the ultimate significance of events. But that is precisely the point: persons who are able to feel comfortable with deadlines and headlines, and who never have an opportunity to think much beyond them, may well make the best journalists.

There remains the delicate matter of narcissism. People with high narcissistic needs tend to inflate their own importance and devalue that of others. According to conventional psychological accounts, the reason for this tendency is relatively low self-esteem. Such people do not take criticism well and often respond with indignant and self-righteous assertions. As Edward R. Murrow is supposed to have said, 'Newspeople don't have thin skins – they have no skins.'[40] Even Gans reported that the subjects of his study harboured grave suspicions regarding both his own work and the audience research done by their own network.[41] As was mentioned above, a pilot study undertaken a few years ago under my direction that was critical of several claims made by the CBC brought a very hostile response: alleged methodological inadequacies were sufficient grounds for threatening a lawsuit.

The conclusion to be drawn from the Lichter study is that, just as one may speak with some justification of a military mentality or of the mentality of policemen, football players, or professors of political science, so too is there a configuration of measurable attributes that can reasonably be said to constitute a journalistic mentality. It is conditioned not merely by explicit beliefs and organizational imperatives but by less articulate motivations as well. The authors of *The Media Elite* conclude that such personality traits are, in fact, useful for 'good, tough, unyielding journalism.' People who are 'both outwardly critical and sensitive toward incoming criticism may be just the driving force needed to pry stories loose from recalcitrant sources, while offering protection from dangerous self-doubt.'[42] Such people may not be nice, but nice guys get scooped.

There is an obvious objection to all this: So what? Does it matter what motivates journalists? Supposing there are interconnections between journalists' personalities and a propensity to produce stories visualizing deviance, what differences does it make? If the news were either 'just the facts' or the whole truth, then it would make no difference who produced it. But it is evidently neither. Accordingly, one is led to conclude that claims about professionalism and metaphors about a nose for news are also indicators of ingrained expectations. Those expectations are, at least in part, structured by personality.

We have considered several of the implications of news understood as the visualization of deviance. But news is also a kind of knowledge. Specifically, it is *produced* knowledge. As Ericson, Baranek, and Chan argued, 'the active production of knowledge is fundamental to the reproduction of society, since social order is possible only because there are shared symbols for collective action.'[43] According to this conception, which has been given rigorous form in the writings of Michel Foucault,[44] knowledge is a kind of tool or technique by which modern society manages itself. It is a 'discursive practice,' not a means to the quiet contemplation of truths experienced as existing in a mode that transcends society. In a technological or 'information' society such as our own, the creation of information and the transformation of it into intersubjective understanding or 'knowledge' is a significant purpose of news.

The production of this contextual knowledge carries with it no implication of truth with respect to realities experienced as transcendent to society, but only that it is believed to be true. In terms used by classical political science, this knowledge is a mode of *doxa*, opinion, not *epistēmē*, science or knowledge.[45] The purpose of news as knowledge in a technological or information society is, therefore, to be useful as a means to control an environment that is understood as standing in need of control.[46] Or, following the formula of Ellul, if the technological society is, politically speaking, an administrative organization designed with the aim of regulating normal behaviour, the information and knowledge that constitute the news are inherently instrumental.[47]

To draw together a few of the threads of the argument to this point: first, news production is not reporting self-evident reality. Second, news is produced from a dialectic of journalist, source, and organization. Third, the product structures reality rather than expresses it on the basis of a 'news discourse' or discursive practice conditioned by a wide range of realities, some of which may be hidden even from the practitioners. In antiquity, opinion, *doxa* – or, if you like, doxic 'knowledge' – was made articulate in conventions. The knowledge/power of the press is likewise guarded and sustained by conventions, or *nomoi*. We have already mentioned Reuven Frank's remark that every news story 'should, without any sacrifice of probity or responsibility, display the attributes of fiction, of drama.' It remains, however, to discover the meaning of the terms 'probity or responsibility.' According to the *conventions* of journalism, probity and responsibility in practice are called objectivity, balance, or fairness.

In her survey of journalists in 1977, Phillips found virtual unanimity (98 per cent agreement) regarding the proposition that 'the norm of objectivity forms the core of the defining logic and mission of news creation.'[48] Moreover, objectivity was understood to be synonymous with balance and fairness. Considering the findings of the Lichter study, that 'source selections, summaries of news stories, and TAT themes tend to be consistent with the social attitudes they express,' it is just as well that objectivity is refined into balance and fairness. The reason is simple, but needs to be stated: conscious opinions about objectivity and, indeed, fairness, 'are reflected to some degree in the ways that they [journalists] subconsciously structure reality.' Accordingly, 'the conscious effort to be objective takes place within a mental picture of the world already conditioned by one's beliefs about it.'[49] In other words, the conscious efforts of a journalist to be objective and fair may be insufficient because the effects of journalists' perspectives are not themselves the result of conscious choices but rather are part of what might be termed the journalistic subculture or world. As Ericson, Baranek, and Chan pointed out, 'cultural templates' frame media accounts of what is in light of what ought to be.[50] Moreover, there is no reason to assume that the organizational imperatives discussed by Epstein systematically contradict the 'cultural' assumptions of the journalists' milieu.

If it be granted that objectivity, as distinct from fairness and balance, is an impossible dream, what is implied by the remaining two conventions? The CBC manual *Journalistic Policy* may serve as a useful starting-point.[51] The Corporation, according to the manual, 'takes no editorial position in its programming.' When remarks by a correspondent or anchor on the significance of topics presented in the news of the day are broadcast, these items are called 'analysis,' not 'commentary.'[52] Fairness is not 'rigid neutrality or mathematical balance,' but equitable treatment of 'the relevant facts and significant points of view.' Likewise, balance is considered in the same kind of language: 'CBC programs dealing with matters of public interest in which differing views are held must supplement the exposition of one point of view with an equitable treatment of other relevant points of view ... Equitable in this context means fair and reasonable, taking into consideration the weight of opinion behind a point of view, as well as its significance or potential significance.'[53] The BBC has a similar document, *Principles and Practice in News and Current Affairs*, and the American Federal Communications Commission has enunciated a quasi-legal 'fairness doctrine.' The problem with these sets of guidelines, norms, or conventions, however, is that they are tautological: fairness means equitable treatment, which means balance, which means fairness. All of which is decided on the basis of relevance, significance, reasonableness, the weight of opinion, and, of course, fairness, balance, and equity. In short, the journalistic self-interpretation of fairness, balance, and equity is far too flexible to be of any use in establishing a coherent meaning or useful criteria.

Let us then consider what scholars have said about journalists' practical implementation of these doctrines, balance and fairness. Gans recounted the familiar description of a balanced program as one that 'presents a diverse collection of stories' and connected this format to the belief of journalists 'that if they fail to maintain political balance, they will be accused of bias, which undermines credibility.'[54] But credibility is a necessity, not an option, for media of secondary orality. Accordingly, as Tuchman argued, 'objectivity' is a 'strategic ritual' subordinate to the requirements of continued existence.[55] But, in that case, it is less a norm to be admired for its justice than the result of calculative cleverness. In any case, nothing is said about the inherent justice or desirability of providing a balanced account. The possibility of a conflict between a balanced and an accurate account cannot be raised within the context of secondary orality. Such questions belong firmly to literate culture.

In consequence of these strategic considerations, then, objectivity, balance, and fairness have become understood in terms of journalists' intentions. Reuven Frank called this self-serving position 'artificial innocence.' The adjective, at least, is accurate. Fairness, said Gans, is also 'a matter of intent, and journalists who believe they have acted fairly can ignore charges to the contrary.'[56] If such a convention were not already flexible enough, Gans added that, 'generally speaking, fairness is determined in accordance with the enduring values, which is why socially and morally disorderly actors need not be treated fairly.'[57] 'Enduring values,' like all values, are also conventional; they change, as all conventions change, and in the end are incapable of providing adequate standards by which to judge soundly.[58] Stripped of the obfuscating language of intention, the doctrine of fairness and balance amounts to this: on the one hand, journalists consider themselves to be fair and balanced when they try to be fair and balanced; on the other, they need not try to be fair with those who are 'socially and morally disorderly.' The restraints imposed by conventional requirements of balance and fairness, one may safely conclude, are anything but onerous.[59]

The other side of the coin is that the audience 'doesn't miss what it doesn't see.'[60] The more positive version of this convention is that television journalists provide audiences with what they need, not what they want. Gans related this convention to the alleged professionalism of journalists who provide a valued service 'for a predominantly lay clientele.'[61] By this imagery, not only are journalists professionals, they are clerical. In the words of a CBC president, writing the preface to the Corporation's handbook of journalistic conventions, 'programming cannot be limited to what the largest audience wants to know; it must include what the public is entitled and needs to know.'[62] Two claims are being made here: first, that audi-

ences have needs, whether they know it or not, and, second, that journalists
are in a position to assess those needs and, obviously, to satisfy them as well.

We are then compelled to raise the commonsensical question by what
right of passage did journalists become capable of such assessments? How is
it that their audience can be conceived as a 'lay clientele' and themselves as
priestly? The answer, most emphatically, is *not* by determining the needs of
their audience by investigation. Indeed, several social scientists have
expressed mild surprise at the distrust by journalists of audience surveys.[63]
The logic that sustains their claim to know audience needs is the prior claim
to be 'knowledge producers.'[64] It would be more accurate to understand
this exalted status to claim secondary orality. There is no reason at all for
those who transmit information to be concerned about feedback from their
audience; their chief concern, very nearly their only concern, is that there
be a public to consume 'information' or, if one prefers, 'knowledge.'

From the ethnographic studies of news-producing organizations, the
meaning of these conventions is not that journalists cynically rationalize
their subterranean motives by using celestial rhetoric. Motives are hardly
ever considered, which is precisely what one would expect in organizations
that adhere strongly to their own conventions. The formula by which the
conventions of fairness and balance is put into practice has been called by
Epstein 'the dialectical model.'[65] The dialectic is a simple one: 'storylines
tend to follow a point-counterpoint format, with correspondents providing
some sort of synthesis, though not necessarily an answer to, the opposing
views in a final comment.'[66] The usual means of signalling the transition is
the conjunction 'but.' Stories often follow this formula: 'Today actor A said
this. *But*, actor B said that.' One may therefore conclude that, in so far as
news consists in visualizing deviance, even the point/counterpoint format is
not neutral. On the contrary, it lends itself to becoming an episode in the
ongoing deviance-and-control morality play. As Ericson, Baranek, and
Chan pointed out, this superficially balanced structure means 'it is inevitable that one side is portrayed negatively via an imputation of deviance from
the other side. The trick of the trade is to ensure that one is on the right
side as much as possible, making the imputation rather than having to
answer for it.'[67] In other words, even the point/counterpoint formula can be
used in a manipulative way. Hence, the importance of what has come to be
known as 'spin.' And 'spin-doctors,' one hardly need add, can be both
sources and journalists.

Most of the time, however, providing a resolution to the 'dialectic' is the
last thing a good journalist wants to do. The reason is not merely that one-
sided treatment violates the conventions, for we have seen that conventions

are flexible. A large number of examples of one-sided treatment indicates that, under exceptional circumstances, a single defensible side is sometimes presented. But these are exceptions to standard practice.[68]

In the absence of self-serving and spurious appeals to canons of balance and fairness, the most obvious reason that the dialectical model is maintained is that it serves the interests of news producers. It does so in two different ways. First, it is dramatic, and drama is a major consideration in news formatting. Second, an indeterminate synthesis of the two sides of the dialectic serves to ensure that the story is a continuing one. An indeterminate synthesis also has the advantage of not requiring correspondents to attempt independently to verify the truth of a source's statements. 'Facts' are essentially what sources say, and 'research,' for journalists, means collecting a large number of quotations from sources; for television in particular, it means selecting the appropriate stock visual from the video library.[69] In neither case does it mean independent or factual verification by the journalist.

The foregoing remarks were directed at the removal of some of the moralizing dissimulation from accounts of news production. The remaining question of newsworthiness may be considered summarily. Nearly all who have studied this topic agree that the criteria of newsworthiness are complex and unsystematic. Not unexpectedly, assignment editors and producers take the route of least resistance, or at least of minimal ambiguity, and ask: 'Who is involved?' not 'What is happening?'[70] The substitution simplifies matters considerably. Moreover, by personalizing news, the possibility of dramatization is also enhanced. Visualization of deviance depends on continuity to establish frames of reference; accordingly, dramatic events are conceived as part of a trend or as 'symptomatic' of something greater than themselves.[71] In all of these attributes, the prime criteria remain deviance and control. What makes a story interesting, and thus subject to simplification, dramatization, personalization, and so on, is that it can be visualized as deviant.[72] What is eminently unnewsworthy is criticism of other journalists. Deviance, by the strongest of conventions, is always social and political, never journalistic.[73]

3 AGENDA SETTING

In section 1 (above), the observation was made that content analysis of the mass media began during the 1930s. In a pioneer study of the 1940 U.S. presidential election, Lazarsfeld, Berelson, and Gaudet found that the effects of 'radio propaganda' on popular beliefs were minimal. All that exposure to media propaganda did was strengthen beliefs and predispositions that were already in existence.[74] Later research confirmed what has come to be known as the 'theory of minimal effects.' Since this early work showed that the messages transmitted by the mass media did not change people's minds and had no measurable effect on voter turnout or voter preference, televised messages were considered as simply another source of information citizens could attend to or not.[75] V.O. Key, one of the most knowledgeable political scientists of his day, summarized the prevailing view: 'Neither radio nor television has been able to grow into an independent source of political information or interpretation. In the main, these instruments have been brought into the pattern of older news media; they are by and large transmitters rather than originators of political intelligence. As such, radio and television have not become institutions of political influence in their own right.'[76]

A decade later, Patterson and McClure restated what had become the received wisdom of a generation of social science: 'the nightly news is too brief to treat fully the complexity of modern politics, too visual to present effectively most events, and too entertainment-minded to tell viewers much worth knowing.' Accordingly, 'most network newscasts are neither very educational nor very powerful communicators.'[77] The description of TV news remains accurate, but the conclusion does not follow, and probably never did.

There are two reasons for questioning this view. The first, discussed in section 1, is that the authors were insufficiently sensitive to the significance of the form of secondary orality. Their conclusion, in effect, stated that TV is a poor newspaper, little more than a headline service. One need not, however, consider the question of form in order to see a second limitation of the earlier orthodoxy. The immediate experience of televised events during the late 1960s and early 1970s showed even social scientists that television had a significant effect on politics. Common-sense observation indicated that citizens generally hold strong views on matters that lie far beyond their direct experience. Ordinary Canadians are concerned, not just with keeping a job, supporting a family, and enjoying the company of their friends, but also with pollution on Baffin Island and the politics of South Africa and Bosnia. They make their political judgments without having visited the Arctic and perhaps with but the shadiest notion of where Sarajevo is. Common sense, as well as the direct experience of the impact of television on, for example, the Vietnam War, led social scientists in the 1970s to the inevitable conclusion that the media had a considerable capability to shape public opinion about political things.

Social science rarely begins with common sense, however. Initial studies were concerned with audience size and credibility as well as with the questions associated with producing news that were discussed above, in section 2. The conclusions, usually tentatively expressed, were in the form of suggestions that there were several unsuspected consequences of television news.[78] This later work, however, remained speculative. More precisely, there was a sense that television had made a difference, but there was no clear conceptual way to describe the difference it made. At about the same time, the concept of 'agenda setting' was introduced into public-policy studies, and was quickly appropriated by media scholars.[79]

In effect, the concept of agenda setting pushed the argument away from the well-known and obvious surface characteristics of the media – triviality, superficiality, and so on – to a concern with their function or purpose, understood in terms of longer-range consequences. Cohen's study, *The Press and Foreign Policy*, made extensive use of the concept. 'The press,' he wrote (and we may add, television), 'is significantly more than a purveyor of information and opinion. It may not be successful much of the time in telling people what to think, but it is stunningly successful in telling its readers [and viewers] what to think *about*.'[80] McCombs and Shaw added to Cohen's argument. Citizens or audiences, they said, learn 'in direct proportion to the emphasis placed on the campaign issues by the mass media.'[81] The approach was further refined through an analysis of the relative effects of print as compared with television and of the direction of the relationship between media priorities and public perceptions.[82]

A further question remained to be clarified: is agenda setting a lengthy process or a one-time affair? If the former, then longitudinal studies are required; if the latter, then cross-sectional studies are sufficient. Those studies adopting the latter assumption alone characteristically show ambiguous results. Those adopting the former indicate more strongly that public opinion tends to follow the media attention paid, over time, to a topic.[83] In a series of cleverly conceived experiments, Iyengar and Kinder have provided a splendid refinement of the agenda-setting approach, and incidentally have clarified some of the ambiguities raised in earlier studies.[84]

According to the agenda-setting hypothesis, issues that are prominently featured on television news become those that the television audience comes to consider as important. On the basis of experimental evidence, content analysis and longitudinal analysis of national public-opinion surveys, the hypothesis was strongly confirmed. 'People who were shown network broadcasts edited to draw attention to a particular problem assigned greater importance to that problem.'[85] By 'greater' the authors mean that subjects, after viewing the edited simulated newscasts about topic X, thought topic X to be more important than they did before being exposed to the experimental information, and that subjects exposed to the simulated newscast thought topic X to be more important than did a control group from whom information regarding topic X was withheld. 'The verdict,' the authors wrote, 'is clear and unequivocal.' All the data – from cross-sectional experimental evidence to longitudinal studies, and over a wide range of issues – were in agreement. 'By attending to some problems and ignoring others, television news shapes the American public's political priorities.'[86] The evidence was so strong that the conclusion may be taken as unqualified fact. There is no reason to think that different results would be obtained from Canadian subjects.

Agreement of the momentary experimental evidence is significant because it means that agenda-setting effects are volatile. Television audiences, therefore, show 'a limited memory for last month's news and a recurrent vulnerability to today's.'[87] Public priorities are altered by television emphasis and altered again when something new is produced. This experimental evidence regarding agenda setting supports Postman's argument that television can produce only novelty and entertainment. Equally important was the finding that TV coverage is 'particularly effective in shaping the judgements of citizens with limited political resources and skills.'[88] In fact, the more removed from participation in politics a person is, the more he or she will be influenced by the agenda-setting power of the media. Audience studies have shown that television news is viewed disproportionately by poorer and less educated citizens.[89]

There is, however, more to television news than the management or manipulation of a comparatively ignorant and poor population endowed with few alternative sources of information and a low sense of political efficacy – in short, the political weaklings of modern society. Highly politically engaged subjects turned out also to be responsive to changes in the media's agenda.[90] The difference between the two groups may in some measure reflect the difference between reception and acceptance of the media agenda. That is, politically uninvolved people may well simply accept the agenda-setting consequences of the media's messages whereas the politically engaged receive the message but do not necessarily accept it. This interpretation was sustained by what the authors called the 'priming effect.'

The priming effect may be understood most easily as the chief consequence of agenda setting. 'By calling attention to some matters while ignoring others, television news influences the standards by which governments, presidents, policies, and candidates for public office are judged.' Priming, accordingly, 'refers to changes in the standards that people use to make political evaluations.'[91] For example, if the television news agenda shifts from unemployment to constitutional problems, the government and political leaders would tend increasingly to be judged on their handling of the latter issue. The assumptions underlying the priming effect are, first, that audiences exhibit selective attention to a few themes, and second, that audiences attend to the most accessible information – that is, to what most easily comes to mind. The expectation that the more attention TV pays to an issue (the more an issue area is primed), the more viewers use that information to make political judgments was strongly supported by the experimental evidence.

Priming is especially important when policy issues are new and information scarce. This particular condition leads to personalization of issues and emphasis on the character of the political actors involved. In terms of considerations of secondary orality, priming enhances the tendency to rely on formular visualizations. In a literary medium, one would speak of clichés in this context. The association of Gorbachev and *perestroika*, of Arafat and the PLO, and of Bishop Tutu and South Africa are examples of priming. One may know nothing of Russian or Middle Eastern or South African politics, but that is no barrier to making strong political judgments on the basis of primed messages. Since, typically, audiences are poorly informed anyway, the priming effect is likely to be enhanced when the news content is generally unfamiliar or its significance is ambiguous.

The victims of agenda setting, as Iyengar and Kinder called them, were people who were unconcerned with public affairs, uneducated, and poor. The victims of priming reflected a somewhat different set of characteristics. Priming was, to begin with, not consistently related to education. As the authors put it, 'against the power of television news, education by itself offers little protection.' What did was partisan attachment. Politically engaged citizens would be as primed by news about the budget or unemployment or inflation as the politically unengaged. The reasons, however, were different. The uninvolved are susceptible to priming for the same reasons they are susceptible to agenda setting, namely, the day-to-day focus of the news or its entertainment effect. The politically involved are susceptible to priming because they are looking to be primed, to have their own views confirmed. Moreover, the politically involved are looking for different things: Conservatives, for example, are usually looking for evidence of poor performance by Liberals, and Liberals for evidence of poor performance by Conservatives. New Democrats, of course, are looking for poor performance by both Liberals and Conservatives. Hardly anyone is primed by a good performance.[92]

Both priming and agenda setting depend for their effects on the nature of the audience as well as on the message transmitted. Audiences are not, therefore, homogeneous, although television acts on the assumption that they are. Indeed, technological consideration and costs, as well as the entertainment effect, make it virtually impossible to operate a network on any other assumption. This observation does not contradict the argument of Meyrowitz concerning the *diffuse* homogenizing effects of television.[93] Rather, it confirms the earlier point that propaganda 'reinforces the public's preferences [but] it does not, and perhaps cannot, change them.' Political persuasion is difficult, 'but agenda-setting and priming are apparently pervasive.' Accordingly, the power of television news 'appears to rest not on persuasion but on commanding the public's attention (agenda-setting) and defining criteria underlying the public's judgements (priming).'[94]

The argument does not lead to the conclusion that journalists have a hidden ideological agenda that is manifest in the agenda-setting and priming effects. There is, in the first place, no evidence that, for example, priming in the area of the budget has any effect in the area of attitudes towards South Africa. Agenda setting and priming do not, therefore, stimulate ideological coherence; nor do they create problems that do not exist or obscure ones that do. Instead, television alters priorities that audiences attach to a plausible and circumscribed set of issues. In the second place, the relationship between news sources and news broadcasters seems to be symbiotic (at best), or even mutually manipulative.

For example, in 1983, the Canadian deputy minister for External Affairs, de Montigny Marchand, paid his respects to the power of the media by observing that they 'consecrated' the existence of foreign events by turning them into news.[95] This complaint has been generalized into a full-fledged doctrine by advocates, chiefly within UNESCO, for a New World Information and Communication Order.[96] The substance of the NWICO complaint is that, by covering only hard news and crises, which they call a 'coups and earthquakes'[97] syndrome, an unbalanced, distorted, biased, etc., picture of foreign (chiefly poor) countries is provided to domestic (chiefly North American and European) audiences. However, the media regularly complain that they are manipulated by governments. As long ago as 1964, McLuhan observed that government by news leak was inherently a part of modern, technologically sophisticated government.[98] More recently, Patricia Karl argued that 'the media are increasingly part of the process (if not the entire process) in the communications between governments and publics about international politics.'[99] Edward Said managed to argue that the media both distorted reality to fit the foreign-policy objectives of their governments, and so were manipulated, and were major factors in setting the foreign-policy agendas of governments.[100]

It is, of course, no contradiction to assert that the media are both manipulators and manipulated. Indeed, the relationship of sources to news organization makes any other relationship highly unlikely. On the one hand, news sources seek access to broadcasters rather than mere coverage, but, on the other, they also seek to deny broadcasters access to their own backstage activities.[101] Moreover, the 'epistemology of television,' as Postman said, with its devotion to image and visualization, means that 'distortion' is coeval with coverage. It ought to come as no surprise to learn that news does not merely document change around the world and inform audiences of external states of affairs. For reasons already discussed, the news, understood as the visualization of deviance, is bound to appear distorted, unbalanced, biased, and so on, to those who wish to project different images.

The conclusion we would draw from the foregoing remarks is, first, that producing news introduces a gap between the event and the report of it. Television news, therefore, cannot be neutral. Second, consideration of the chief consequences of television news – namely, agenda setting and priming – reinforces the first conclusion.

4   METHOD AND DATA

In section 1 (above), the argument was made that, even though TV broadcasts were filled with sights and sounds, using content-analysis techniques on television audio transcripts was a legitimate research procedure. Something may be lost by ignoring the quality of the music that accompanies the opening of the network news; gestures and intonation and camera angle are important but subsidiary considerations, and elaborate and subtle theories are available to account for these topics. The purpose of this study, however, is less sophisticated. We are looking at a product, TV news, that was carefully engineered. We assume that the engineers and technicians were competent and thus that the musical cues, video footage, tone of voice of correspondents and anchors, camera angles, and so on reinforced one another and supported the verbal message. To use a west-coast image, it is as if we were seining for salmon, not herring. The mesh is sufficiently large to allow the herring to escape, should any be caught inside our purse.

The term 'content analysis' usually refers to a set of techniques that enable information to be categorized systematically and impartially. A review of the standard manuals, monographs, or resources dealing with content analysis[102] indicated that there exist a few general rules applicable to all such studies, but that each particular study must be tailored to the topic under consideration. The general rules concern such requirements that coding categories be exhaustive, independent, mutually exclusive, and derived from a single principle.[103] Beyond that, however, it is possible to minimize the influence of the idiosyncratic dispositions of coders only by making as explicit as possible the rules by which coding decisions were to be made. The aim of explicit decision rules is to maximize *reliability*.

Content analysis that is totally reliable could be undertaken by computers. Unfortunately, the results of such an analysis would not be very interesting. The other concern of content analysis – namely, *validity* – deals with the question of interesting or significant information. Judgments regarding significant information, however, are not independent of the dispositions of coders or of information available to them. Indeed, considerations of reliability and validity are often at cross-purposes. Deciding how much reliability should be sacrificed in order to consider non-trivial questions invariably reflects the researcher's strategic consideration of the relative importance of the two concepts.

For example, a word-count of the term, 'NATO' would produce highly reliable but utterly trivial data. An analysis of stories dealing with NATO that included a judgment by the coder as to whether NATO policies were accurately portrayed might produce less reliable data, but they would be much more interesting. Content analysis that is focally concerned with validity is indistinguishable from careful reading. This is why Leo Strauss, who was nothing if not a careful reader, sometimes described his own technique of textual analysis as content analysis.

The usual method, described in books with the term 'content analysis' in their titles, might more accurately be described as quantitative content analysis. The objective of such studies is to produce reliable statistical profiles, guided by the assumption that statistical reliability is an indicator of validity.[104] These data are then interpreted in an expository form in order to convey a meaning. The objective, in common-sense language, is to write a narrative about human practices. Such an objective is not dissimilar from conventional storytelling by historians or novelists. The discursive form, however, is often different.

The data used in this study came from nearly 250 broadcasts, aired between June 1987 and June 1988 over the CBC. The procedure was tedious but not complex. News and public-affairs shows were taped and transcribed. Initially transcripts of both the CBC and CTV were subjected to a quantitative content analysis using a coding instrument developed and refined over several months and focused on peace and security stories. Very few statistically significant remarks were obtained, which is one reason I did not reproduce those data here.[105] Another is that, while quantitative political science has a charm of its own, that charm is exercised chiefly over academics who are good in arithmetic, not citizens guided by common sense, and this book was written for the latter. A third reason is that, to be frank, quantitative studies are too abstract to be of much interest to any but abstracted intelligences. In any event, the following chapters are concerned with what we shall call 'qualitative' rather than 'quantitative' content analysis.[106] Qualitative content analysis considers the text of a TV news broadcast more or less the way a poem or a philosophical discourse would be treated by a skilled and competent reader. One must pay attention to what is said and how it is said. One must know enough about a topic to know when things that might have been said, or even that should have been said, were not said. In the language of Michael Polanyi, qualitative content analysis employs connoisseurship.[107]

Three long-running stories are discussed: the Soviet Union, the Reagan–Gorbachev summit talks, and Africa. In each of the following chapters, virtually all the stories that were recorded are analysed. An occasional anchoronly mention of an event may, however, have been ignored. Considerable evidence is reproduced before I offer an analysis of it, and I assume at the outset that anyone dealing with the same data would come to similar conclusions. That is, after all, one of the meanings of 'empirical.' One should bear in mind, however, that the results of content analysis, whether quantitative or qualitative, are not meant to end disputed interpretations. It is enough perhaps to expect that my argument will reduce (to some extent) the confusion of questions of opinion with questions of fact. What is certainly true is that no interpretation, disputed or not, can take place in the absence of agreement on what is or is not a fact. On the one hand, the evidence presented and analysed here may help in the constitution of reasonable discussion regarding the significance of television in the conduct of Canadian public life. On the other hand, it may simply annoy my fellow academics and amuse my fellow citizens.

I should add that this study does not presume to be the final word on the significance of the constructed mediation of reality by television. I certainly believe that the conclusions can be extended beyond the CBC and beyond the time period and the stories covered, but the evidence presented in the following chapters can be treated and understood on its own. It will become clear soon enough that the sins of omission referred to in the title of this book may be summarily indicated by an ideological label. But it is not my intention simply to label the CBC as left-wing or anti-American. Regarding the motives of producers, reporters, and anchors, I, like everyone else, am completely in the dark. So, to recall what I indicated in the preface, I am presenting evidence – that's all. I am analysing it – that's all. If somebody finds the results of my analysis of the evidence unsatisfying, he or she is as obliged to indicate, as I would be grateful to learn, where I went wrong. And finally, it is inevitable, because I did not examine *every* story aired over a twelve-month period, that I missed some significant stories or story series. But again, readers who find the analysis as presented to be unsatisfactory can help the progress of science by correcting my innocent omissisons.

In the meantime, the proof of the pudding is in the eating; so now we turn to the CBC's visualization of the USSR.

CHAPTER TWO

Back in the USSR

This chapter is concerned with the visualization of the USSR by the CBC television news. I begin with an analysis of the CBC's account of domestic life and then consider their version of some of the difficulties encountered by the then Soviet Union in Armenia and Afghanistan. The procedure used here is more or less that employed in the following chapters as well. First, I present the text of the transcript, or else a paraphrase or summary of it. Second, I undertake an analysis of the visualization implicit in the text. Third, I offer an interpretation of the significance of the visualization. Occasionally, when CBC accounts of events stray significantly from more or less well-known facts or from accounts in other standard sources, such as *The New York Times*, I draw attention to the matter and discuss or speculate upon the significance of the selected presentation of reality. Following a procedure more or less like the one just outlined constitutes the substance of the qualitative content analysis adopted in this study.

5 VISIONS OF SOVIET LIFE

Coverage by the CBC of domestic stories of life in the USSR may be divided into three general categories. The first was concerned with what might be termed ordinary news, the second was centred on the novelty of *glasnost*, and the third dealt with more diverting aspects of changes in Soviet social life. Unlike the process of visualizing news in Canada, the United States, or other Western nations, the point/counterpoint formula could not normally be employed. If there was to be any dramatic structure at all, it would have to come either from the universal appeal of the events that are broadcast as news or from analytical commentary by the correspondent or anchor. As there was relatively little of the latter, accounts of events were often diffused without additional clues or interpretative guidance as to their significance. This does not mean, however, that news focused on the USSR was without a consistent structure. On the contrary, stories were visualized consistently in such a way that the Soviet Union was presented as being very much 'like us.' Such differences as were emphasized tended to indicate that the Soviet Union was a 'progressive' kind of place, its leaders concerned very much with establishing 'peace,' its difficulties temporary. Obvious external or elemental differences, such as the absence of genuine elections, the existence of a secret police, the concentration camps, and restrictive emigration policy, were ignored, played down, or euphemized into innocuous variations of normalcy. In short, the substantive political and, indeed, cultural differences between the political regimes established by communism in the USSR and those set up by liberal democracy in the West were minimized.

The category 'ordinary news' contained little by way of explicit visualization. The first such story we recorded was an anchor-only report on the trial of Soviet officials charged with violating safety procedures at Chernobyl and thereby contributing to the explosion and fire at the nuclear reactor in that city (7 Jul. 1987).[1] According to the officials who had been charged, their equipment was faulty. The trial was reported as if it were, in principle, similar to a trial in Canada. In fact, most of the three-week trial was held *in camera*. The top three 'officials,' the plant director and two subordinates, were sentenced to ten years in a labour camp.[2] A second Chernobyl story (31 Jan. 1988) was also an anchor-only report from official and anonymous sources.

Peter Mansbridge: A senior Soviet medical specialist says it's now safe for people who used to live around the Chernobyl nuclear plant to return home. He says the area has been made liveable again since the explosion there two years ago. More than a hundred thousand people were evacuated from the area when one of the plant's reactors blew up [31 Jan. 1988].[3]

In this story, nothing was said about faulty equipment or reactor design, or about safety procedures or criteria by which the Chernobyl area was declared safe; nor was the trial of Soviet officials mentioned.

A second trial story concerned the execution of an eighty-year-old man convicted of being a guard at Treblinka:

The news agency Tass says the death sentence on Igor Fedorenko has been carried out. It didn't say when or where. In 1984, Fedorenko became the first accused Nazi war criminal ever extradited from the United States to the Soviet Union. The Soviet court convicted him, last year, of treason and mass murder [27 Jul. 1987].

In other news of Soviet criminal behaviour, there was a report on 'a bloody hijacking attempt':

It happened yesterday. The Soviet news agency Tass says a group of armed criminals took over a domestic Aeroflot flight bound for Leningrad. Tass said a flight attendant and two passengers were killed, along with most of the hijackers. The report did not say how many hijackers had commandeered the plane [9 Mar. 1988].[4]

No comment was made on the relative scarcity of information or of corroboration of what would elsewhere have been a major and dramatic event. Whatever Tass said was so authoritative that no further investigation was needed. Of course, none was possible either, but that point was never mentioned.[5]

Coverage of space flights also reflected official Soviet policy. On 22 July 1987, Knowlton Nash reported:

A space capsule carrying two Soviet cosmonauts blasted off from Central Asia and into orbit today, and there was a third man with them, an army colonel from Damascus, who becomes Syria's first man in space. The Syrian will photograph his homeland during three passes over the desert and the Euphrates River Valley. It's hoped the pictures he gets will help solve Syria's ancient irrigation problems. During their ten-day mission, the trio will dock with the space station and will meet other cosmonauts who've been up there since February.[6]

Several aspects of this visualization of the Soviet space flight should be noted. First, no military purposes were associated with any aspect of the Soviet space program. Second, it had an international flavour: a Syrian was aboard. A June 1988 report also emphasized the international aspect: Bulgarians, Afghans, and Frenchmen would be accompanying Soviet cosmonauts on future flights. Moreover, the Syrian had a useful job to do while in space: he would take pictures. These pictures would have nothing to do with such questionable activities as spying on the enemies of his country. On the contrary, it was hoped that they would help solve the ancient problem of irrigating the Syrian desert.

To appreciate the significance of this visualization of the Syrian cosmonaut, consider how the following (imaginary) press release from NASA would have been greeted:

Aboard the space shuttle Xanadu, launched today, was the first Israeli astronaut, an army colonel from Jerusalem. The Israeli will photograph his homeland during three passes over the desert and the Dead Sea. It's hoped the pictures he gets will help solve Israel's ancient irrigation problems. During their ten-day mission the shuttle will dock with the space station Greenpeace Harvester, and will meet other astronauts who've been up there since February.

Some of the following questions would, no doubt, have been posed, if not answered: Who was this colonel? Was he an intelligence officer? What else was he photographing? How will his photographs help solve the ancient irrigation problem? What other ways can the ancient irrigation problem be solved? Can it be done on the ground, or do you have to go into space to do it? Why could the guest astronaut/cosmonaut not ask his hosts to take the pictures for him? Why not use a satellite? What else were they doing for ten days? what is the space station for? Who is in it? What are they doing? In the actual story of the Syrian and the Soviets, none of these questions was raised. Audiences were expected to take the story as given.

The only other space story that was sampled probably belongs in the category of diverting trivia.

Knowlton Nash: There's monkey business going on in space, and the Soviet Union isn't very happy about it. The monkey is on board a Soviet satellite launched last week for an experiment on weightlessness. The monkey was strapped down, but he's managed to free one arm, and now he's pressing every button and pulling every knob within reach. And he's jeopardizing the whole mission. The Soviets say they may have to bring the satellite back earlier than expected. The monkey's name is Yerosha. In English, that means 'troublemaker' [7 Oct. 1987].

Soviet politics were described by terms used in Canadian politics. There was no attempt to situate Soviet practices or the use of words by communists in any other context. For instance, the temporary eclipse of Boris Yeltsin's career was described as follows:

Sheldon Turcott: The Soviets are revealing more details about the firing of Boris Yeltsin. He's the former Communist Party boss of Moscow, a strong reformer. He was dismissed yesterday for criticizing the slow pace of change. Today, the party newspaper, *Pravda*, printed what it called excerpts from the meeting where Yeltsin was fired. Speakers are quoted, accusing Yeltsin of huge crimes and of trying to split the leadership. And Soviet leader Mikhail Gorbachev said Yeltsin was destroyed by his personal ambition [13 Nov. 1987].[7]

First, one must notice the language used to describe what happened to Yeltsin. He was not purged, but *fired* (twice) or *dismissed*, like a waitress from a truck-stop. Second, common sense might wonder how a 'strong reformer' could legitimately be accused of 'huge crimes.' And if the accusation was illegitimate, did this mean that his criticism of the slow pace of change was legitimate? Particularly ominous, at least in the context of Soviet politics, was Gorbachev's remark that Yeltsin 'was destroyed by his personal ambition.' These matters, however, depend for their resolution on the visualization of Gorbachev, considered below in sections 10 and 11 (chapter 4).

The second category of Soviet news expressed the theme '*Glasnost* is good for you.'[8] A transition story, which visualized the USSR as changing in a 'progressive' direction, concerned the 1988 May Day parade:

Peter Mansbridge: It's May Day, a day of rallies and parades to honour the workers of the world, especially the Communist world, where the biggest celebration of all took place. Moscow's Red Square was a sea of flags and banners and balloons, with none of the military hardware usually on display. It seemed more a celebration of Soviet leader Mikhail Gorbachev's policies of *glasnost*. And it was cheered on by an apparently united Politburo, including Igor Ligachev, who was rumoured to have been demoted. Also in the crowd were Western diplomats, who have boycotted May Day ceremonies since the Soviet Union invaded Afghanistan in 1979. [1 May 1988]

In this visualization, *glasnost* meant the following things: 1 / an end to Soviet sabre rattling (no more 'military hardware' on parade); 2 / a united Politburo (Ligachev was forgiven; Yeltsin, we recall, destroyed himself through ambition, like Shakespeare's Julius Caesar): and 3 / a reintegration of the Soviet Union into the comity of nations (Western diplomats attended the parade). The imagery was continued into the area of Soviet foreign policy as well, as is indicated in chapter 3.

A second story, concerning the church in the Soviet Union or, more generally, the relationship between Christianity and communism, had to be more delicately handled for several reasons. First, one of the aspects of Solzhenitsyn's account of the USSR that Westerners have found difficult to understand or to accept is his view of Russian Orthodox Christianity. The reasons, no doubt, lie in the distinctive forms of Western and Eastern Christianity, the origins of which lie in antiquity. Within Russian Orthodoxy, there is a further distinction to be made between the Russian Orthodox church abroad and the church that had been recognized in the USSR by the Soviet government. Relations between the two Russian churches were complex; relations between each of the churches and the Soviet government were considerably simpler. The Russian Orthodox church abroad had no official relations with the Soviet government. Relations between the Russian Orthodox church and the Soviet government could be described in several ways, all of which are variants on traditional Eastern Caesaropapism. All of these matters require considerable sensitivity in their presentation and analysis.[9] Even more so, the relationship between Christian and Communist spirituality does not lend itself to easy generalization or dramatic presentation. In July 1987, the following account was broadcast on one aspect of this question.

Nash began his introduction as follows: a Russian Orthodox church has been present in the Holy Land for nearly a century and a half. For the first time in twenty years a Soviet government delegation visited Israel to 'survey' church property 'estimated to be worth more than a hundred million dollars.' However, 'efforts to document the property are complicated by the fact that there are really two Russian Orthodox churches; one in Israel and one on the West Bank. As Don Murray reports, they're locked in a bitter battle for recognition' (27 Jul. 1987). Murray visualized the story as one of great complexity: 'Religion, any religion in Israel, is complicated.' He expressed the complexity by means of an unusual metaphor.

Don Murray: Diplomacy dons many robes and it's one of history's small but acute ironies that for twenty years these have been the robes worn by the Soviet Union in Israel. The vestments of the Russian Orthodox church in the so-called Russian compound in Jerusalem. In 1948, in return for recognition by Moscow of the state of Israel, Israel recognized the claim of the Moscow Patriarch, loyal and submissive to the Kremlin, to this and other properties in the newborn state.

Behind the metaphor of robes and vestments was a fairly simple story: the USSR, after twenty years without diplomatic ties, wished to inspect its Israeli property.

Murray then provided a Soviet sound-bite:

Yevgeny Antipov – Soviet Delegation: We came here with two limited, uh, tasks. Uh, first is, uh, to make an inventory of all the Soviet property here in Israel, and ...

The 'second task' was not mentioned. Instead, Murray provided details of the complicated story of Russian Orthodoxy in Israel. The church whose property was being surveyed was in the Russian compound in Jerusalem.

Don Murray: Two kilometres away, on the Mount of Olives, stands the enemy, the Russian Orthodox church abroad, or the White Russian church, as it's known here. Its priests and followers call themselves the true spiritual and legal heirs of the patri-archs and members of the Czar's family, who a century ago bought the land and built the churches in Palestine. Revolution, Russia, 1917, sent the church into exile. And in 1948, while Israel recognized the recently revived Moscow church, the Red church, Jordan recognized the claims of the White church to properties on the West Bank. Today Israel controls the West Bank. But the White church, legally unrecog-nized by Israel, still runs its properties.

Murray next provided a sound-bite from a White church priest:

Father Vladimir Descaron: We think that, uh, our properties are secure.

Don Murray: For the record, he says his hierarchy and the Red church can live side by side. The mask of conciliation soon drops, however. For Father Vladimir, the Red church is still the enemy.

Father Vladimir: They are a complete tool in the hands of the Soviet government. They know that themselves.

Earlier Murray had characterized the Red church as 'loyal and submissive to the Kremlin.' Father Vladimir authenticated this visualization, but his credibility was immediately undermined. Murray indicated the priest was an angry man, and thus not to be trusted. The priest's anger, he said, 'is born of fear that Moscow, if it once again recognizes Israel, will renew its publicly stated claim to White church lands on the West Bank.' On the other side, the White church had a claim on lands owned by the Red church. No attempt to weigh the various claims was made. What Murray did do, however, was indicate the existence of conflict, and conflict was then presented as the dramatic focus of the visualization.

Murray's wrap-up was not so much a reinforcement of the theme of how complicated it all was, as an expression of the complication by a contradic-tory, not to say incoherent, summary. In the midst of these conflicting claims, he said,

stands the Israeli government, arguing this is an internal church matter that it can't, and won't, adjudicate. And so liturgy is accompanied by litigation. In Israel, the war-ring patriarchates battle on, singing the same hymns, chanting the same prayers to almost empty churches. At root, this is a war not about property, but about the past.

About which side may lay rightful claim to the tradition of a thousand-year-old church. A church which today casts only a small shadow on its former self, both inside Russia and abroad. Don Murray, CBC News, Jerusalem.

If the Israeli government wouldn't adjudicate, how could the liturgy be accompanied by litigation? 'Liturgy and litigation' looks like limpid alliteration. At this point, the visualization of 'complicated' religion in Israel was replaced by more bellicose imagery. When Father Vladimir's 'mask of conciliation' was ripped away by CBC correspondent Don Murray, the new mask was revealed: 'warring patriarchates battle on.' But their conflict was futile: the churches were empty, and 'at root' they were not fighting over property anyway. This was a shift: property had been the main topic around which the enmity, the claims, and the imaginary litigation had been visualized. The change made both Red and White churches look ridiculous.

If they had been fighting over property, that, at least, would make sense. It might not have been particularly dignified, but it would have expressed the introductory 'irony' of the Soviet Union wearing diplomatic robes and church vestments at the same time. The sartorial complications were ignored along with the possibility of fighting over a real possession. The two churches, according to Murray, were really fighting over 'the past' and about laying claims 'to the tradition of a thousand-year-old church.' The futility of such a battle was emphasized by the unimportance of the contestants. The church cast 'only a small shadow of its former self.' The final image of this complicated visualization was plain: these two puny churches were squabbling over the past because they had nothing to do in the present. History had passed them by, and they were performing a ridiculous charade thousands of kilometres from their homeland. Even so, the Soviet agents were taking inventory of the hundred million dollars' worth of Israeli property.

A few weeks later, in early August, Michael McIver provided a report from Moscow on the place of the church in Soviet life. Knowlton Nash again provided the introductory visualization.

Knowlton Nash: Organized religion in the Soviet Union. It gets very little support from the state. In fact there have been times when the state has been violently hostile. Yet, the Russian Orthodox church has survived it all. For almost a thousand years.

McIver continued the theme of survival in his opening remarks and explained how it happened.

Michael McIver: The true believers, the life blood of the Russian Orthodox church. Part of the reason the church has survived 999 years. But there's more to survival in a Communist state than believers and the haunting chants of the service. The church is also at the very heart of Russian identity. The Orthodox church was a key force in a consolidation of Russia and the development of its written language, social attitudes, art, and even Russian nationalism.

The identification of the church with Russian ethnic identity, culture, and history as well as with Christianity, and its visualization as consisting of true believers and haunting chants, entailed an ambivalent relationship to the state in so far as Christianity, including its Russian Orthodox form, represents something beyond ethnic identity or political power. Russian Orthodox Christianity, as other Christian denominations, has a world-transcendent direction. Of greater immediate importance, McIver's account presupposed a distinction, which he introduced in the context of foreign-policy analysis as well, between *Russian* and *Soviet*.

Prior to the Bolshevik Revolution, the territory controlled by the Russian Empire was more or less identical to that later controlled by the Soviet government. 'This,' McIver continued,

may explain the roller-coaster ride in church/state relations since the revolution. Stalin first tried to wipe out the church and its clergy, then later revived it. Khrushchev cracked down on the church again. Today, Mikhail Gorbachev is more lenient. Even though church operations are still strictly controlled by very restrictive laws, and its activities are closely monitored by the state.

The 'very little support' of Nash's introduction had become, according to McIver, active persecution in the recent past and strict control under the more lenient Gorbachev. A sound-bite from Metropolitan Pitirim indicated that the church was satisfied with Gorbachev's leniency: 'we've very big opportunities for our church work.' By this visualization, church/state relations were going well, and Gorbachev's leniency was effective.

When things are going well, however, there is no story. And, in fact, church/state relations in the Soviet Union only *seemed* to be satisfactory. McIver was able to locate a spokesperson for 'dissidents,' Alexander Ogorodnikov, and so construct a story where he could employ the usual point/counterpoint technique. Apart from giving his name and additional general information that confirmed the status of the source as a 'dissident,' no attempt was made to indicate the source's *bona fides*.[10] The source, it seems, dissented from the church, not the state. He was of the opinion that the

Orthodox hierarchy were satisfied, according to McIver, 'because the Church leadership has sold out. That serving God and ordinary people, is no longer its top priority.'

Alexander Ogorodnikov – Dissident [voice of translator]: I think the church hierarchy has a lot of compromises in its history, and at the moment is very afraid and represents the interests of the State before those of the church.

But if the 'dissidents' were correct, then perhaps Gorbachev would not be quite so lenient as he was presented. After all, church/state conflict had been visualized as endemic to Soviet life. Now, we know of the importance of maintaining a consistent image in order to ensure credibility, and Gorbachev had consistently been visualized as a reformer. How, then, to account for 'dissident' criticism of the church?

Michael McIver: Ogorodnikov and his friends praise Gorbachev for trying to make Soviet society more open, more democratic. Ogorodnikov himself was recently freed from a labour camp, after serving eight years of a fourteen-year sentence for his radical church views. But these views haven't changed. The dissidents are still demanding the church be given back most of its pre-revolutionary rights.

A sound-bite from Ogorodnikov confirmed this: *Glasnost* would be incomplete, he said, 'if it doesn't touch the church.'

'Dissident' criticism of the church was combined with support for Gorbachev. The image of Gorbachev the reformer remained intact: he was said to have released Ogorodnikov from a 'labour camp' prior to the completion of his sentence. Ogorodnikov merely wished to extend a Gorbachev-style reform to the church. His assertion carried with it the implication that perhaps the church was allied with the 'conservative' members of the Politburo (the hard-line Communists) in opposition to Gorbachev's 'reforms.' As for the nature or content of Ogorodnikov's radicalism, he demanded that the church's pre-revolutionary rights be restored. Nothing at all was said about what these rights might be; nothing was said, for example, about restoring monastic property or converting museums back into churches. But Ogorodnikov was not interested in the church as an institution anyway.

Michael McIver: The top priorities are an end to all state control of church affairs and the right to teach religion anywhere, including in public schools. Now only a child's parents can legally provide religious education, and only in the home. Church leaders say they can live with that.

Metropolitan Pitirim [voice of translator]: Of course, everyone at school must be edu-cated in the beliefs of the state, and there is no antagonism between the church and the state. Even the constitution prohibits hate between believers and non-believers.

The 'radical,' Ogorodnikov, was concerned with education, but the church, according to this visualization, was content with the *status quo*. This con-firmed the imagery of having sold out to the state without having at the same time visualized the state as oppressive. The dissent of the 'dissidents' was not from the state, grown lenient under the ever-reforming Gorbachev, but from the church.

Lest one conclude that Ogorodnikov had painted too perfect a picture or that his testimony was incredible, McIver concluded by reintroducing the earlier distinction between *Soviet* and *Russian*, fringed now with deliberate ambiguities.

Michael McIver: But some believers still have problems. Not officially from the Kremlin, but from elsewhere.

Woman on street [voice of translator]: From one point, we are not prosecuted, but from the other one, I have to hide because I am a believer, and that depends where a person looks.

McIver had said that the 'problems' believers might encounter did not come 'officially from the Kremlin, but from elsewhere.' He didn't say whence, but the woman interviewed seemed to say that she was persecuted because she was a believer. The next sequence did not make matters any clearer.

Michael McIver: But other believers don't care. Their faith is Russian and the Russian church is too strong to let them be intimidated.

Woman #2 [voice of translator]: It is easy because a spirit believes.

Man on street [voice of translator]: I just don't have to be quiet about it. But I am understand perhaps someone have to. But I think this is just a question of person freedom that everyone has to, just to admit, and just be free.

The sources were not particularly coherent, but, *ex hypothesi*, were intended to sustain McIver's visualization. The man seemed to be saying that he, per-sonally, had no difficulties worshipping, but that he understood that perhaps others were not so fortunate. If this man were Russian Orthodox, his reference was probably to Baptists, a Christian sect that had been widely persecuted in the USSR. McIver made no effort to find out about these 'others.' In his wrap-up he reiterated the initial visualization.

Michael McIver: The Communists have discovered that the church is too central to the Russian identity, too close to the heart of what really is Mother Russia to be stamped out, which is why the deep faith of its believers, and the major compromises made by its leaders have helped the church survive to celebrate its thousandth anniversary. It's not healthy, but it survives. Michael McIver, CBC News, Moscow.

Several other stories from the USSR confirmed the significance of *glasnost*. On 18 January 1988, the CBC covered the story of Joseph Begun, initially identified by Nash as 'a human-rights champion,' who was allowed to leave the Soviet Union for Israel. Begun said he was happy at being able to fulfil his dream. The next night, Nash told the story again.

Knowlton Nash: Joseph Begun, the man who won a seventeen-year battle to leave the Soviet Union, arrived tonight in triumph in Tel Aviv. Before he got his exit visa, Begun served three years in prison and nine years in exile in Siberia. The long-time dissident and his family got a joyous welcome. As he held one of his grandchildren, Begun said he was the happiest man in the world. He'd been granted an exit visa as long ago as September, but he stayed in Moscow until the Soviet authorities finally agreed to let his entire family go too.

This was the only story of a Jewish émigré to Israel that we recorded. There were, however, two stories that covered the *return* of 'dissidents' to the USSR.

On 24 August 1987, Peter Mansbridge told of 'the Soviet dissident David Goldfarb,' who had been allowed into theUnited States for medical treatment. Now, he

wants to do what most released dissidents never do, go back home. He says it isn't because of political reasons or being disillusioned with life in the West. It's because the emotional pull of family ties in Moscow is just too much. Goldfarb, a top scientist, had struggled for years for the moment last fall when he arrived in New York. But now he and his wife are finding that life without their daughter and her family is unbearable, and Moscow won't let them out.

Nothing was said of the wickedness of this specific Soviet policy nor of there being anything at all reprehensible in refusing to allow Soviet citizens to leave that country, nor why anyone, Jewish or not, might wish to leave in the first place, unless being a 'dissident' meant you also wished to emigrate. But then one wonders why there are 'dissidents' in the first place. Where do they come from? Are they produced, so to speak, by Soviet government policy? No hints can be found on the CBC. They are simply there, part of the Soviet scene, normal and, indeed, expected. In a sound-bite, Goldfarb said: 'They cannot come here, so we decided to go there,' as if that were the most ordinary thing in the world. Mansbridge indicated *indirectly* that Goldfarb's position was unusual.

Peter Mansbridge: Goldfarb is risking his health and his freedom to see the daughter he misses. He'll formally apply, tomorrow, for a visa. The Soviet embassy says Moscow will have to decide.

Common sense might have anticipated a more dramatic visualization: Goldfarb's personal suffering was increased by deliberate Soviet government policy. In the face of this policy, Goldfarb chose to risk his health and his freedom to be reunited with his daughter. No visualization was made of this painful family drama, or of the cause of that pain – namely, Soviet policy. However, nothing was said either about the treatment he had received in New York, or whether it was finished. Finally, nothing was said about the details of Goldfarb's putting his health at risk: What was his illness?[11] Why could it not be treated in the USSR?

The other immigration story surfaced in connection with the aforementioned July 1987 visit of the Soviet officials to Israel on their inspection tour of church property. Correspondent Don Murray mentioned the flow of Soviet Jews to Israel in the body of his report, along with speculation on the purpose of the visit by the officials. In his introduction, however, Peter Mansbridge quoted, without additional comment, a remarkable statement from a Soviet source.

Peter Mansbridge: The head of the first Soviet delegation to visit Israel in twenty years said today he's been approached by Israelis who want to go back to the Soviet Union. This is a reversal of the usual direction of Jewish emigration, but Yevgeny Antipov didn't deny that thousands of Soviet Jews want to settle in Israel.

Presumably the only thing that is stopping a mass exodus of Jews from Israel to the USSR is the reluctance of Moscow to accept them, which was, after all, Goldfarb's alleged problem.

Three other Soviet stories indicated the goodness of *glasnost*. In August 1987, the CBC reported on an unusual phone-in show.

Knowlton Nash: *Glasnost* is the name of Mikhail Gorbachev's new policy of openness, and there's been a remarkable demonstration of it on Soviet television: a phone-in program on the use of Soviet troops in Afghanistan. A panel answered questions on the Afghanistan war that would have been unthinkable just a few months ago.

Russian official [voice of translator]: It's the most painful question, and it's no accident that the Twenty-seventh Communist Party Congress called Afghanistan a bleeding wound.

Knowlton Nash: Phones lit up as viewers called in to express concern about the loss of life. A military adviser answered.

Military adviser [voice of translator]: There are no wars in which people do not die. We have losses there too. That's indisputable. Our soldiers, carrying out their inter-nationalist duty, demonstrate courage and heroism, and, of course, often die.

Knowlton Nash: The public response to the phone-in voiced deep concern about Afghanistan, although the questions that were asked did seem to be more penetrat-ing than the answers. And that's *The National* for Thursday, August 20th. For CBC News, I'm Knowlton Nash.

According to Nash's visualization, a phone-in show in the Soviet Union was 'remarkable.' There was no corroboration by the CBC Moscow correspon-dent that the televised performance was, in fact, comparable with a Western phone-in show. Instead, there was Nash's account, plus a Soviet feed. Given the ease of faking such a sequence, the CBC showed considerable trust in Soviet TV by presenting the sequence at face value.

Two other stories, which were even more remarkable, were presented by the CBC without even a hint that there might be anything at all suspect in using the material made available by Soviet authorities. On 2 December 1987, Knowlton Nash announced:

Soviet authorities have given what's being called a sensational example of Mikhail Gorbachev's new policy of *glasnost* or openness. Members of a French television crew were allowed to take pictures inside a Soviet labour camp. It's the first autho-rized glimpse the West has ever had of how prisoners work, eat, and sleep behind the gates of a Gulag penal colony. A thin scattering of snow dusted this Gulag southeast of Moscow just a few days before this month's Washington superpower summit. The prisoners are described by the Soviets as anti-social elements, misfits, and thieves. Alexander Solzhenitsyn called them the forgotten and the damned. They spend their years in an assembly shop, or in a sawmill making crates to carry vegetables. In the dining hall, they removed their hats, but they didn't take off their coats. Thin fish soup with noodles was served. Prisoners picked out the bones. The members of the camera crew weren't allowed to talk to the prisoners or to see the mentally ill. The brief look at one day in the life of a Gulag ended with the well-lit dormitory and its double bunked beds where the prisoners spend ten hours every day. It was here the camera crew saw the face of human misery as men faced up to a new year in camp. The visit ended with a look at the pictures on the walls that were put there by prisoners past and present.

In describing the country that invented the Potemkin village, the naïvety of the account by CBC script writers regarding to the admittance of Western media is remarkable. First, the facilities of the Gulag are called labour camps, not concentration camps. This usage conforms to the Soviet penal code, though it hardly describes the reality. Second, no reason was given for the French television crew being allowed in 'just a few days before this month's Washington superpower summit.' Could it be that the two events were related? Third, the implicit point/counterpoint of Soviet officials and Solzhenitsyn is simply bizarre. In his book, *The Gulag Archipelago*, Solzhenitsyn described at length the distinct kinds of *zek*. Some indeed were thieves, and they were employed very effectively by the Gulag administration to police the non-thieves. And what are 'anti-social elements?' Who are these 'misfits'? In the language of common sense they are innocent human beings. No attention was paid to the otherwise inexplicable (and so, 'normal') jurisprudence that found it reasonable to throw 'misfits' or 'anti-social elements' into concentration camps. Even the briefest visualization of how the *zeks* got there might have reduced the complicity of the CBC in the 'face of human misery' they presented.[12]

The third story, equally amazing in its own way, concerned the staff of the KGB:

Soviet citizens have something new to read in their newspapers, a column by the KGB. Soviet spy masters are coming in from the cold with a regular feature about agency aims and activities. Going public is a first in the KGB's secretive history and the latest twist in the Soviet campaign of *glasnost* [14 Apr. 1988].

According to this visualization, *glasnost* has transformed the organs of state terror into the Ann Landers of *Pravda*. The most peculiar thing about this story is that the CBC intended its audience to believe it.

The third category of stories, dealing with domestic life in the USSR, was concerned with essentially trivial items. The first appeared on 13 October 1987. Nash provided the introduction:

Knowlton Nash: The Soviet Union has a new law that cracks down on the abuse of liquor. The law raised the legal drinking age from eighteen to twenty-one, allowed liquor stores to open for only five hours a day, and increased penalties for being drunk in public. And the police have been encouraged to catch drunk drivers. Our Moscow correspondent, Michael McIver, reports.

In McIver's visualization,

cars were valuable possessions, traffic was light, and the number of accidents is astounding. It's so high, they started talking about it on network newscasts. In the first eight months of this year there have been 151,000 accidents, 165,000 people injured, and 23,000 killed. And alcohol is the biggest cause.

Despite a 'national advertising campaign,' higher penalties for drunk driving, and restricted access to alcohol,

the number of alcohol-related accidents has declined only slightly. A random spot check on a Soviet highway. The passenger in this car is sober; the driver isn't. On the floor, a bag full of vodka bottles.

Police #1 [voice of translator]: Why did you give the wheel to a person who is drunk?

Passenger [voice of translator]: I didn't know he was drunk.

Police #1: How can that be? His breath is so bad you can't stand near him. How could you not know?

Michael McIver: Such encounters are not uncommon.

Police #2 [voice of translator]: How much did you drink today?

Man #2 [voice of translator]: Nothing.

Police #2: Nothing? What are you talking about? You smell of alcohol.

Man #2: I was drunk yesterday.

Police #2: You were drunk yesterday? How much did you drink and why?

Man #2: It was my birthday.

McIver supplied the conclusion to this Potemkin video: a breathalizer test indicated he was still drunk.

In point of fact, alcoholism was a matter of major social and economic concern to the Soviet authorities.[13] McIver's visualization confirmed the major strategic message: the Soviets are really just like us. And where they differ, they are striving to become like us.

Michael McIver: But alcohol isn't the only problem. Police say the generally poor condition of the roads is another major cause of accidents. They're full of dips and holes and, usually, even the worst ones aren't marked. One night a woman I know drove into one on a main street that was two metres deep, and it didn't even have a warning sign in front of it. As for pedestrians, well, many of them consider oncoming traffic and crosswalks to be totally irrelevant. It can be breathtaking to watch the risks some of them take. Perhaps the reason for all this, a police official said recently, is that the boom in car ownership is happening so quickly here that people, and those responsible for the roads, to many of those who drive and walk on them, have not yet quite adjusted to the automotive age. Michael McIver, CBC News, Moscow.

On *The Journal*, 6 November 1987, David Gilmour reviewed *A Day in the Life of the Soviet Union, May 15, 1987*, which consisted of the results of one hundred photographers' efforts during the specified twenty-four hours. Some of them, he said,

shot morning calisthenics and children getting an out-of-season tan; others looked, with nostalgia, for Tolstoy's Russia. Getting permission to unleash that many cameras in a country as self-protecting as the USSR took years.

Of course, no reason for the 'self-protection' of the Soviet Union was offered. Instead a sound-bite from 'Canadian photographer, Andrew Stewicky' was provided. He was introduced as having 'shot from before dawn to late at night, capturing the faces, the moods, of the Soviet Republic of Uzbekistan, on the Turkish border, where the Islamic religion is still practised.'

Andrew Stewicky – Photographer: And the place where I was, was very, very small. It show. They always look at me like some stranger going around. So, I speak a little bit Russian, so I talk with them, they ask me what I am doing here, why I am shooting them, so I explain about this project, but not too many people know about it.

David Gilmour: Photography is a competitive business, and this is the photograph of Stewicky's which finally made it into the book. *A Day in the Life of the Soviet Union* will be available in bookstores this week.

Like any picture book, it will be available soon in bookstores near you, which again indicated how normal the USSR really was.

On 21 January 1988, *The Journal* broadcast two stories on the Soviet Union, both of which emphasized the honesty and forthrightness of the Soviet government. One dealt with the failure of Gorbachev's attempt to reduce alcohol consumption.

Susan Harada: The campaign wasn't working and Mikhail Gorbachev has to admit it. In 1985 the Soviet leader cut back sales of liquor, hoping to make citizens healthier and more hard working. The results? Long line-ups for vodka, and a booming black market. The solution? Two hundred new wine and beer stores are opening in Moscow.

No attempt was made to indicate the obvious meaning of the facts reported: the economic laws of supply and demand can override government decisions regarding public health and productivity. Instead, 'Gorbachev' was visualized as having to admit that a basically good campaign was being frustrated. No attempt was made to visualize the cause of his frustrations, and certainly nothing was said to indicate the existence of a connection between alcoholism and Soviet life.

The second story dealt with homeless children.

Susan Harada: *The Journal Diary* for January 21st. The Soviets have known for decades that they were not living in Paradise. Now their government is admitting it. Some of the admissions have been very painful. One involves Soviet children. Invisible children, or invisible until recently. Not talked about, the homeless, the orphaned. *Glasnost* has made them visible again. The Soviets now say their first social priority is the care of more than a million homeless children.

The theme of the Soviet Workers' Paradise is an old one; according to Harada, it has long been known to be fraudulent. The evidence under *glas-*

nost has nothing to do with the apparatus of state terror, the problems it has caused or the difficulties of dismantling it. Rather the non-paradisal existence of Soviet citizens was made clearly evident by the presence of orphans. This is why we are to believe it is their first social priority. Harada went on to say that Raisa Gorbachev herself

has lent her support to the new Lenin's Children's Fund, an organization that has run completely against the Soviet grain by soliciting donations from around the world. Moscow Children's Home Number Five, home for 135 pre-schoolers, neglected, abused, abandoned. Some by very young women. The Soviets are particularly worried about a recent rise in the number of abandoned children. Some experts think it indicates a basic deterioration of the Soviet family.

One wonders where these children came from. Perhaps from the very young women? And if there is a basic deterioration, why is it taking place? Is there something wrong with the *Sovietness* of the family in the USSR, or are families deteriorating everywhere, including in the Soviet Union? Some such questions did occur to the person who wrote Harada's script, since the next part of her report provided an account of how, despite all this pain and family deterioration,

Lenin's vision of a balanced workforce has been achieved. Half of all Soviet workers are female. But that has naturally changed the way Soviet children are raised. Olga is an architect, like thousands of other Soviet women. Soviet men steer well clear of housework and child care. And if she married, she'd be a mother, a worker, and a maid.

Olga [voice of translator]: There are too many responsibilities. We work just like the men, then we look after the apartment, and then the child. It's too difficult to care for a child and a husband.

First of all, there could be nothing wrong with Lenin's vision: half the workers are female, just as half the population is female. Accordingly, it must be the sexism of Soviet men that lies at the heart of the deterioration of the Soviet family. Women, especially very young ones, who have not, one assumes, attained the position Olga has, would rather abandon their infants than marry and have to take care of a husband *and* a child. By implication a normal Soviet family, untainted with sexism, consisted in a single female parent with a child in day-care. Such a vision of normalcy lies behind an otherwise incoherent wrap-up:

Susan Harada: The Soviets have always thought of themselves as people who particularly treasure children. It seems now they must face the fact that they have trea-
sured their own, and ignored the pain and fear of a million others.

Normal Soviets love children; likewise, normal Soviet citizens share or
rather embody Lenin's vision of a 'balanced' workforce. Owing to the
deplorable but also unmentionable sexism of Soviet men, these normal men
and women must face the painful fact of a million orphans. Who could
doubt their ability to do so?

On a lighter note, CBC viewers were informed a month later that Astro
Pizza, on sale in Moscow, 'is doing a booming business outside sports stadi-
ums in the Soviet capital' (*The Journal*, 17 Feb. 1988). On 2 May 1988,
Susan Harada noted that not only were Pepsi and pizza available, but
McDonald's was opening twenty restaurants in Moscow.

Susan Harada: The Soviets aren't noted for their fast food so the business of the
golden arches should be brisk. The advance word has been good. McDonald's was
recently praised in a Soviet TV documentary for its quality, efficiency, and for its policy of hiring young people. The first McDonald's will be for foreigners only. Moscovites will have to put off their Big Mac attacks until late next year. The first outlets
for locals will be located on Gorky Street, just a stone's throw from the Kremlin.
Burgers will sell for two rubles, about four dollars, Canadian.

Two weeks later, *Venture* did a major report, as Robert Scully put it, on 'the
notion that the Golden Arches should stretch from the Polish border to the
Caspian Sea.' Apparently, McDonald's had expected to be present at the
1980 Moscow Olympics. According to George Cohon, the president of
McDonald's Restaurants of Canada, which was going to operate the Soviet
outlets,

those talks broke down. Kept reading their press-on thing, you know, be persistent,
be determined. We started in the early 'eighties to try to have a permanent presence,
and it wasn't until last year when, when *glasnot*, *dereshtroka* [his pronunciations],
openness, restructuring, came into play, that we were able to really make some headway and sign the ...

Robert Scully: So, in a nutshell, no Gorbachev, no Bolshoi Mac. If he hasn't been
there ...

George Cohon: Well, we woulda hung in, I mean, I, I would like to think that, you know, the project was, uh, important enough to us as a corporation and to me as an individual that we woulda kept going, but I think that, that if you, if you say what Gorbachev has done, and the mood there, um, it sure had sped up the process, and ...

Robert Scully: We also have a bit of a, a, um, I guess a cliché view of the Soviet economy. To us it's all queues in front of empty stores and shortages, and that's not very fair, but there's some truth to it. And, uh, won't there be what the economists call a perverse effect; I mean, the shortage'll displace itself. People will line up in front of your restaurant and, and there won't be any Macs.

George Cohon: Well, I think the McDonald's in Moscow will be the highest-volume McDonald's in the world.

The 'cliché view of the Soviet economy,' whether 'fair' or not, presented a real problem to McDonald's. How to ensure that they could get the right quality of food, so that the Big Mac tastes the same in Moscow as it does in Toronto, or Vancouver, New York, or Rio?

Robert Scully: So you'll have to get the meat before the grocery stores then, because they do run out.

George Cohon: Well, they've got 280 million people there. The question of whether they have enough meat to supply 20 McDonald's. I don't think it'd be much of a problem. The important thing is that the quality of the meat is, is 100 per cent pure beef, that the bun is baked the proper way, that the, uh, that the packaging is right. All those things that exist at McDonald's around the world are important to us.

According to this visualization, the cliché view of the Soviet economy was irrelevant: McDonald's would get its beef.

There was another problem or another cliché about investing in the USSR.

Robert Scully: Now, they're a 51 per cent partner, uh, you're the 49 per cent partner, but you've said that you're not too worried about taking out profits now. You want to reinvest, as you've done elsewhere, so you'll end up with a pretty big chain in a few years. But what if the Gorbachev mood or the system changes? You, you'll be on the hook with this huge asset that the system could take back from you.

Cohon wasn't worried. Business was risky everywhere

George Cohon: I guess anywhere you go in the world you, you know, we reinvest. In this country, as an example, we have 550 restaurants, and we'd still reinvest with 550. I guess that's a risk anywhere you go in the world, but there are companies that have dealt in the USSR for years and years, and I guess systems change, and, and head people change, but once they make a contract, I am inclined to think that I can trust them, and it'll be a partnership.

Scully drew the obvious conclusion: the Soviet Union was open for business.

Robert Scully: There are a lot of Canadian business people, some of them watching us right now, who'd love to trade with the Soviet Union. We have good relations. We share a lot of geography. But, uh, if it takes twelve years at a shot, they're not going to want to go. So what could you tell them?

George Cohon: One thing is, don't get discouraged, I guess. I would, I would just press on. I'd be persistent, and I think the mood is changing now. They're open for business, they want to do business, and I, in jest, but I'm sort of serious, call it burger diplomacy. I think if companies like McDonald's do business with them, then the world'll be a better place to live in. For all the Canadian businessmen that are out there, trying to do a deal, hang in, I think you'll get it done. Just work at it.

It is no exaggeration to suggest that the president of McDonald's was a script-writer's dream. He saw no problems involved in starting up a fast-food restaurant chain in the Soviet Union that would market a product identical to that produced in Rio and Vancouver. There were no problems being in a minority partnership with the Soviet government. Persistence at the fine art of burger diplomacy has made the world a better place.

As if to add sweetness to perfection, on *The National* for 12 June 1988, Peter Mansbridge introduced a report, taken from CBS, of a Soviet beauty contest, 'complete with bathing suit competitions,' despite the fact, according to Mansbridge, that such contests 'are losing favour in the West.'

Burt Quint [CBS]: Julia Markava says her mama doesn't like what she's doing tonight and she's glad her boyfriend is out of town. But for Julia and the other contestants in Moscow's first beauty contest, this is *perestroika*, part of the restructuring of Soviet life, and these women, students, teachers, economists, housewives, are beating the trail to the world of Western-style beauty. Their maps, the foreign films and magazines, are becoming more available. The girls' steps are uncertain, but they certainly are enthusiastic. In this country, equality means women work full-time in the toughest jobs and get no help at home from the menfolk. On the other hand, the state-controlled media praises the pageant for demonstrating that Soviet women are not just strong and active and decisive, that they must be beautiful as well. As this man says, as though discovering a new socialist truth.

Man #1 [voice of translator]: Men like to look at beautiful women. If a women is beautiful, she should be able to show it.

Burt Quint: And they did on Moscow Television Tonight. Tonight, Miss Moscow, and if this kind of thing catches on, who knows, maybe tomorrow, the world.

Beauty contests, McDonald's, Pepsi, pizza, drunk drivers, sexism, advertising and check-stop, these are the images of *glasnost* that the CBC supplied its audience. On policy matters, audiences were told that *glasnost* has transformed the KGB and the Gulag, and that the church would do well to catch up to the great reformer, Gorbachev. Those persistent but negative sides of Soviet life were either clichés, and so could be ignored, or were rapidly ending. During the period studied, two areas of trouble remained, Afghanistan and the rebellions of ethnic minorities in the Soviet Union.

6   IMPERIAL HEADACHES

One of the perennial problems of imperial politics consists in reconciling the universalist aspirations of empire with the particularist identifications of its several constituent communities. The available options are, in fact, somewhat limited. In antiquity, the crisis of the Athenian Empire consisted, in part, of the irreconcilability of domestic democratic politics with a foreign policy that was indistinguishable from tyranny. Alexander sought to unify Greek and Asiatic through the symbolic mass marriage of Persians and Macedonians. The Romans were more successful in so far as they were able to identify Roman law with the Stoic symbolism of natural law, and Roman citizenship with Stoic cosmopolitanism. The universalism of Western medieval Christianity achieved an even better symbolic expression of universality in so far as the church represented the world-transcendent aspirations of Catholic humanity. From its inception, however, the church was strained as much by the problem of the 'nations,' the *gentes*, as by doctrinal differences.

Later claims to universality suffered under the insuperable handicap of having to deal with experiences that, with Christianity, were left in God's hands, to deal with as he saw fit, after humans had died. Salvation, that is,

was by divine grace in death. One of the consequences for politics was to
deprive pragmatic human action of ultimate significance. Of course, this
way of dealing with the relationship between religious universality and
political particularity ended with what we conventionally call the Middle
Ages, and even then the various Christian compromises in both the Orthodox East and the Latin West had been under attack by sectarian activists.

Considered in this light, the modern solution has been, characteristically,
to do one of two things, neither of which has proved to be particularly satisfactory. The first has been to inflate one particularity, usually that of a specific nation, into a carrier of universality. Several Messianic nationalisms
and versions of a vertical mosaic were invented to deal with this problem.
The second and more recent attempt at reconciliation of universal and particular has been ideological rather than religious. In place of world-transcendent aspirations to posthumous salvation by divine grace, ideological
sectarians attempt to extend grace to themselves, as Nietzsche put it, and to
undertake their own salvific activity. Of these new and ersatz religious
movements, the human beings living in the territory once controlled by the
USSR have had to endure two: pan-Slavism and communism. Resistance typically has combined ethnic and religious elements. Difficulties within the
Soviet Empire prior to its collapse were, so to speak, part of a long tradition.

During the course of this study, there were riots and murders in Armenia
and Azerbaijan, and war continued in Afghanistan. Coverage of the first
topic emphasized the violence and ethnic conflict. The first story in our
sample, however, dealt with another ethnic hostage to communist fortune,
the Crimean Tatars.

Knowlton Nash: There was an unprecedented meeting today at the Kremlin. The
Soviet president, Andrei Gromyko, met for more than two hours with a delegation
of Crimean Tatars. A quarter of a million Tatars were deported from their homeland
by Josef Stalin in 1944. They were accused of collaborating with the Nazi invaders.
Now, they want their homeland back. Today's meeting with Gromyko came after
authorities allowed the Tatars to hold a weekend of protest near Red Square (27 Jul.
1987).

The impact of this story had nothing to do with the fate of the Crimean
Tatars, and everything to do with the allegedly new regime, with *glasnost*
and Gorbachev. The meeting was 'unprecedented,' and earlier the Tatars
had been allowed to hold a protest. Nothing was said to indicate the atro-
ciousness of 'Stalin's' act, or who accused them of collaborating, or whether

it was true that they collaborated and, if true, how many did so and why. That there might be a genuinely dramatic story connected to the fate of the Crimean Tatars never seems to have occurred to anyone at the CBC.[14]

The Armenia story began on 25 February 1988 with an anchor-only report by Peter Mansbridge.

Peter Mansbridge: There are reports tonight that Soviet tanks and troops have been sent to parts of the Soviet Republic of Armenia to stop demonstrations there. For days, thousands of people have been protesting in Armenia over a disputed area in a neighbouring republic. Witnesses in the capital city, Yerevan, say soldiers and tanks have taken up positions there and in one other city. Soviet officials confirm the protests are going on, but won't give any other details.

A week later, Mansbridge introduced a report from Michael McIver.

Peter Mansbridge: The ethnic rioting which took place in the Soviet Union over the weekend was apparently even more violent than anyone expected. It's the first official comment since the rioting took place. The Soviet news agency, Tass, today said thirty-one people were killed. The trouble's been going on for nearly a month and was sparked by a dispute over the boundary between Armenia and Azerbaijan. Our Moscow correspondent, Michael McIver, reports.

McIver's report from Moscow, not Azerbaijan, was a more lengthy version of Mansbridge's introduction. The information was taken directly from Soviet TV, which in turn consisted of an anchor-only reading of a Tass report.

Michael McIver: The TV news anchorman simply read the official news agency Tass story. That was it. No elaboration. No original reporting, even though thirty-one people have died in the worst known unrest in the Soviet Union since the early 'twenties.

The visualization of these events as 'ethnic rioting' or 'ethnic unrest' established the angle that was subsequently developed. However, Peter Mansbridge summarizing Michael McIver summarizing Soviet TV reading Tass is not a story. The story was that the Soviet television audience was informed of anything. 'Still,' said McIver, 'it was the first time since Monday [three days earlier] that ordinary Soviets have been told anything at all about the riots in Sumgait.' He went on to provide a background summary of recent events. Sumgait is where Azerbaijanis went on a rampage in response to massive peaceful demonstrations in neighbouring Armenia last week. There, hundreds of thousands of people went into the streets to demand their republic be reunited with Nagorno–Karabakhskaya. Nagorno–Karabakhskaya was severed from Armenia in 1923 and made part of Azerbaijan, even though most of the people in the region are Armenian. The riots in Sumgait, which erupted on Sunday, were finally suppressed when troops with armoured cars moved in and a curfew was imposed. But, before order could be restored, unconfirmed eyewitness reports say, one family of seven was among the murdered, women were raped, and there was widespread looting. Michael McIver, CBC News, Moscow.

Common sense might wonder why Nagorno–Karabakh was severed from Armenia in 1923. Why were the Azerbaijanis rioting in response to a peaceful demonstration in another Soviet state? What kind of a town was Sumgait? The focus, however, was on discontinuous, contextless events, followed by a dramatic visualization of troops moving in to restore order, but too late to prevent rape and rapine. It was a splendid example of Postman's 'Now this ... ' technique of trivialization.

On 9 March 1988, Peter Mansbridge provided another anchor-only report.

Peter Mansbridge: Mikhail Gorbachev says he won't be making any change in the status of a Soviet Republic that was the scene of violent rioting last month. But the Soviet leader did tell the Communist Party today that an investigation is under way into the clashes that shook Azerbaijan. Soviet authorities are now reporting that the rioting left thirty-two people dead.

Mansbridge did not say why Gorbachev wouldn't be making any changes. The next night, Mansbridge's report was accompanied by 'pictures smuggled out of the Soviet Union' purporting to show 'tens of thousands of people protesting in the streets.' Again he mentioned that the Armenians living in Azerbaijan wanted to join the Armenian republic. He did not say why, nor did he attempt to indicate what this 'tension' signified. On 13 March 1988, Mansbridge reported a peaceful demonstration in Moscow. As in the earlier reports, he mentioned that thirty-two people had been killed in Azerbaijan.

Two days later, McIver provided another report, this one twice as long as his earlier third-hand version taken from Tass. Mansbridge provided the introduction and reiterated the earlier visualization. These had been 'ethnic riots.'

Peter Mansbridge: A top Soviet law official says gangs of young Azerbaijanis commit-ted terrible crimes against Armenians during ethnic riots last month. The Soviet deputy prosecutor general says the disorder in Azerbaijan was massive. More than thirty people died. The clashes involve a region of Azerbaijan inhabited mostly by ethnic Armenians, who want the area reunited with Armenia. The CBC and the TF-1 network of France have obtained exclusive videotape of the aftermath of the unrest. Our Moscow correspondent, Michael McIver, tells us what it shows.

What it showed was as obvious as it was dramatic – namely, the effects of violence.

Michael McIver: This videotape graphically documents the consequences of what must have been widespread disturbances in Stepanakert, Nagorno–Karabakh. Dam-aged buildings, some of them gutted by fire. Vandalized buses. Cars, with their win-dows smashed. Authorities have acknowledged that there was racial trouble in Stepanakert, but have refused to give many details. Judging by this video, the vio-lence was more brutal and widespread than previously believed.

Resident #1 [voice of translator]: I'm seventy-four years old and they knocked all my teeth out.

Resident #2 [voice of translator]: They hit me round the head until I lost conscious-ness, and then they broke my legs.

McIver then described the violence more generally and provided a visual-ization of the meaning in accord with Mansbridge's introduction.

Michael McIver: Homes were looted and set on fire. One woman even displayed a charred picture of Lenin, to show that the vandals have spared very little. Armenian Christian residents of Nagorno–Karabakh, who make up 75 per cent of the popula-tion in that mountainous region of Azerbaijan, have demonstrated in unity with hun-dreds of thousands of people in neighbouring Armenia, in late February. They were demanding Nagorno–Karabakh be severed from Azerbaijan and reunited with Arme-nia. These demonstrations provoked a violent response from Muslim Azerbaijanis, who attacked Armenians from Sumgait and other cities and towns in Azerbaijan, including, it's clear from this tape, Stepanakert. Altogether thirty-four people died, according to Soviet authorities. Unofficial reports say the death toll is far higher.

McIver then provided an introduction of his own, and presented more violence.

Michael McIver: Eyewitnesses filtering into Moscow tell of terrible atrocities.

Man [voice of translator]: I came across a young woman lying on the ground, who had been recently married. Her stomach had been torn open and the baby torn out.

Michael McIver: These horror stories cannot be independently confirmed. The whole area is sealed off to foreign reporters. In order to cool tensions, the Kremlin sent Peter Demachev, a member of the ruling Politburo to Stepanakert. He tried to address a huge rally in the main square of the city, but as the tape shows, the densely packed crowd jeered him, and tried to shout him down – an extraordinary thing to happen to a Politburo member. Armenians, without exception, insist they support the Soviet leader. They say they're angry with the top party bosses in Azerbaijan, and with the national media based in Moscow, which has given only a sketchy, incomplete picture of events here.

Man [voice of translator]: What they're informing us on the TV is all wrong. I want us to be brothers. Why don't they tell the truth to Gorbachev? We're for truth, and I believe in the Russian people and that they will follow us.

Michael McIver: The Kremlin's got the seemingly impossible task to try and resolve the Nagorno–Karabakh crisis in a way that will satisfy both ethnic groups. If it fails, there could be more trouble. Planning is already under way in Armenia for a general strike at the end of this month, and if that happens, it could touch off another violent response from Azerbaijanis. Michael McIver, CBC News, Moscow.

The emphasis remained on the 'horror stories' that illustrated the ethnic crisis, but why the crisis occurred or what it meant was still a mystery. Of the several topics that might have shed light on these events but were not discussed, the following may serve as an illustration: Why did Armenian Christians and Muslim Azerbaijanis not get along? No mention was made of the fact that the two places where riots took place, Sumgait and Stepanakert, were new cities established during the 1950s and 1960s, and populated by comparatively deracinated inhabitants.[15] The support by Armenians of the Soviet leader was presented as a paradox since they also shouted down a Politburo member and criticized the 'top party bosses in Azerbaijan.' No mention was made of the ethnic composition of those 'top party bosses.' Why were the Armenians angry at Moscow's TV coverage? It is particularly regrettable that no attempt was made to explicate the remark 'I want us to be brothers,' because it expressed so well the problem of ruling any multinational empire, communist or not. McIver's wrap-up summa-

rized nothing but indicated that the story of contextless and enigmatic violence would continue, so stay tuned.

Two weeks later, on 31 March 1988, *The Journal* discussed the events in
Armenia and Azerbaijan. The focus of the visualization was less on the reason for the conflict, which simply repeated the video material from McIver's
report, as on its novelty. Initially, therefore, the story was *getting* the story,
and not its contents.

Paul Griffin introduced the sequence:

There's something happening deep in the Soviet Union that's virtually unprecedented in the nation's history. Details are sketchy, but in the last month revealing
videotape has been smuggled out. The story is about Soviet Armenians, Christians,
who are under the authority of the predominantly Muslim Republic of Azerbaijan.
The Armenians complain of racial discrimination, and oppression. Perhaps surprisingly, they've engaged in mass protests – unheard of in a state where social unrest
has been suppressed for seventy years. From our London bureau, Anne McMillan
has this report.

Anne McMillan agreed:

It's an unprecedented display of dissent in a country whose centralized Communist
autocracy has traditionally come down hard on any kind of protest.

She found the wonderfully named Dr Pravda to add authority to the visualization.

Dr Alexander Pravda, Director, Royal Institute for International Affairs: It's quite
remarkable. It's the first time we've ever had any kind of film from an area of protest
in the Soviet Union. Before, we've always had these areas immediately sealed off,
not just from foreign journalists, but also from outsiders as a whole. You never had
film of this kind being smuggled out, before.

McMillan then summarized the previous reports regarding the ethnic conflicts and the Stepanakert heckling of Politburo member Demachev. At last,
the CBC found a way to account for the ethnic riots without opening up the
question of ethnic diversity, historical hatreds, or other matters that might
indicate the complexity of political reality: the cause of the disorders was
glasnost.

Anne McMillan: It may seem surprising that so many of the protesters carry pictures of Mikhail Gorbachev, and it's his policy of *glasnost* that inspired these people to believe that the Kremlin was at least ready to respond to their demands.

Dr Pravda once again obligingly agreed.

Dr Alex Pravda: What *glasnost* has done is to have created a climate in which people's expectations, expectations of Armenians, in this case, have been raised, and they'd actually thought that by putting their case to Moscow and by coming out on the streets, they could make an impact on a much more flexible government than has existed hitherto.

McMillan again reminded the audience of the recent violence, and pointed to the more general problem faced by Soviet rulers.

Anne McMillan: For the Soviet authorities, the trouble in Nagorno–Karabakh is the tip of a dangerous iceberg. The Armenians are not the only racial group demanding changes in the Soviet Union. Gorbachev has said no to them, because he knows any concessions could open the floodgates for other dissatisfied groups.

Dr Alex Pravda: This, of course, is the largest single and the most intractable problem which faces any Soviet ruler. How to keep control of a heterogeneous empire with a hundred nationalities, where Russians barely form a majority of the population. They're now at 51 per cent and going down fast. So that any symptom of non-Russian protesting in any sense against Moscow, always, I think, puts a great deal of anxiety into the Soviet leader.

Anne McMillan: In order to defuse the Armenian situation, last week Gorbachev announced cultural changes in Nagorno–Karabakhskaya. For example, he said Armenian would become an official language, and a special radio station would be set up for the Armenian population. Whether these limited reforms will satisfy the crowds of protestors remains to be seen. It's a test case, which the Kremlin and the world will be watching closely. For *The Journal*, I'm Anne McMillan.

McMillan's final presentation was a much more adequate description of the realities of Soviet and Trans-Caucasian politics than anything previously presented. It remains surprising, however, that it took the CBC a month to find an 'authorized knower' who could present an account of events that was anything more than superficial cliché. It is surprising, moreover, because the events *were* dramatic and the location *was* exotic, at least to Canadians. Here was one case where events did not have to be extensively retouched to create the 'news of the day' as an entertaining and interesting bit of television.

The remaining four stories on Armenia and Azerbaijan (24 Apr. and 19, 20, 21 May) reverted to the earlier mode, anchor-only talk stories about ethnic demonstrations, protests, rioting, and violence.

The other important difficulty encountered by the Soviet Union was in the southeastern marches of its empire, in Afghanistan. The first stories we recorded on Afghanistan appeared on 8 February. By that time, there was considerable evidence of the increased capability of the mujahedeen to fight the Soviet armed forces. In March and April 1987, the Afghans had attacked across the Oxus River into the Soviet Union.[16] In May, a Soviet *Spetsnaz*, or special forces unit, had been defeated at Paktia, and in June, an Afghan Army offensive in the southeast of the country had been defeated, accompanied by many desertions to the mujahedeen.[17] Regular reports of fighting continued throughout the summer and into the fall, along with reports of car bombs in Kabul.[18] Late in November, President Najibullah called a meeting of the Loya Jirgah, or Grand Assembly, in order to push his program of 'national reconciliation.' This event was protected by a very large Soviet security operation and, in anticipation of the Reagan–Gorbachev summit, was important for public relations as well. In response, the mujahedeen mounted a rocket attack on the capital.[19] It was repeated a few weeks later.[20] Meanwhile, a Soviet-led counter-attack on the mountain town of Khost, near the Pakistan border, southeast of Kabul, was well underway. The fighting went on into January 1988.[21] At the initial announcement of the Khost offensive, the spokesman for the Soviet foreign ministry, Gennadi Gerasimov, went out of his way to say that U.S.-made Stinger anti-aircraft missiles had shut down the Khost airport and specifically mentioned how they had been used to shoot down Antonov-26 transport planes.[22] U.S. and U.N. officials were of the view that Soviet military offensive was a prelude to negotiating a withdrawal.[23]

In his Christmas Eve press conference, Gerasimov mentioned the most decisive weapon in the mujahedeen arsenal – the Stinger missiles. A Stinger is a 35-pound (16-kilogram), shoulder-borne, heat-seeking anti-aircraft missile with a vertical range of 4,900 yards (4,500 metres) and a cross-terrain range of 5–6 miles (8–10 kilometres).[24] It flies at Mach 2.2, and had an estimated hit-ratio in Afghanistan of between 40 and 60 per cent. The first batch of Stingers arrived in the fall of 1986. Reports on the number of Stinger deliveries ranged from twenty to a hundred a month during the fall and winter of 1986–7.[25] By mid-1987, they were proving highly effective against the Soviet heavily armed MI-24 helicopters, known as 'flying tanks,' as well as against fixed-wing jets.[26] Some accounts claimed between one and two Soviet aircraft a day were being shot down by Stingers.[27] In any event, it seems clear that the story of the Stingers is, so to speak, the untold story of the Soviet defeat.

The focus of the CBC stories on Afghanistan was on what might euphemistically be called 'the peace process.' Nothing whatever was said of Soviet defeats leading up to the announcement made by Mikhail Gorbachev at the so-called proximity talks held in Geneva.[28]

On 8 February, Nash provided an anchor-only report.

Knowlton Nash: Mikhail Gorbachev says he's ready to start pulling Soviet troops out of Afghanistan beginning on May 15th. But he said in a statement today that the withdrawal would go ahead only if there's a final peace agreement by the middle of March. Soviet television interrupted a movie tonight to read Gorbachev's announcement to the Soviet people. Gorbachev said the withdrawal from Afghanistan could be completed in ten months if Afghanistan rebels and the Afghanistan government can reach a final accord at talks going on now in Geneva. The Soviets have been in Afghanistan since 1979. They are believed to have more than a hundred thousand troops in the country.

Three things may be noted about this report: the withdrawal was not a retreat, and even less was it the result of military activity by the Afghan resistance. Second, since it was highly unlikely that a peace agreement would be worked out in six weeks, Gorbachev's announcement clearly was a signal of something.[29] Third, it was a shrewd move by Gorbachev in so far as it promised nothing with respect to the major concern of the mujahedeen – namely, self-determination for the Afghan people – but left the impression that a window of opportunity had been opened that would slam shut on 15 May if the United States and Pakistan refused to cooperate. The CBC exercised uncharacteristic restraint in declining to speculate on what this announcement, which was important enough to interrupt a movie on Soviet TV, might mean.

This story was followed by a summary of a statement by General Manuel Noriega that he wanted U.S. troops out of Panama. One of the strategic techniques used in television news production is linking stories together. The linkage here was in the form of parallel language rather than substance. Where Gorbachev was going to pull troops out of Afghanistan, presumably as a gesture of goodwill or because he was a kind man, Noriega 'says the U.S. is an offensive power and its presence violates the Panama Canal Treaty.'

The difficulties Noriega had encountered with the U.S. Drug Enforcement Agency were mentioned, followed by a statistic on U.S. troop strength. The Soviets were believed to have a hundred thousand troops in Afghanistan, and 'there are ten thousand American troops in Panama.' Both stories ended with a response from the U.S. State Department. Regarding Afghanistan, 'the State Department said the announcement is a positive step, but they're waiting to hear more details.' Regarding Panama, 'the U.S. State Department has had no comment on Noriega's position.' The effect of juxtaposing the two stories this way was to sustain the visualization of moral equivalence between the USSR and the United States, while at the same time giving the edge, so to speak, to the Soviets. After all, they were withdrawing.

Unfortunately things did not go according to the plan announced by Gorbachev in February. There followed a series of apologies. On 15 March, Peter Mansbridge made the announcement

Peter Mansbridge: The Soviet Union has delayed plans to pull its troops out of Afghanistan. The Soviets have said the withdrawal will start on May the 15th, provided a peace accord could be reached in Geneva by today. But, there's no peace agreement yet. Moscow says the pull-out from Afghanistan will not begin until two months after any peace accord is signed.30

Three weeks later, on 8 April, hopes had risen. Nash provided the opening visualization.

Knowlton Nash: An agreement has been reached that could lead to peace in Afghanistan and the withdrawal of Soviet troops. The deal was announced this morning in Geneva at talks mediated by the United Nations. Soviet leader Mikhail Gorbachev said later the agreement now means his troops will start pulling out of Afghanistan on May 15th. A White House spokesman says he's delighted and hopeful, but the end of the war may not come quickly. The Afghan rebels were not involved in the peace talks and they say they'll keep on fighting. Terry Milewski reports from Washington.

The agreement 'could' lead to peace, Nash said; but it would not be easy, inasmuch as the Afghan rebels, who were actually doing the fighting, were, on the one hand, said not to be involved, but, on the other, had said they would keep it up until the question of Afghan self-determination was settled. Gorbachev's statement, which Mansbridge had also noted on 15 March, had been made on 8 February, and had gone nowhere. It was simply

a pious but fraudulent hope, a bit of old Soviet information or disinformation made credible by being mentioned just before the views of a White
House spokesman were summarized.[31] In point of fact, the Geneva talks
had stalled because the Americans continued to insist on symmetrical disengagement, and the Soviets continued to resist this precondition on the
grounds that, if they withdrew their troops, but continued to supply the
Afghan army while allowing the Americans to supply the mujahedeen, the
latter would prevail. This would indicate clearly that the Afghanistan government existed solely because of the presence of Soviet troops. By early
April, it was clear that, soon enough, the Soviets would have to agree. The
greatest resistance to meeting the U.S. demands came from President
Najibullah.[32]

Terry Milewski began his report with the same piece of Soviet information, now inflated into an *expectation* that they would 'begin leaving.'

Terry Milewski: More than eight years after they arrived, Soviet troops are expected
to begin leaving Afghanistan next month without achieving their objective, a stable
pro-Soviet regime.

By this account, the Soviets 'arrived' rather than invaded; they failed to
achieve their objective, rather than being defeated in their invasion.
Milewski did not dwell on these unhappy outcomes for Soviet policy but
turned immediately to the universally more exciting topic of fighting and
the costs involved.

Terry Milewski: The cost has been enormous for the Russian troops facing a determined mujahedeen resistance armed with American weapons, and for the Afghan
people, millions of whom are in exile. And now, there is still no cease-fire to a civil
war which brought the Russians in and will go on without them. The U.S. will continue to supply the mujahedeen, and the Soviets will continue to supply their man in
Kabul. But observers expect Najibullah will not survive for long without troops to
prop him up.

The oddity of a civil war that 'brought the Russians in' was overshadowed
by the suggestion of a parallel role of the two outside powers. The Soviets
had 'their man' in Kabul and the United States had 'their' men, the mujahedeen, whom they supplied with arms that cost so many Russian (not Soviet)
lives.

There followed the usual sound-bites to confirm the expectation of continued and increased disorder if the Soviets were to leave. A former U.S.

ambassador expected a collapse of the Soviet-backed regime followed by a 'bloodbath.'

Robert Neumann, former U.S. ambassador: Ah, the question is not whether there will be a bloodbath. There will be a blood bath. The question is how deep, how many, and how long.

What made this outcome the more regrettable, according to the CBC's visualization, was the apparent legitimacy of Soviet interests in Afghanistan. Milewski found an Afghan refugee in Toronto who opposed the agreement as not being in the 'national interest of the Afghan people. It is not representing the Afghan side and, it is giving the Soviet Union a sort of colonialist power over Afghanistan. Afghanistan would always remain under the Soviet influence.' If Afghanistan would otherwise have remained always under Soviet influence, their leaving was a major concession. They were conceding to the Americans, of course, not the Afghans.

Terry Milewski: The Reagan administration was also cautious about that, although it did welcome the agreement. Chief of Staff Howard Baker said he wants to see the fine print on the question of continued Soviet military support to the Kabul regime.

Chief of Staff Howard Baker: Those are details we'll have to examine carefully, but, if it is what it appears to be, it appears to be a very major achievement indeed.

Terry Milewski: For the White House, the Afghan agreement is a definite political bonus because it makes the prospect that much brighter for the Moscow summit at the end of May. For eight years, the United States has made an improvement in relations conditional upon a Soviet pull-out from Afghanistan. If indeed that happens, the improving relations could bring a treaty on strategic arms. Terry Milewski, CBC News, Washington.

The completed visualization of the Soviet defeat in Afghanistan indicated, in the end, that they had walked the extra mile in order to improve relations with the United States. They were willing to leave even without a cease-fire (because the nefarious Americans were supplying 'their' side, the mujahedeen, with weapons). Perhaps this extra effort would improve the possibility of a treaty on strategic arms.

Two days later, the cruelty of the American-backed 'rebels' and 'guerrillas' was indicated in a report by Nash; it was considered important enough to be given the third position in the news line-up.

Knowlton Nash: Government radio in Afghanistan says twenty-nine people were killed today when Afghan rebels shot down a passenger plane near the Soviet border. Radio Kabul said the plane was on a domestic flight when guerrillas fired on it with anti-aircraft rockets.

There is no question that the war in Afghanistan was conducted with considerable ferocity and disregard for conventions whose purpose is to reduce unnecessary suffering, especially by non-combatants. There is also no question that fighting in Afghanistan, either among Afghans or between them and outsiders, has historically or traditionally been vicious. And, finally, there is no doubt that using anti-aircraft missiles on civilian airliners is a nasty business. At the same time, however, one must note that no context was supplied by the CBC. The Canadian audience, therefore, would have to do so. Would they think that the 'passenger plane' might be used to transport Soviet troops, or would they think of an Air Canada 'passenger plane' or some such domestic aircraft being blown out of the sky by murderous guerrillas? A second point: we recorded nothing of what the Soviet occupation had done to the countryside and no story of Soviet atrocities.[33] We found no account, for instance, of exploding dolls used to maim Afghan children and dropped by Soviet helicopters, or of the enormous minefields laid by Soviet troops and what would happen to them when the Soviet armed forces left.[34]

On 14 April, Knowlton Nash announced:

An historic accord setting the stage for a Soviet pull-out from Afghanistan was signed in Geneva today. The accord outlined a step-by-step withdrawal of Soviet troops beginning May 15th. But it does not mean an end to the fighting. Afghan rebels did not attend today's ceremonies, and they say they'll keep on fighting until they've overthrown the Soviet-backed government in Afghanistan. Claude Adams reports.

Adams reported that 'the accords won't end the civil war that's claimed nearly a million lives, [but] they do point to a possible conclusion.' How? Well, nobody could say. The secretary general of the U.N. did, however, provide a useful and sublimely meaningless sound-bite: 'They represent a major stride in the effort to bring peace to Afghanistan and ensure reprieve for these people.'

Adams never did identify who actually signed the accord (Afghanistan, Pakistan, the USSR, and the United States) but passed on quickly to his visualization of the future course of events. The Russians would withdraw their hundred thousand troops, and five million refugees 'will be able to come home.' Out go the Soviets, in come the Afghans. Nothing was said about the sort of a home they were likely to find after years of Soviet occupation.

As for the United States and the USSR, blame was apportioned with equality and impartiality. First of all, the Soviets had *not* been defeated.

Claude Adams: Soviet foreign minister Eduard Shevardnadze denied today the troops were being pulled out because of Soviet inability to win the war. He said Soviet troops had helped the Afghans in a difficult moment, and they were leaving with a sense of duty accomplished.

Unfortunately, since the people against whom the Soviet troops were fighting had not been a party to the accords, it was necessary for the USSR to keep the Kabul government supplied with weapons. Besides, Adams went on,

the Americans have matched this with increased support of the Afghan guerrillas. These superpower arms shipments aren't affected by the Geneva Accord signed today.

George Shultz – U.S. Secretary of State: As the Soviet Union asserts its right to supply arms to those whom it supports in Afghanistan, we do as well.

Claude Adams: Shultz said the U.S. will scale down its support only if the Soviets do. Notably absent from the peace table were the Afghan resistance fighters. From their bases in Pakistan, their leaders called the Geneva peace process a waste of time because it continued to recognize the Communist-backed regime in Kabul. Nevertheless, that regime isn't expected to survive very long once the Soviets withdraw. Claude Adams, CBC News, Geneva.

The next night, 15 April, *The Journal* gave extensive coverage to what Barbara Frum introduced as 'an astonishing agreement aimed at ending the long war in Afghanistan.' The accord, she said, 'creates hope,' but her co-anchor provided a sobering counterpoint:

Paul Griffin: But along with hope arising from the historic achievements of East/West cooperation, there's scepticism. The accord is supposed to pave the way for peace, but already guerrilla fighters in Afghanistan have rejected the plan and vow to continue their fight.

No reason was given for the rejection of this achievement of East/West cooperation, nor was any explanation offered as to why the mujahedeen had not been a party to the Geneva talks. The implication, however, was clear: the mujahedeen were unreasonable in holding up the 'peace process.' According to Griffin's visualization,

the Soviets rolled their forces into Afghanistan to secure the country's fledgling Communist government. But progress towards Soviet withdrawal has accelerated in the past few months. Final obstacles to the agreement were removed in a historic meeting last week in the Soviet city of Tashkent between Mikhail Gorbachev and Afghan party leader Najibullah.

Again the Soviets did not invade; they rolled their forces in. The most natural thing in the world for such forces to do was to 'secure the fledgling Communist government.' One wonders why 'progress towards Soviet withdrawal has accelerated in the past few months.' In reality or in fact, this 'progress' was not unconnected to the activities of the mujahedeen, to the success of the Stinger missiles, and to the U.S. demands for symmetrical disengagement. According to the CBC, however, the 'historic meeting' at Tashkent and the 'astonishing agreement' were visualized as reasons for hope. Nothing the mujahedeen had done would interfere with the consistent, if somewhat fantastic, imagery of the USSR as the world's great peacemaker. On the other side, 'scepticism' was laid at the feet of the United States and the Afghan rebels. The sound-bite from U.S. Secretary of State Shultz was replayed to emphasize the point, along with one from an Afghan spokesman.

Paul Griffin: So, it appears that Afghanistan's war is far from over, and a long awaited agreement is only the first step to peace.

Now, the agreement was visualized as having resulted from Soviet goodwill and their long-standing desire for peace. If they had, in fact, taken the first step, then surely it was up to the Americans and the mujahedeen to take the second.

To discuss the Soviet 'pull-out and the peace plan,' Barbara Frum engaged a journalist writing for a British newspaper and an American employee of the Carnegie Endowment for International Peace. She began by asking the American a question:

Barbara Frum: Selig Harrison, after he signed yesterday's treaty, Soviet foreign minister Eduard Shevardnadze said the USSR accomplished its mission. What did they come away with after eight and a half years of occupation?

Selig Harrison – Carnegie Endowment for International Peace: I don't think they've gotten very much out of it; on the other hand, I don't think that they've been defeated in the strict military sense that they were forced to withdraw at this particular time under direct military pressure. Ah, it's really been a stalemate.

The way out of the 'stalemate,' he said, was to accept this U.N. deal,

which was a face-saving kind of an arrangement. It didn't ah, it didn't require them to abandon the Kabul government and ah, it was a deal which ah, helped them to get out in as graceful a way as possible.[35]

Such realistic or hard-nosed speech about international affairs, especially as touched the Soviet Union, was not often heard by CBC audiences. Frum then intervened and directed a question to the other authorized knower. She also changed the subject. Can the Soviet puppet, Najibullah, survive, she asked, without Soviet troops?

Arthur Kent – London Observer: Over a long term, no. But if the Soviets ah, stage a partial withdrawal, pull back ah, most of their forces to the northern provinces of Afghanistan behind the Hindu Kush mountain range, which bisects the country, and continues substantial arms shipments to Kabul and to government forces in the south, they can frustrate the mujahedeen groups based in Pakistan long enough for perhaps President Najib to garner some measure of political respectability in the world, prove that he can at least hold out for a number of months and, who knows, ah, perhaps invite again as a, as the Soviet foreign minister Eduard Shevardnadze pointed out yesterday, ah invite the Soviets back to protect them against outside interference.

This kind of discussion of *Realpolitik* was also rare; again Frum changed the subject, this time to a safe speculative question about the future of the country. Harrison, the American, confirmed the earlier CBC visualization that the Afghan refugees would come in as the Soviets left. Kent disagreed:

they will not return as long as there is a Communist government in Kabul which can be helped by the Soviets in terms of aerial bombardment because they are not eager to subject their families once again to what we saw in the early years of the war, and, indeed, as recently as January 1988, when I was in Azadran Valley. Flights of eight Soviet SU24s bombing a valley within ten miles of the Pakistan border three times a day. The Soviets are very determined to sustain this government, as you yourself pointed out, and as long as it is there, the Afghan refugees will fear Soviet and Kabul government air force reprisal against the civilian population.

Frum immediately turned back to Harrison and asked him about the possibility of sending a U.N. peacekeeping force, perhaps including Canadians. All Harrison could do was point out the obvious, that no such force was contemplated under the U.N. agreement.[36] Kent was then asked for his predictions and, quite sensibly, he said he expected a 'very long period of instability,' first, because the mujahedeen sought to destroy the Kabul regime, which the Soviets did not wish to see happen, and second, because, apart from their opposition to Kabul, the mujahedeen were united on little else. Lest one be left with a sobering appraisal and no one to blame, co-anchor Griffin provided a postscript or trailer.

Paul Griffin: Less than twenty-four hours after the signing of the accord, the Soviet news agency, Tass, accused the United States of trying to ruin them, by continuing to supply arms to the rebels. In a moment, we'll be back with Friday Night Arts and Entertainment with David Gilmour.

The CBC's visualization of the conflict in Afghanistan was neatly summarized by Nash on 29 April 1988 in his introduction to a story concerned with Afghan refugees in Canada for emergency medical treatment.

Knowlton Nash: In just over two weeks, Soviet troops will begin leaving Afghanistan. They've been there for nine years, backing up the Afghan government in the civil war against Moslem rebels.

The conflict was a civil war; the USSR did not invade but arrived, rolled in, or simply showed up to help the Afghan government. They were leaving, thanks to the U.N. accord, and, owing to U.S. support for the rebels, sometimes visualized as Muslim fundamentalists, there would likely be a great deal of bloodshed when the Soviets were gone.

On 12 May 1988, a new angle was introduced: Pakistanis were making money from the war. Peter Mansbridge began with the usual introductory visualization and then added the new one.

Peter Mansbridge: In just a few days, the Soviet Union will start pulling its troops out of Afghanistan. They've been there since 1979 helping the Afghan government fight an indecisive war against Moslem rebels. The war has had a profound effect in neighbouring Pakistan. Thousands of Afghan refugees have poured across the border to escape the fighting. Afghan and Soviet planes have attacked rebel bases there. But, for some, the war has meant a lot of money for the family business, especially when that business is dealing in arms. Our Asia correspondent, Tom Kennedy, reports.

Kennedy reported from Darra, a small town in the Northwest Frontier Province of Pakistan that for over a century has produced copies of European weapons.

Tom Kennedy: In the last century, it was the carbines of the British. Today, it's the sub-machine-guns of the Soviet Union. You can also buy Russian-made machine-guns and rocket launchers. These were captured from Soviet soldiers in Afghanistan. The war has been good for the arms merchants, and the peace accord in Afghanistan doesn't seem to have changed that. Demand for weapons is up, and so are prices. Shop owners say that, during the peace negotiations in Geneva last March, Afghan refugees here in Pakistan began selling their weapons, believing they'd soon be moving their families home. But that's changed. Today they're arming themselves ... Just like the stock market, the arms market gives a reasonable idea of people's mood, and the mood here is that the fighting in Afghanistan is not over. Tom Kennedy, CBC News, Darra, Pakistan.

The kindest thing one might say about this vision of Third World merchants of death is that it was inaccurate. The personal weapon of choice of the mujahedeen has always been the long-range Lee-Enfield .303 clone, not the short-range Soviet AK47.

The next stage in the drama was concerned with the actual exit of Soviet troops. Despite the persistent visualization by the CBC, invading armies do not simply 'leave.' Tourists leave; armies retreat. Sometimes the retreat is orderly, and sometimes not. When it is orderly, the reason is most often because it is strong enough to discourage attack by the enemy. There is usually no reason for the enemy to allow them to 'leave,' and to think that the mujahedeen would allow the Soviet armed forces to do so is simply fantastic. Any self-respecting Afghan resistance fighter would like to kill as many retreating Soviets as possible, to say nothing of the government they supported in Kabul.

Nash led off *The National* for 14 May 1988 with the following introduction:

Knowlton Nash: Good evening. A truck bomb went off in the heart of Kabul today, less than twenty-four hours before Soviet troops begin pulling out of Afghanistan. Sixteen people died in the bombing. A few hours later, four more people were killed in a rocket attack on the city's suburbs. The mujahedeen rebels are making it clear that, even as the Soviets prepare to leave, the fighting is far from over. The CBC's Michael McIver reports from Kabul.

Nash appeared surprised that the rebels would make things clear in that, way, as if it somehow was not fair. McIver, the Moscow correspondent, likewise found the behaviour of the mujahedeen in poor taste.

Michael McIver: In spite of Soviet armour at key intersections in Kabul, in spite of the watchful presence of Soviet troops in the city, in spite of careful checks by Afghan security forces, the mujahedeen guerrillas still penetrate the defences. Early this morning, a truck bomb destroyed this mud-and-straw house, killing everyone inside, and some nearby. A brother of one man who was killed searches the ruins for family mementoes.

Visuals of a destroyed 'mud-and-straw house' and of a man searching the rubble 'for family mementoes' gave the visualization a deeply pathetic hue. How awful that the murderous mujahedeen would blow up mud-and-straw houses and cause such grief to families! For a perspective on these terrible events, McIver turned to the Commander of Soviet Forces, General Boris Boronov. According to this source, McIver reported,

it's the rebels who are responsible for the killing of innocents. 'We came in peace,' General Boris Boronov told a news conference. Rejecting evidence to the contrary, he claims Soviet forces have never attacked civilians or bombed villages in Afghanistan. 'Our mission completed,' he says, 'Soviet forces leave, wishing success, happiness, and peace to the Afghan side.' Soviets, right up to the military commander here, insist they're not retreating. They say they're leaving because their job is done, or to put it in the jargon that's used here in Kabul, they say they've fulfilled their internationalist duty in assisting a peace-loving, friendly nation. And nearly every Soviet soldier denies they invaded Afghanistan in the first place. Intervention? What intervention, he's saying. We were invited to come here. It was our duty to bring peace to a friend.

In this sequence, McIver indicated there was evidence of Soviet killings of civilians; he did, moreover, actually employ the words *invasion* and *retreat*. But he did so in a context of denial: the Soviet commander rejected evidence of Soviet killings of civilians and denied they ever invaded. Perhaps McIver believed what he was saying; perhaps he was merely making diplomatic statements in order to ensure he would be able to remain in the country.

The closing sequence was similarly ambiguous. It was clear to most people that if, in fact, bringing peace had been the Soviet mission, it was not a success. McIver visualized the devastation the Soviets caused through the eyes of Soviet soldiers keen on going home or leaving.

Michael McIver: The peace of this Soviet military base on the outskirts of Kabul was suddenly shattered by an incoming rocket and an artillery response. But the short duel didn't seem to affect the ordinary routine of the base. Even an army band that was staging a little show for visiting journalists didn't miss a beat. The song is called 'Afghanistan, My Soul Is Hurting.' But the hurt will ease for these troops in four or five months. That's when their unit goes home. But with no sign of an end to the war, the hurt will last a good deal longer for the country they're leaving behind. Michael McIver, CBC News, at a Soviet military base, near Kabul.

According to this visualization the Soviets, and not just the Afghans, suffered. The audience was, in effect, invited to sympathize with the invaders. The army band played a lugubrious tune, even under fire from the enemy; their 'hurt' would soon be over; they were going home. Now, thinking of their 'hurt,' the audience was invited to think of the longer-lasting 'hurt' of the country they were leaving. The audience was not invited to relate the 'hurt' of Afghanistan to the cause of it – namely, the Soviet troops who were 'leaving.' Instead, they were simply invited to feel a kind of generalized compassion for all these 'hurt' people.

The second story in the 14 May line-up was also on Afghanistan. Nash set the stage and thereby established the discourse of normalcy.

Knowlton Nash: Afghan president Najibullah said today, he isn't worried about hanging onto power once the Soviet soldiers leave. But the thousands of Moslem rebels, who have been fighting the Afghan and Soviet armies for almost nine years, disagree. As our Asian correspondent, Tom Kennedy, reports, the rebels are stockpiling tons of arms and ammunition for what they hope is a final stage of the war.

Nash's 'but' established the mujahedeen as deviant, as contesting the authorized visualization. The appropriate way to deal with deviant discourse is, naturally enough, to dispute it or indicate its untrustworthiness. This is what Kennedy did.

'For ten years,' he began, 'the mujahedeen objective was to defeat the Soviet Army.' By the standard CBC account, they had failed to do so; how, then, could they succeed in their next objective, 'to overthrow the country's Communist regime'? Kennedy's visualization was as follows. First, 'when Russians are finally gone from Afghanistan, the mujahedeen will no longer be able to depend on outside military aid, so for the past month they've been building up supplies all along the border with Pakistan.' He did not explain how the Soviet departure would impair supplies to the mujahedeen, but it was no doubt true that they, like all armies, were concerned with logistics. The problem, as Kennedy saw, was to determine just how vital the question of continued supply was. They were open to attack, of course, but more important, 'the Soviets know that supplies could become the mujahedeen's biggest problem. Supplies are not a problem, says this mujahedeen leader: "I have enough explosives to blow up every house in Kabul." But not all commanders believe they have enough supplies.' A suitable sound-bite followed, and Kennedy provided the conclusion: 'most mujahedeen are hoping the war will end quickly.' His point was not humanitarian, but suggested rather that a protracted conflict could not be won by the mujahedeen.

In the next sequence Kennedy first showed they were not entirely misguided in their hopes: 'They say morale in the Afghan army is bad. Many soldiers are deserting. Here are six deserters. They gave themselves up just a few hours before these pictures were taken.' Kennedy then provided a translation of appropriate sentiments voiced by one of the deserters: 'But the rest of the Afghan Army probably won't collapse so easily. And if the war does not end quickly, the mujahedeen will need foreign supplies and their vital bases in Pakistan.' True, there had been desertions, but if there were not mass desertions, the question of supplies will again be crucial. And where would they be obtained? According to the Geneva Accord, foreign disengagement was supposed to take place, but, as Kennedy went on to say, 'Pakistan implies, if the superpowers stay involved in the conflict, it will too.'

Zain Norrani – Pakistani foreign minister: The freedom fighters will continue to receive assistance right up to Afghanistan from whatever channels, whatever sources, they've been receiving in the past.

Tom Kennedy: Including Pakistan.

Zain Norrani: Well, that's up to you to guess.

Tom Kennedy: But if the superpowers do stick to the peace agreement, this could be the last of the mujahedeen supplies. The Kabul strategy now is to try to negotiate with the mujahedeen to come up with a government suitable to all. The mujahedeen strategy will probably be a desperate push for a final quick and total victory. Tom Kennedy, CBC News, on the Afghanistan border.

Apart from indicating that the foreign minister of Pakistan was a slippery customer, Kennedy's wrap-up reconfirmed that the mujahedeen were the source of the deviant discourse. Supplies and logistics were the key, according to Kennedy, and since Kabul had more, and the mujahedeen were about to be cut off (he thought), their only hope was a 'desperate push for a final quick and total victory.' Since no guerrilla army is likely to be successful under such circumstances (indeed, no guerrilla commander would be likely to do something so stupid as what Kennedy visualized), the implication of his remarks was that the mujahedeen would succumb to the Kabul strategy.

The next day, 15 May, the first two stories were again on Afghanistan. In his introduction, Peter Mansbridge used the word *retreat* to describe the Soviet exit. It was the first time in our sample that the term was used unambiguously by the CBC. He ended his remarks, however, by providing his audience with the Soviet meaning of events as well as with the obvious facts: 'Although the Soviets say they're not leaving as losers, it is the first time the Soviet Union has abandoned a Communist ally. The CBC's Michael McIver reports from Afghanistan.' McIver's report showed some splendid visuals of a 'goodbye performance' and a 'public-relations exercise' by Soviet troops leaving Jalalabad for Kabul. For the first time, a CBC correspondent showed sustained scepticism regarding Soviet accounts of their activities. He ended his report, however, by combining the official Soviet version with the regrettably discordant facts.

Michael McIver: Soviets insist this is neither a retreat nor a defeat. But whatever you want to call it, it is in the end of an era. Until now, Soviet policy has been to expand its influence and outright control. But today, the first time in years, Soviet troops are under orders to march toward home, and not away from it. Michael McIver, CBC News, on the Jalalabad Road, near Kabul.

The second story in the line-up was also concerned more with the facts than with speculative visualization. As Mansbridge said in his introduction, 'the Soviet pull-out by no means resolves the problems of Afghanistan.' In particular, the refugees in Pakistan could not simply walk in as the Soviets walked out. This amounted to a considerable change in the hydraulic imagery that had been offered earlier. A closer examination of the problem indicated that more than 'fierce anti-communism' or 'Islamic fundamentalism' prevented the refugees from going home to live in peace under the Communist regime in Kabul:

Tom Kennedy: But some camp officials say, that in reality refugees are less concerned with politics than they are with the state of their farms, and most farms are in ruins. Afghanistan's agricultural infrastructure will take years to rebuild. There are thousands of land mines, like this one, that may only be found when people step on them. Aid workers believe that if all Afghan refugees were returned home now, it would be a disaster.

Anders Fenga – Swedish relief worker: They can't even produce enough to, to support the people which are in there now. And if, uh, millions of refugees are just going in in a flood wave over that border, it will be famine.

Kennedy's initial 'but' again indicated that what followed was the deviant, minority, or non-official account. Yet, the manifest truth or commonsensical factuality of what the relief worker said changed for a brief moment one correspondent's visualization. His wrap-up summarized what the previous sound-bite indicated.

Tom Kennedy: The Khyber Pass, between Afghanistan and Pakistan, one of history's great crossroads. Hundreds of thousands of refugees fled Afghanistan through here, and eventually they'll use it to go back. But not today. There are no refugees on the road down there, and probably won't be for some time yet. The United Nations and aid organizations believe that peace, if it is ever achieved, in Afghanistan, will be just the beginning. It will take years for the country to recover enough to support its population. Tom Kennedy, CBC News, in the Khyber Pass.

This fit of realistic appraisal did not recur in our sample. As is indicated below, the remaining stories on Afghanistan sustained the earlier version.

The next day, 16 May, McIver followed the retreat of the same troops who had performed the 'public-relations exercise' in Jalalabad the day before. This time, however, no such language was used. Mansbridge's introduction set the tone: 'Another step in the Soviet withdrawal from Afghanistan.' The 'public-relations exercise' and 'goodbye performance' of 15 May had become 'an official thank-you and farewell from Afghan president Najibullah and his troops.' McIver was less reverential. He began by mentioning the sparse crowds that watched the Soviet armour move through the streets of Kabul: 'they were barely out of town and onto the Salang Road running north to the border when they had to stop for an official farewell. These battle-hardened veterans, already tired from the first leg of their journey from Jalalabad to Kabul yesterday, managed to work up just enough energy for a cheer for Afghan/Soviet solidarity.' For three hours, the troops listened to President Najib say goodbye and 'assure everyone that the Soviets had not come to occupy Afghanistan' but to help. The commander, General Boronov, grew emotional, but 'an ordinary Soviet soldier,'

Sergei Milavonov, 'cut through all the official jargon.' In a sound-bite, Milavanov said that 'Afghanistan is for the Afghans; they should be the ones to try and solve its many problems.' This was followed by a clip of General Boronov, who said it was time to go home.

Michael McIver: Finally the soldiers saddled up ... And after yet another pause, this one for a photo session, they headed out into the mountains, in the most dangerous leg of their journey home. Michael McIver, CBC News, on the Salang Road.

The wrap-up provided a last romantic visualization. The commander had said it was time to go home; the troops had listened patiently to long hours of 'official jargon,' a splendid euphemism; finally, they saddled up and rode off into the dangerous sunset after a last photo-op. One would almost think these were our boys coming home.

Later, on *The Journal*, Afghanistan led off the program. The first sequence consisted of a guest performance by Peter Marshall of the BBC on 'what lies ahead for Afghanistan.' Some shocking new language was introduced in his opening words:

Peter Marshall: As the Red Army moves out, a new era begins. The superpower, the Soviet Union, is in retreat.

From facts he moved quickly to prediction:

Within nine months, all 115,000 of its troops will be gone. Now the doctrine 'what we have, we hold' has been erased. Similar departures from South Asia and Africa could follow.

Despite the visualization of a general retreat of Soviet power, there remained the civil war in Afghanistan. The 'regime the Soviets have been propping up' sat behind its defences in Kabul, and the mujahedeen controlled most of the countryside. One mujahedeen commander provided an optimistic sound-bite that Najib would be gone within a year.

Peter Marshall: Others aren't so sure. The mujahedeen are indominable as guerrilla fighters, but in eight years of war, they've never taken a Soviet garrison. They're still ridden with factional rivalries, and pulling together to take the whole country could yet be beyond them.

An authorized knower, Anthony Hyman, confirmed Marshall's doubts.

Marshall then named the several factions, and a second authorized knower, Julian Gearing, confirmed their divisions. The most obstreperous of the factional leaders – identified, not surprisingly, as a 'hard-line fundamentalist,' and 'favourite of Pakistan' – was asked not about mujahedeen factionalism, but about the future of the Kabul regime.

Peter Marshall: How long will the, the Marxist regime survive without the Soviet troops?

Gulbaddin Heckmatyar: Not for few days. It is difficult after Russian withdrawal that, ah, Najib government survive.

This provided Marshal with an occasion for 'balance' and a portrait of Najib, 'a robust character, physically huge, nicknamed the Ox, and tough,' who 'was installed two years ago, ostensibly to pave the way for peace, but also to reconcile feuding factions within the government.' Najib, the huge peacemaker, was also, as Hyman pointed out, a medical doctor who has never actually practised medicine – an Afghan Che Guevara, one might say.

Anthony Hyman: He was always a party organizer and he's made his reputation in the 1980s as the head and organizer of the Afghan secret police. That's to say he's feared, and to that extent he's respected in Afghanistan.

Marshall then suggested that Najib's troops were unreliable and that the Kabul government had plans to retreat to the north near the Soviet border to provide 'a bulwark against Afghanistan's Islamic fervour.' The possibility that the Soviet invasion was intended as a response to Islam was not elaborated. Instead, there followed a familiar visualization of refugees in Pakistan and their 'spoiled and dangerous' fields at home.

Marshall's wrap-up was a summary visualization that Afghanistan was simply a mess. There was no attempt to assign responsibility for making it that way.

Peter Marshall: So the price of war for the Afghans has been appalling. Perhaps a million, maybe more have died. But the Soviet Union, too, has lost thousands, and they'll have more to bury yet. Will you allow the Soviet forces safe passage as they leave?

Allahuddin Khan [voice of translator]: We have no agreement signed with the Soviets. There are no cease fire. We will continue our attacks on them until the last Soviet soldiers leaves Afghanistan.

Anthony Hyman: I think it's quite clear that the Soviet Union has achieved very little and has had many disappointments in Afghanistan. They haven't um, swept away the opposition as they expected. They haven't ah, made the government so, given it an entrenched position that it can't be bought out. And, they haven't won the reputation for, for, for protecting their friends either because ah, obviously the problems of Afghanistan is such that um, no one can predict what its future is going to be.

Peter Marshall: Kabul today. The invaders, hugely relieved, prepare to go. The 'great game' was Kipling's phrase for adventures in Afghanistan. Mr Gorbachev has made reference to the bleeding wound. After years of war, it's clear which description is the more apt.

In the second sequence, a conversation between Barbara Frum and Arthur Kent, a journalist who 'has been covering the war in Afghanistan since it began' and a *Journal* regular, repeated the Soviet version, even while calling it a 'public relations opportunity.' Frum asked Kent if it had been successful. One wonders what that could possibly mean. If the whole business had, in fact, been public-relations, it would have been successful only if nobody saw it that way. Frum therefore implied that the CBC was not fooled by Soviet PR; thus, what they did visualize must be the real story.

Kent began by saying the troops that McIver had watched move out constituted a 'very symbolic movement of one regiment, twelve hundred men, two hundred vehicles.' But, he immediately added, it

has, indeed, given some weight to the expectation that the Soviets will come through with their promise to remove half their 115,000 troops by the end of the three-month ah, period agreed in Geneva, with the entirety going no later than February 19th of ah, 1989. However, I must say that there is some degree of scepticism. Certainly among the international press corps who feel that ah, perhaps events so far have just been too slickly stage-managed. Everything is falling into place ah, however the Soviets are, are not willing to discuss figures.

Neither was Frum. Nor did she ask Kent what to make of the entire process. She turned instead to the more speculative question of the mujahedeen strategy: Did they have one? Kent responded by praising the Soviet Union, that is, by providing a visualization that confirmed their public-relations line.

Arthur Kent: Well, I think we're going to find out that in the next days and weeks, certainly weeks, whether the resistance can pull together and respond to what has been a brilliant diplomatic and political ah, shift by the Soviets in ah, deciding to leave Afghanistan and putting upon it a gloss of victory. In fact, all we've heard from the Soviets this week is the fact that they are not withdrawing. They are not retreating. They have completed their internationalist duty. They have helped sustain a communist regime in Afghanistan against external interference and that indeed they are leaving in honour.

And, as for the mujahedeen, Kent thought they would continue fighting. Frum then asked what the Soviets were leaving behind 'in the hands of Najib in the way of weapons, equipment and funds to keep that army loyal to him?' Kent replied that they had been shipping in supplies by air.

Peter Kent: Also, it should be noted that when you're with President Najib, his bodyguards are Soviet, KGB, Special Servicemen, and ah, the closest advisers in his government indeed are Soviet ah, officials and soldiers. The state of Afghanistan, as such, does not ah, exert an independent foreign policy nor domestic policy. It is only within that Soviet protective cocoon that Mohammad Najib clings to power. The Soviets have thus far shown no sign, no sign of weakening their resolve to keep him in office and in power in Kabul.

With that frank recital of facts, Barbara Frum ended the discussion.

The final two stories (19 and 21 May) were anchor-only reports. These spoke of the continued withdrawal of Soviet troops. On 19 May, Peter Mansbridge allowed that the Soviets had *invaded* Afghanistan in 1979 rather than 'arriving' or 'rolling' in. On 21 May, Sheldon Turcott summed up the CBC visualization of events.

Sheldon Turcott: Armoured columns of Soviet tanks and troop carriers lumbered through Kabul this week as the Soviet Union began its military withdrawal from Afghanistan. For eight and a half years Soviet forces have backed up the Afghan army in the civil war against anti-Communist rebels. The Russians were happy to be going home.

The last sequence in our sample showed a 'rousing welcome' given to the first soldiers to cross 'the Oxus River into Soviet territory.' They had made it. It was as if our boys were home and safe.

If the Soviet embassy in Ottawa kept tabs on the CBC's coverage of their country, they would doubtless be pleased with the result. It seems clear that the CBC made allowances for the more unsavoury aspects of Soviet politics. One reason for this gentle treatment, no doubt, is that exposure of the

Soviet Union to the normal standards of 'investigative journalism' as practised in North America would quickly enough get the correspondent
arrested or expelled. At the same time, however, the CBC never once mentioned the difficulties their correspondents encountered in producing their
visualizations.

CHAPTER THREE

New Thinking about the Summit

7 MEDIA SHERPAS

In December 1987, President Reagan and General Secretary Gorbachev met in Washington; the following June, they met again in Moscow. Summit meetings combine all the constituent elements of news. They are dramatic and personal, and can be visualized as having apocalyptic importance. They are also splendid occasions for priming and agenda setting. In this section, we consider the visualization by the CBC of the relations between the two countries, especially as they were exemplified in the coverage of the two leaders.

We encountered the visualization of Gorbachev in the analysis presented in chapter 2. We are primed, therefore, to encounter a progressive reformer. The symbols *glasnost* and *perestroika* were readily invoked to convey a sense of general and political well-being in Soviet life. Gorbachev had courted difficulties with his bold policy for change, by this account, and had encountered them in Armenia and Azerbaijan. At the same time, the CBC presented him as a man ennobled by his forthright dealings with these domestic difficulties. In Afghanistan, he was nothing less than the great peacemaker. It would, I believe, be fair to say that the CBC presented Gorbachev and his actions in a very favourable light. The same cannot be said for the visualization of President Reagan.

On 12 June 1987, Reagan was on a state visit to West Germany and visited Berlin on the occasion of the 750th anniversary of the founding of the city. Nash provided the introduction.

Knowlton Nash: Ronald Reagan went to the Berlin Wall today, and he appealed to the Soviet Union to tear the wall down. It's divided East and West Berlin for more than twenty-five years. But Reagan told a crowd today that, if Moscow is serious about change, the wall will disappear. Joe Schlesinger reports.

The wall has done more than 'divide' East and West Berlin. Centre Street divides east and west Calgary much as Yonge Street divides east and west Toronto. The Berlin Wall sealed off East Berlin from West Berlin and interrupted the one-way human traffic between the two Germanys. Joe Schlesinger did not remind CBC viewers of such things, but treated Reagan's visit as a public-relations gesture that didn't quite come off.

Joe Schlesinger: For Ronald Reagan, it was a dream setting. The Berlin Wall. Guards and guns to keeping people back on the other side. He came ...

Ronald Reagan: ... the third time for me to see it.

Joe Schlesinger: He saw ...

Ronald Reagan: I think it's an ugly scar.

Joe Schlesinger: And he threw a challenge to the leader of everything beyond the wall, Mikhail Gorbachev.

Ronald Reagan: General Secretary Gorbachev, if you seek peace, if you seek prosperity for the Soviet Union and Eastern Europe, if you seek liberalization, come here to this gate. Mr. Gorbachev, open this gate. Mr Gorbachev, tear down this wall. *Es gibt ein Berlin.*

Joe Schlesinger: There is, he said, only one Berlin. It was no match for John Kennedy's famous words.

John Kennedy: *Ich bin ein Berliner.*

Reagan's rhetoric expressed a real problem that the Soviet Union and Eastern Europe were facing: the prosperity and technological productivity of Western Europe and North America, which were sought after by people living in the East Bloc, were connected to the liberalism of Western politics. Recently, the workers at the Lenin Shipyards in Gdansk had reminded the Communist leaders of Poland, in Eastern Europe, that economic productivity and political reform, or even political revolution, were two aspects of the same process.

Reagan's connection of political liberalization to economic prosperity came at a time when the USSR earned between $30 billion and $35 billion, in hard currency, which was about half what General Motors earned in sales. In 1988, about 30 per cent of its hard-currency 'earnings' were in the form of Western European credits. The economics of Eastern Europe were in need of enormous capital infusion in order to enable them to maintain even a modest industrial base, and capital was (and is) available only from outside sources. The general disarray of Communist economies can be found in statistics as well. Soviet life expectancy is about the same as that in Jamaica or Panama. Twenty per cent of the population live below the Soviet-established subsistence level; one-sixth of the population share an apartment with an unrelated family. Medical services are taking a declining share of the national budget. Alcoholism, air and water pollution, and poor health and safety standards are continuing problems. In terms of computer technology, the USSR hardly appears in the data.[1]

One may question the connection between political liberalism and technological or industrial productivity, at least in the abstract. But considered concretely, in the case of the Soviet Union and Eastern Europe in the closing decades of this century, it seems pretty clear that communism is the political word for bankruptcy. Even if that is an exaggeration, it is at least plausible that the USSR was getting rid of its major loss-leaders, such as Angola, Afghanistan, and a grossly overblown military establishment, in order to avert a complete economic and political collapse. In other words, whatever the reality indicated by *glasnost* and *perestroika*, some sort of change and restructuring had become necessary at this point in Soviet history.

To appreciate the significance of the substantive content of Reagan's remarks in Berlin – indeed, to establish some kind of perspective on Gorbachev's rhetoric and its visualization by the CBC – it might be useful to suggest a longer-range historical context. It is not news that the Russian legacy inherited by the Soviet Union was highly autocratic; it is also commonplace to observe that autocracies have, on occasion, transformed themselves into liberal democracies. Liberalization of the USSR should not be excluded simply because of the Soviet Union's autocratic heritage. What is in need of explanation, however, is the persistence of autocratic structures in the Russian civilizational area long after they dissolved in Central and Western Europe.

One widely accepted account argues that three still unresolved questions persist from Russian into Soviet history.[2] The pre-modern regime in Russia, as elsewhere, was ruled from the top down. At the start of Russia's modern era, with Peter the Great (1689–1725), military defeat inspired the opening of his famous 'window to the West.' If Russia was to avoid defeat in war, it had to modernize, that is, to copy certain features of Western organization and technology. As Peter's empire expanded, it required more military power, and so more money. Funds could be obtained, with effort, from the agrarian economy. From the start, therefore, the 'military question' was connected to the 'economic question.' Successful military expansion introduced the third structural problem, the 'nationalities question.' When, in the West, nationality became the basis of state sovereignty, the legitimacy of the multinational Russian Empire was called into question.

It has been argued that had the First World War not occurred, the transition to liberal democracy by way of economic expansion might well have taken place. However that may be, the Bolshevik *coup d'état* in October 1917 ended that option. Moreover, their two revolutionary slogans, 'Peace, Bread, and Land' and 'National Self-Determination,' addressed the military, economic, and nationalities questions, respectively. The Civil War reversed the military and nationality policies, and collectivization reversed the economic one. By the 1930s, then, Soviet Russia had reverted to a regime that had re-established the three basic problems of the imperial autocracy. Owing to the establishment of rule by terror that was justified by ideology, Stalin was able to command even greater changes than Peter the Great had managed to.

De-Stalinization and the rise to power of a new generation have resulted in any number of accounts of the liberalism of Andropov, former head of the KGB, and of Gorbachev. What is often overlooked in these novelties is the question of how Gorbachev was dealing with the threefold structural dilemma of Soviet life. First, the economic question: *Can* a socialist economy be sufficiently productive that a widespread and significant rise in consumer activity is possible? Many Soviet as well as Western economists doubt it, so that the real question amounts to whether the Soviet Union is capable of privatizing agriculture. Second, the nationalities question remains: how to maintain the territorial integrity of the USSR (or the revived Russian Empire) without recourse to terror is not obvious. Third, with respect to the military question, it is by no means clear that guns and butter are fungible. And, even if they were, it is certainly questionable whether Soviet leaders could take the risk of reducing the military establishment in the face of nationalist agitation in Eastern Europe and outside the Russian states of the union. Mentioning these long-term factors of Soviet imperial politics does not, of course, mean that reform from the top or by command is impossible. It has taken place elsewhere. It does mean, however, that such changes are constrained.

In his remarks in Berlin, President Reagan was, in his way, engaging to support Gorbachev in his undertaking. Like the general secretary, the U.S. president was also engaged in 'new thinking' – *novoye myshleniye*, as Gorbachev put it. The central element of 'new thinking' is the substitution of the concept 'survival of humanity' for the concept 'class struggle.' None of this was ever mentioned on the CBC. According to Schlesinger's visualization, the most important thing about Reagan's 'challenge' was that it was not as stirring as Kennedy's. He compared the receptions accorded the two presidents as well.

Joe Schlesinger: But it's a different Berlin now. There were angry demonstrations last night against Reagan's visit where Kennedy's trip in '63 drew only cheers. And there were similar demonstrations earlier in the week on the other side of the wall against the restrictiveness of the East German regime. So in a way, Berlin is united in the restlessness with which the young view their future.

In closing, Schlesinger returned to the theme of 'challenge.'

Joe Schlesinger: It was Ronald Reagan's toughest challenge yet to Mikhail Gorbachev. In the past, on issues such as the elimination of medium-range nuclear weapons from Europe, Gorbachev accepted the Western challenge, and then turned it around and used it to his own advantage. Accepting this dare, though, and tearing down the Berlin Wall, would alter the political landscape as much as building it did a quarter of a century ago. Joe Schlesinger, CBC News, Berlin.

Within the 'challenge' metaphor was contained another meaning, the equivalence of challenger and challenged. Gorbachev had accepted earlier challenges, to his own advantage. This one was more than a challenge; it was a 'dare.' But the moral equality of the two sides, the moral symmetry necessary for the 'challenge' imagery to make sense, was maintained. The audience had been primed already by reports of 'restlessness' on both sides of the Wall. According to this visualization, then, building the Wall and tearing it down were more alike than different. Both were major alterations in the political landscape. By the same logic, being thrown in jail and being let out of jail would be more alike than different: both are major alterations in one's personal landscape.

Nash continued the landscape imagery with his trailer.

Knowlton Nash: But Moscow has already made it clear that the political landscape is not going to change any time soon. The Soviet news agency, Tass, denounced

Reagan's speech. Tass said Reagan had been provocative and war-mongering. The Soviets said Reagan's speech was delivered in the spirit of the Cold War.

If one understands the term 'Cold War' to refer to the domination of Eastern Europe by force of arms, Tass was exactly wrong: Reagan's 'dare' was for the Soviets to end the Cold War.

In the same anchor-only segment, Nash reported on the Intermediate-Range Nuclear Forces (INF) negotiations.[3]

Knowlton Nash: There were some signs of an agreement between East and West today. The NATO Allies told the Americans they can go ahead and sign a treaty with the Soviets on reducing nuclear missiles in Europe. It's expected to be ready this fall. The approval came at the end of a two-day meeting in Iceland of the NATO foreign ministers, including Canada's Joe Clark. They endorsed the so-called zero-zero option. The Americans and the Soviets would both get rid of their medium- and short-range missiles on European soil. But NATO said West Germany should keep some of its short-range weapons.

Neither in this story nor in subsequent CBC visualizations was the role of nuclear weapons in NATO, and especially in the Federal Republic, brought into focus or coherently explained. This report of NATO agreement on the zero-zero option, we must note, was factual and restrained.

The next story that we recorded was on 22 July, when Gorbachev accepted the zero-zero option to which NATO had agreed at the June meeting.[4] The emphasis was rather different.

Knowlton Nash: Mikhail Gorbachev had made a major new offer to the United States on arms control. The Soviet leader says he's ready to scrap all Soviet medium-range missiles in both Europe and all of Asia, if the Americans do the same in Europe and not put any new missiles in Alaska. It's an offer that took the White House by surprise. Gorbachev said he's ready to agree to what's known as the 'double-zero option' during an interview with an Indonesian newspaper editor. The United States welcomed the offer, but it's cautious about it.

From this report, Gorbachev was visualized as the initiator. In fact, according to the 12 June story, Gorbachev was responding to the U.S. offer.[5] In this visualization, the Americans were surprised and cautious. The sound-bite that followed, however, indicated neither surprise nor caution.

Kenneth Adelman – Director, U.S. Arms Control and Disarmament Agency: I would say to the Soviets, welcome aboard. It's about time that they have agreed with the president to eliminate an entire class of weapons systems.

Knowlton Nash: When the Geneva arms talks resume tomorrow, the proposal will be formally presented by the Soviet negotiating team.

In fact, the Americans had every reason to be confident that the INF negotiations would be a success. For reasons discussed above, *perestroika* and *glasnost* also indicated that the Soviets were aware of the relationship between their economic difficulties and their military expenses.

The deal was completed in mid September. On 18 September, *The National* and *The Journal* both led off with stories on the topic. Nash was impressed equally with the novelty of the event and its extent.

Knowlton Nash: Good evening. It's never happened before. For the first time since the superpowers began building nuclear weapons, the total number of warheads will go down. And it's no small reduction. 1,047 medium- and shorter-range missiles will be scrapped. That's every one of those types of missiles.

Coverage began with a report from Terry Milewski, who immediately provided a contrasting visualization.

Terry Milewski: Many thought that a president famous for his anti-Soviet rhetoric would never do it, but, today, Ronald Reagan gave his blessing to an arms deal with Moscow.

A forty-seven-word Reagan sound-bite followed; it contained the information that the two governments had reached an agreement in principle and that the details would be worked out before the Summit. In contrast to the visualization of the U.S. president as anti-Soviet, the Soviet foreign minister was party to a great historical event.

Terry Milewski: For the Soviet foreign minister, this was history.

Eduard Shevardnadze [voice of translator]: For the first time in the history of the existence of nuclear weapons, of the existence of what I would call the nuclear face-off between the Soviet Union and the United States of America, it has been possible to agree on the elimination of two classes of nuclear weapons. This is a beginning, certainly a beginning which we hope has to be and will be followed by a continuation.

Milewski then provided details and concluded:

Terry Milewski: There is no doubt that today's agreement is an impressive achievement. However, it does leave untouched a vast amount of firepower on both sides. In fact, only 5 per cent of the superpower's nuclear arsenals will be affected at all. That leaves unanswered the crucial questions in arms control today. What about the 95 per cent? The vast stockpiles of long-range strategic missiles on both sides, on land, on bombers, and in submarines. And beyond that, what about the future, Star Wars, and the prospect of weapons in space? Well, both sides say they're working on it.

There followed three sound-bites from the American 'side.' A somewhat hesitant George Shultz, U.S. secretary of state, said it was a start. A U.S. senator and 'prominent defence expert,' Sam Nunn, agreed but raised the issue of conventional parity.

Senator Sam Nunn – Chairman, Armed Services Committee: I think if you look at this agreement alone, it is a positive step forward. But we have to ask, what happens to the conventional balance, the non-nuclear? We have to ask whether we have conventional-force improvements and conventional arms control coming alone, because we in the West depend on nuclear weapons to compensate for conventional disadvantages.

Shultz hesitated; Nunn made explicit the reasons for U.S. prudence. Milewski ended his presentation with a third sound-bite, from President Reagan's 'evil empire' speech, introducing the clip with a remark about how things had changed. The impact of Reagan's powerful words – 'They are the focus of evil in the world' – was to suggest precisely that things had not changed. In fact what had changed was the Soviet position, in that it came closer to the position established in 1981 by the United States: that is, the 'concessions' by the Soviet Union amounted to a legitimization of the long-standing U.S. position regarding the strategic imbalance favourable to the USSR in consequence of the Soviet deployment of SS-20 missiles. Neither this important fact, nor other areas where the U.S. position was agreed to, were ever mentioned.[6]

The second story visualized the Moscow response. Unfortunately, as Nash said, 'Soviet radio and television gave only limited coverage to the

arms talks, and revealed very few details. More from Michael McIver.'
McIver was baffled.

Michael McIver: Fifteen minutes into the program comes the story that there's been
an historic breakthrough in nuclear disarmament. And it's told in an understated,
matter-of-fact way. The joint Shultz–Shevardnadze statement is read by the
announcer, as is Reagan's statement. Then, some videotape of Shevardnadze's news
conference in Washington is shown. There's been no analysis, no self-congratula-
tions. And from the Kremlin itself, absolutely nothing. A surprisingly muted
approach, considering the Kremlin does have a good deal to crow about.

Part of the reason for McIver's surprise, no doubt, was a result of the different purpose of television in the USSR. As he said in his introduction, 'BPEMR,
the main Soviet TV newscast, conveys Kremlin priorities to the people.'
Whatever that means, it is something other than entertainment. McIver,
therefore, repackaged the 'understated, matter-of-fact' presentation and did
some crowing on behalf of the Soviets.

Michael McIver: Gorbachev and his team wanted this agreement and made big concessions to get it. This ability to compromise at crucial points is a key factor why the
negotiations have been a success. Gorbachev has made it clear he views an intermediate-range treaty as only a first step in the disarmament process.

There followed a sound-bite from Vladimir Bogachev, identified as a military analyst for Tass, who provided a choice piece of disinformation.

Vladimir Bogachev - Tass Military Analyst: We are going to maintain only as many
forces that are necessary, absolutely necessary, just to defend our country.

To appreciate the significance of Bogachev's sound-bite and the endorsation
of it by the CBC as being relevant to their visualization of events, one should,
perhaps, recall some facts: the tremendous conventional superiority of Warsaw Treaty Organization (WTO) forces, as Senator Nunn had indicated a few
minutes earlier, was the reason why NATO deployed nuclear weapons in
Europe in the first place.[7] If Bogachev was telling the truth, one wonders
why the Warsaw Pact conventional-force levels were maintained at such a
high level: twice as many tanks, nearly four times the armoured personnel
carriers, more than three times the artillery, and so on. To suggest that the
WTO forces served primarily the purpose of defence was, simply stated,
ridiculous. NATO forces were hardly *capable* of invading Eastern Europe,

even if they wished to do so; that is, WTO conventional superiority, in the absence of a NATO nuclear deterrent, would be destabilizing unless NATO increased its conventional military levels to match, or the WTO forces were reduced to approximate the NATO force levels. These arguments and doctrines are simple, and they are well known. The CBC has never made them the centre of its visualization of WTO/NATO relations.

McIver then provided a wrap-up.

Michael McIver: And on another level, the Kremlin claims it wants to put superpower relations on a less confrontational, more business-like footing, and the tentative agreement is definitely a big step in this direction. Yet, so far, there's been no trumpeting from the walls of the Kremlin. In fact, there's been nothing but silence. Michael McIver, CBC News, Moscow

McIver must have been more than mildly puzzled by the 'silence' of the Kremlin. No doubt the inhabitants of that place would be grateful to the CBC for doing their crowing and trumpeting for them, but why was it necessary? To put it another way: Why were McIver and the CBC not more curious about the fact that the Soviets said one thing to the Western media – Shevardnadze's historic event – and another to their own people?

Nash then provided an introduction to the reception by the Europeans of the event that had never happened before. They welcomed the agreement, of course, but they also muted their trumpets because, as Nash said, 'a treaty would mean Europe would have to find other ways to protect itself.' Sheila MacVicar began the report by recalling the anti-nuclear protests of the past.

Sheila MacVicar: There were sit-ins in Germany, huge rallys in Italy, night-time marches in Belgium. But the American nuclear missiles came and stayed, the huge demonstrations faded away. And today, at Greenham Common, the British peace movement's most enduring protest, only a few women are left. Today's announcement, they said, was a beginning, but not nearly enough.

Woman protester: It's like you and all your friends are sitting in an armoury, you know, with all this, all these submachine-guns, and pistols, and rifles and stuff pointed at you. And then someone says, look, look, we've taken the bullets out of one gun, you know.

The initial visualization of 'Western Europe' was of a disarmament protester at Greenham Common. The discourse of normalcy having been established, MacVicar then turned to government responses.

Sheila MacVicar: In spite of the huge protest, Margaret Thatcher's British government has always argued that the American intermediate-range weapons must stay, until the Soviets were ready to give up theirs. The possibility of an accord now is seen here as a vindication of that policy of hanging tough.

The lonely women at Greenham Common have suddenly become a huge protest, and the British government policy has been simplified into one of simple nuclear balance. Both versions of events constitute substantial modifications of reality.

The British foreign secretary and the secretary general of NATO then provided sound-bites to confirm the usefulness of 'hanging tough.' MacVicar next turned to visualize the German reaction.

Sheila MacVicar: For those in West Germany closest to the firing line, and in the middle of any future battlefield, the news that at least some of the missiles there might soon be gone was welcomed.

Woman on street: I think such agreement would be wonderful.

Man on street: I don't like to have nuclear weapons around me.

This technique is known as the doughnut. The implication of the metaphor is that what is in the middle is nothing. The protesting ladies at Greenham Common and the German gentleman who doesn't like nuclear weapons provided the main elements of her visualization of the 'European' reaction. In her trailer, MacVicar introduced a quite separate theme.

Sheila MacVicar: But some Europeans see this agreement as the beginning of the decoupling of their security from the United States. This agreement will increase fears that the American government could more easily abandon Europe, and that's why European governments will spend more time talking about how to better defend themselves. Sheila MacVicar, CBC News, London.

Nothing further was said of these alarming possibilities.

Coverage continued on *The Journal*. Nash had said the agreement was spectacular in its unprecedentedness; for Frum, it answered the deep emotional needs of an entire generation of humanity.

Barbara Frum: For forty years now, the world has longed for an end to the dangerous nuclear stand-off between the superpowers. Today, the United States and the

Soviet Union took the first small step toward disarmament. More than a thousand missiles in Europe and Asia will be dismantled. And there may be further agreements on the horizon. But this process, as welcome as it is, presents its own dangers and uncertainties. We begin tonight with Bruce Garvey reporting on the ambivalence that greeted today's news.

The ambivalence was, in reality, a consequence of the aforementioned disparity between WTO and NATO conventional forces. Garvey mentioned this problem and added another of his own.

Bruce Garvey: But, perhaps, there's one central question that's more bothersome than all the rest. It's this: Is this confluence of superpower interest nothing more than an economic breathing space for the hard pressed nations? And, at the same time, a cosmetic finale to Ronald Reagan's presidency? With cautious optimism, we all hope it's considerably more. For *The Journal*, I'm Bruce Garvey.

Since Garvey did not elaborate on what this odd remark might mean, it is difficult to say much about it beyond the obvious: one should beware of 'a cosmetic finale to Ronald Reagan's presidency.' That is, since Reagan was such a devious (or such a superficial) man, he couldn't really have meant (or thought through) the implications of the INF Treaty. Hence, no more than 'cautious optimism' was warranted.

In the second story, Frum engaged in conversation with three 'authorized knowers,' Stephen Cohen, of Princeton, a *Journal* regular; Dimitri Simes, of the Carnegie Endowment for International Peace; and Christof Bertram, a German journalist and strategic analyst.[8] Frum began.

Barbara Frum: For all its faults, today's agreement has raised great expectations.

Her opening phrase indicated the premise 'nothing is perfect; but the context for our discussion is that the agreement has raised great expectations.' The theme of great expectations was a theme of progress that sustained visualizations of an improved world.

Frum turned for confirmation of this visualization, first, to Professor Cohen.

Barbara Frum: Stephen Cohen, what's ahead in your view? Is this the start of something big, even a new relationship between the superpowers?

Cohen let his imagination soar.

Stephen Cohen – Princeton University: If the announcement today, ah, is, ah, a sign of what's to come, if they continue to negotiate, and particularly about a test ban moratorium, a test ban on nuclear testing as they suggest, it could be historic. It could be the end of the nuclear arms race. That would be the best possible outcome.

Normal discourse had been established twice, by Frum's introduction and by Cohen's reading the event as a 'sign of what's to come.' Frum indicated that the second speaker, Simes, would be deviant, and he obliged by making an enigmatic dissent.

Barbara Frum: Dimitri Simes, are you as optimistic as that?

Dimitri Simes – Carnegie Endowment for International Peace: Ah, I am optimistic that, ah, Steve is wrong and it will not lead to any meaningful arms-control agreements. I am perfectly comfortable with the deal that they're about to negotiate, because it is so meaningless militarily, but symbolic politically. But too much of arms control, like too much of a good thing, may be damaging to our health. Fortunately, it's not in the cards.

What could Simes have meant? He was optimistic that Cohen was wrong? He was pleased that it would not lead to any meaningful arms-control agreements? He was comfortable because the deal was meaningless militarily but symbolic politically? Too much arms control can be damaging to our health? The man spoke in paradoxes! Any interviewer faced with such peculiar statements or donnish double-talk would, one would have thought, asked for a clarification. But Frum knew her man. She knew from his answer, if not from prior intelligence, that Simes did not share her vision or experience of a great rise in expectations. She did not accept his gambit, boldly offered, but pressed on, with at least a show of greater boldness, to the German. But her confidence in progress was no longer quite so secure, and she allowed for qualifications in her questions.

Barbara Frum: Mr Bertram, how are Europeans in general, if it's possible to generalize like that, reacting? There was a, a significant deal that West Germany had to make here, for example, to make this possible. Do they think they're buying something that, that they're going to like, ahead?

Her 'if it's possible to generalize like that,' her ambiguous and flabby following sentences, may have indicated that other things were on her mind: specifically, Simes was a loose cannon.

Did the Germans like it? Bertram, quite prudently, said they had mixed feelings: the ordinary man in the street was happy enough, but 'there are worries in the chancelleries and ministries, in the defence establishment, whether weakening nuclear deterrence, ah, will not, ah, undermine security.'

Frum had just been informed that her visualization of great expectations, while shared with ordinary Germans, was based on ignorance. Bertram, like Simes, had spoken within a discourse of deviance. Like Simes, he spoke in paradoxes: weakening nuclear deterrence can undermine security? What could this mean? The only thing to do was get back to Cohen. At least he shared Frum's enthusiasms about the future.

Barbara Frum: Let me go back to the most enthusiastic of all you; Stephen Cohen, you are the most positive. Why aren't people more excited? Why is there so much nervous waiting and seeing?

Stephen Cohen: Well, I think we're at a dangerous moment. I, I'm not, I'm enthusiastic if the deal goes through. If the negotiations continue to, the treaty is ratified, to they go on talking about a test ban, to they go on address the problem of the long-range missiles. The reason that I'm enthusiastic and positive is, is that for the first time in history, the two countries have agreed to throw away perfectly usable nuclear weapons. Weapons that, in which both had a lot of political capital. In this country, in the United States, that means that the discussion of arms control and the elimination of whole categories of nuclear weapons, has now been legitimized by the most right-wing president in American history, on this issue. That means the political spectrum has broadened up, the discussion will broaden, and more possibilities now become politically feasible.

Cohen was enthusiastic because he had great hopes for future disarmament; he entertained such hopes because he was of the opinion that disarmament meant peace, and he favoured peace. Second, he was of the opinion that, by and large, the right was not in favour of peace. Thus, if 'the most right-wing president in American history' had been able to legitimize the discussion of arms control, a more moderate, that is, a less right-wing, president could do so much more, especially if the political spectrum was 'broadened up.'

Frum apparently found Cohen's vision and hope to be reasonable. She turned back to Simes, now with an edge of aggression in her voice.

Barbara Frum: Dimitri Simes, what are you objecting to tonight? Are you saying, this is only good if it proceeds and there's more? Or are you saying something else?

Simes, however, remained uncooperative.

Dimitri Simes: Barbara, as a matter of fact, I am in favour of this agreement. I think it is the wrong agreement at the right time. Militarily it is meaningless, but politically it will prove that if you persevere, if you don't accept Russian 'nyet' for an answer, if you deploy your weapons, you can strike a better deal with the Soviet Union. It is a first, modest step. We're reducing less than 4 per cent of nuclear weapons. And this 4 per cent solution should not be perceived as a beginning of a new era in the U.S./ Soviet relationship. Unless something much more meaningful happens, it is a foot-note to history, and there is no reason for euphoria.

Simes's reply said, in effect, your visualization of great expectations is fool-ish: slow down and think about what actually has been accomplished.

Of course, there was no time for that on *The Journal*. Back to Bertram. He had explained that 'European ambivalence' had resulted from the igno-rant but decent hopes of the man in the street, and the knowledgeable but prudent doubts of responsible politicians, statesmen and leaders. Frum changed the terms of his ambivalence.

Barbara Frum: Mr Bertram, in Europe, are people ambivalent because they are not sure what Gorbachev's true intentions are or because they see that peace breaking out here is somehow a threat to the Western Alliance?

The first part of her question raised the matter of prudence in international politics; the second part seems, on the surface, unintelligible. After all, NATO was established in response to certain very specific Soviet actions in order, precisely, to help ensure peace through strength, stability, and prosperity. Bertram's reply ignored the possibility of a threat to NATO and focused on the manageable question of prudence.

Christof Bertram: I think they are ambivalent because they are not quite sure what Mr Gorbachev is after and they are not quite sure what Mr Reagan is after. After all, what is Mr Gorbachev doing? Ah, he has been pursuing a traditional Soviet policy of getting nuclear weapons out of Western Europe. Is he thinking of new things? Is this a more constructive approach, now that Mr Gorbachev is there, than his prede-cessors had pursued? The ambivalence on the American side, is that people in Europe have come to doubt the strategic wisdom of President Reagan. They were profoundly opposed to his idea of Star Wars. They were profoundly worried when, roughly a year ago at Reykjavik, he seemed to be willing to give away all strategic missiles. What follows from this, is it the traditional Soviet policy that we're seeing or something much better, more constructive, more cooperative?

Bertram was surely correct to indicate that the Soviets had indeed been pursuing the traditional policy of getting nuclear weapons out of Western Europe. And the reason had several times been stated: by doing so, they would have a strategic superiority by virtue of their great advantage in conventional forces. Bertram, with equal prudence, allowed that there *may* be something more. And, on the other side, the faith of the Europeans in the United States had been shaken because, for a brief moment, it looked as if President Reagan would, in fact, remove U.S. nuclear weapons from Europe. This kind of common-sense remark was 'balanced' by more of Cohen's visions.

Barbara Frum: Which do you think, Stephen Cohen? You've just returned from there. What, what did you pick up?

Cohen recast her question into one that he liked better. He had picked up a great deal.

Stephen Cohen: Well, you asked the question, 'What is Gorbachev up to?' I can tell you what Gorbachev is up to. He is up to an attempt to carry out a historic reform of the Soviet Union. And this foreign policy, in fundamental ways, is the foreign policy of domestic reform. As for the conventional weapons, it's a very serious issue. It's, the opponents of this treaty, particularly the United States, Senator Nunn, Les Aspen today, are going to attack this treaty on the grounds that it leaves the Soviet Union with a preponderance of conventional forces in Europe. But, it is very important that, on two occasions in the last four or five months, Gorbachev has strongly hinted that he is prepared to carry out unilateral reductions, however symbolic, in Soviet forces in Eastern Europe. And that is something that should be pursued with great vigour. There is no reason why this administration shouldn't continue to talk, with a little more imagination now, about mutual reductions in Europe.

Cohen's answer disposed of the problem of conventional superiority, at least to Frum's satisfaction. After all, Gorbachev has been giving strong hints that he was going to reduce conventional forces anyway. All that was needed was 'a little more imagination.' Cohen had shown his audience what was involved.

Frum returned to Simes and asked him 'What do you think is Mr Gorbachev up to. And what is he likely to do next?"

Dimitri Simes: Well, ah, Barbara, unlike Stephen Cohen, I do not know what Mr Gorbachev is up to. I cannot read his mind.

Stephen Cohen: You can. You need to read his speeches, Dimitri; that would be a good beginning.

Dimitri Simes: Well, I have to say, Steve, with all due respect, Mr Gorbachev's speeches are not entirely credible in my view. You would not recommend that I took literally Mr Reagan's speeches. I certainly am not going to take literally Gorbachev's speeches.

Unlike Cohen, Simes was a member of the single-standard school of political analysis. 'Covenants without the sword are but words,' said Hobbes. Mind reading and speech reading should be accompanied by a reading of events. Simes pointed this out.

Dimitri Simes: What I do know, is that Mr Gorbachev pursues a number of traditional Soviet policies. In the Third World, he increase[d] military assistance to a variety of countries. I do not see that his nuclear-arms-control platform is somehow a part of broad and new thinking which would be more congenial to the West. But I do repeat, Steve, let me finish, but I do repeat, that I think that we have to talk to Gorbachev, we have to experiment, we have to give him a chance. I'm not in favour of chronic nay-think. All I'm saying now is that this is a very modest agreement, which in itself doesn't tell us very much about Gorbachev's intentions. Let's ... let's wait and see.

Frum had time for one last topic.

Barbara Frum: Okay, gentlemen, I've got so little time left. I want to do a quick survey of what you think this means for NATO and the Western Alliance. Mr Bertram, any, any fears on that side?

Bertram had no fears; like Simes he wanted to wait and see.

Barbara Frum: Dimitri Simes?

Dimitri Simes: I completely agree with Christof. What is done is done. We should claim political victory. We should, ah, indicate that we are willing to talk to Gorbachev further. But we should understand this agreement was somewhat, ill ... ill-conceived. We're dealing with a very serious leader in Moscow, and we should discuss with NATO allies any new strategic proposals. We should not laugh. We should be serious. And before talking to Gorbachev, we should be determining first what we really want of him.

Bertram was asked for his fears; Simes was asked nothing specific. Cohen, however, was offered another chance to treat the audience to his visions, or at least to provide some entertainment.

Barbara Frum: Stephen Cohen, have prospects for more been enhanced by this deal, or been reduced, do you think? Some fear that the leverage of putting it all in one basket has been reduced?

Stephen Cohen: Let me, ah, unsettle Dimitri completely. I predict that if this agreement is not accompanied by additional agreement, particularly political accords, not just weapons accords, but political accords, this agreement will never reach fruit at ... fruition. They're talking about removing those missiles over a period of three to five years. When you think of all the political conflicts between the two countries, you see that this is a fragile agreement. So, I hope, and I suspect there will be, given goodwill in the United States and in the Soviet Union, more accords to come.

Barbara Frum: Gentlemen, I thank you all.

Throughout the discussion, Frum persistently returned to her 'great expectations' theme. When this visualization was contradicted by alternative accounts, or by prudential considerations, or by mere facts, she changed the topic. This procedure can be considered a variation on Postman's 'Now this ... ' technique. The result was less to trivialize events than to attempt a specific kind of priming. Cohen was the authority who most closely fit the 'great expectations' visualization, and he was given opportunities to expand it. The other two were given no follow-up opportunities to explain their occasionally gnomic remarks. Frum's formula may simply have been designed to produce entertaining TV. It is a considerable stretch of journalistic convention to call the whole performance a balanced analysis of a significant event in international affairs.

These preliminary visualizations of the major actors indicated that the CBC continued to portray Gorbachev as the great reformer and peacemaker. Reagan, in contrast, was the great anti-communist, the right-winger, the deviant opponent of progress with silly notions of an evil empire. The 'great communicator' was compared unfavourably as a communicator with President Kennedy, but no attention was paid to the substance of his remarks. Tass was quoted *verbatim*, and no questions were raised about the legitimacy of its stories. So far as the CBC was concerned, it was a reliable and authoritative source. No effort was expended to explain in detail, or even with a minimum of coherence, what the basic elements of NATO strategy were. Accordingly, the meaning of the INF agreement was never clearly presented. Sources who attempted to indicate what it might mean did so in spite of the questions asked by CBC interviewers.

8 SELLING THE CAUSE IN WASHINGTON

A month or so before Reagan and Gorbachev were scheduled to meet, coverage of the Soviet leader grew more intense. *The Journal* for 3 November began with a stirring introduction. 'Message from Moscow: down with Stalin, up with reform. Mikhail Gorbachev rallies the masses.' The cult of personality, so prominent a feature of Stalinism, was present still in the CBC's image of Gorbachev. Only now he was a 'reformer.' Whatever that word might mean in the Soviet context, it was considered progressive and, so to speak, a good thing.[9] This perspective was indicated in the words of Barbara Frum's lead-in.

Barbara Frum: Ever since Mikhail Gorbachev appeared on the scene two and a half years ago, the Western world has been fascinated by the Soviet leader's style. He introduced a new word into our vocabulary, *glasnost*. In English, that means 'openness.' How it translates into Soviet policy, most of us aren't yet sure.

Gorbachev simply 'appeared on the scene' and, according to this visualization, has been fascinating us all with his 'style.' The CBC did not display much concern for where, *in fact*, Gorbachev came from, nor for any serious concern of how *any* words get 'translated' into policy. There is, of course, plenty of evidence on both questions.

Instead, the audience was treated to a genuinely fascinating performance by co-anchor Bill Cameron.

Bill Cameron: But in his speech yesterday, marking the seventieth anniversary of the Russian Revolution, Gorbachev may have given us a clue. The Soviet leader made history by denouncing Stalin and praising Khrushchev. Gorbachev is the first Soviet leader to talk publicly about Stalin's crimes. Not all of them; he didn't acknowledge that Stalin's regime took millions of lives. Gorbachev said it was thousands, but he left no doubt about who was responsible for the huge purges of the 1930s. He said, 'The guilt of Stalin before the party and the people is enormous and unforgivable. This is a lesson for all generations.' Then Gorbachev turned to the present. He said it was important to fight people who opposed *perestroika*, restructuring. This is a fight on two fronts. On one side, there are the conservatives who think *perestroika* threatens what Gorbachev calls their selfish interests. On the other, there are the radicals who think reform is moving too slowly. Gorbachev said, 'It should be clear that one cannot leap over essential stages and try to accomplish everything at one go.' That was a warning to people like party leader Boris Yeltsin who wants reform to move faster, and it is said, has offered to quit if it doesn't. Finally, Gorbachev talked about Soviet/American relations. He said that the world expects concrete results of the approaching summit meetings. And he said once again that the Americans would have to negotiate on Star Wars. He promised to work unremittingly for a palpable breakthrough in reducing strategic offensive armaments and barring weapons from outer space. Many historians say that Mikhail Gorbachev is the first real post-Stalinist leader in the Soviet Union. His policy of *glasnost*, of openness, may finally have buried Joseph Stalin once and for all.

According to Cameron's visualization, Gorbachev located himself as an heir of Khrushchev and opponent of Stalin. 'Stalinism,' it may be safe to say, is a trope for all that is excessive, evil, and murderous, about communism. The first 'clue' about how *glasnost* translates into policy, by this view, is that it is not Stalinism.

But what is Stalinism? According to Cameron's visualization, it is a criminal regime that murdered millions of people, which is not quite what Gorbachev said. In the context of mass murder, Gorbachev's 'thousands' was simply a lie, and it was known, at least by his audience, to be a lie. Khrushchev, once a loyal henchman of Stalin, also denounced him, but he did so in a 'secret speech,' before the Twentieth Party Congress. In that context, the loyal servant of Stalin blamed his former master for crimes that implicated himself and many members of his audience. Gorbachev was also an heir of Khrushchev in the mode of his denunciation of Stalin. To contemplate the significance of Cameron's visualization of Gorbachev, consider the speech having been given by a German denouncing the other great mass murderer of the twentieth century for killing 'thousands' of Jews and, in the process, damaging the political effectiveness of the German nation.

In fact, such imaginative efforts are not required. Neither Gorbachev nor Khrushchev was addressing historians eager to set the record straight. Stalin's 'excesses' had hurt the *party*, and it was the party that both men addressed. Notwithstanding the visualization of Cameron or of his script writer, no one in his live audience would be likely to misinterpret Gorbachev's warning: 'This is a lesson for all generations.' That is, Gorbachev was delivering a lesson for the *present* generation of party officials.

Cameron's visualization, however, indicated that Gorbachev was criticizing Stalin: 'Then Gorbachev turned to the present.' In fact, he never had left it, and neither, for that matter, had Cameron's performance. Accepting, however, the visualization of Gorbachev as a man morally distressed by the acts that were literally a thousand times worse than he allowed, we must, at the same time, overlook the fact that Gorbachev adopted the classic Stalinist line: there are right deviationists and there are left deviationists, and only the middle course, which is the speaker's course, would prevail. Stalin's 'right deviationists' had become Gorbachev's 'selfish conservatives.' Stalin's 'left deviationists' had become Gorbachev's 'radicals'; Trotsky had become Yeltsin. No member of the audience being addressed would be in any doubt about the role adopted by Gorbachev.

The final topic of Gorbachev's speech also has a firm Stalinist precedent. 'Capitalist encirclement,' in Stalin's day, justified 'socialism in one country' as a temporary measure until the wave of history rolled up the beach once again in the great revolution. Gorbachev's version of this old old Bolshevik theme was to invoke the expectations of the world. This recondite symbol may be considered the modern Bolshevik's equivalent of the revolutionary yearnings of the workers of the world. The equivalent to capitalist encirclement in this tableau was the SDI of President Reagan.

If it is true, as Cameron said, that 'many historians' share his visualization of Gorbachev as the 'first real post-Stalinist leader' of the USSR, it is also true that they must also share a highly defective understanding of Stalin and Stalinism. The reason is simple enough: the great virtue of Stalinism, as of all ideologies that are serious about being ideologies, is that it can be transformed into its opposite in the twinkling of an eye.[10] Cameron's closing remark, that Gorbachev's 'policy of *glasnost*, of openness, may finally have buried Joseph Stalin once and for all,' is meaningless. It visualizes a 'breakthrough' in arms reduction as being connected to a kinder, gentler Soviet Union.

The CBC then turned to two 'authorized knowers' to sustain the visualization. The first was a 'Soviet commentator,' Joe Adamov. He was of the opinion that 'the force of inertia from the old times' was strong enough to prevent the Soviet Union from doing 'something different.' Barbara Frum allowed as she was 'interested in, in what he's trying to do here.'

Mr Adamov: Well, I think, you see, we do not want any blank spots in our history. Uh, the subject of the Stalin period was more or less taboo in our media for a long time and uh, Mr Khrushchev ...

Barbara Frum: Why? Why?

Mr Adamov: ... partly lifted the curtain. Why? Because, ah, it was that way under

Stalin. And, as I said, the inertia kept going. And Khrushchev, I think, was a very brave man for having actually said what he did say about that period.

Frum then asked, somewhat indiscreetly, 'How much rewriting of the history books is going to be required if all truth is to be known?' And Adamov replied that 'practically everything is known now.' She had not taken Adamov's hint:

Barbara Frum: Mr Adamov, did he go as far on Stalin as you expected? Could he have gone farther yet? What's still holding him back from the complete truth?

Mr Adamov: Well, I don't see what else he could have said. You see, a lot of things bind you.

One of the things that 'bound' Gorbachev was his opposition, not Yeltsin this time, but 'the middle-level administrators.' The people, however, were 100 per cent in favour of *glasnost* and *perestroika*, according to Adamov.

The second 'authorized knower' was Stephen Cohen. As expected, he confirmed many of Adamov's points, which in turn sustained Cameron's visualization of an embattled reformer intent on bold changes.

On 17 November, *The Journal* was entirely devoted to a production called 'The Birth of a Superpower,' a title that recalls the U.S. film *Birth of a Nation* and underlined the doctrine of moral equivalence between the 'superpowers.'

The initial visualization of the seventieth anniversary of the Bolshevik Revolution was one of contrast.

Bill Cameron: Seventy years ago, there was no Soviet Union, just a war-weary, violently divided old nation called Russia. Today, the USSR is one of the most powerful, remarkable, most often damned nations on earth. In 1917, Russia was a living laboratory of social change. In the space of a few months, revolution moved it from a feudal state ruled by Tsars to the beginnings of a modern phenomenon that now sends Mikhail Gorbachev to bargain with the most powerful man on earth.

The dramatic imagery of contrast was continued with historical examples. In Marxist language, the CBC presented its audience with the 'historical contradictions' of pre-Bolshevik or Tsarist Russia. The gracious and agreeable life of the aristocracy existed alongside the most advanced verbal and artistic forms of modernity, and both of these with the less agreeable and gracious experiences of peasants, and then of soldiers on the Eastern Front.

Permeating, leavening, and perhaps even expressing these contradictions, was the notion that the nation was 'making progress.' According to the Marxist accounts of such matters, historical contradictions must be resolved: they are fatal in every sense of the word.

In keeping with what can only be called a Marxist visualization, a historian told the audience that 'history suggests' that revolutions occur under such circumstances. Another professor assured the audience that it was 'in the cards from the turn of the century onwards.' Cameron expanded the visualization.

Bill Cameron: February 1917, Petrograd, formerly St Petersburg. The German Army is outside and there is a developing rebellion inside. It is the beginning of the revolution. Maybe it started in a bread line. Hunger finally transmuted into overwhelming anger. Suddenly, there were demonstrations in the centre of the city, huge ones. Thousands of workers, and then soldiers from units stationed in Petrograd. It was almost instantaneous and it spread across the country. Everywhere the Tsar's officials were realizing the Romanov regime was over. After a week, the Tsar abdicated. He'd been overthrown in a leaderless outpouring of hatred, rage, and then hope. Everyone on the streets knew it; this wasn't a *coup* or a *putsch*. It was a breaking of chains. A spontaneous, massive turn of the national wheel.

Yet another authorized knower, Michael Ignatieff, confirmed the imagery of revolution through historical inevitability: his grandfather, who had served the Tsar, 'just knew in his bones that it was over.'[11] Cameron went farther: everyone knew that 'the past was abolished' and that 'Russia was inventing itself every day.'

One would think that, if Russia was inventing itself daily, there would be many opportunities and many alternative outcomes, not a single inevitable fate lying before it. Another historian was introduced to inform the audience that 'the provisional government never stood a chance.' Like the transmutations and instantaneous spreadings and leaderless outpourings visualized by Cameron, the 'Soviets,' too, 'spread throughout the country.' None of the leaders of the provisional government, by this account, was capable of ruling.

Bill Cameron: That spring and summer of 1917 in Petrograd were very competitive. The party activists were in the streets, making converts, stealing members from other parties, talking, arguing. And somehow, it was the Bolsheviks who were saying things most people wanted to hear.

More specifically, it was Lenin and Trotsky. 'When Trotsky spoke,' said
Cameron, 'the Soviets listened. Bolshevik strength was growing.' They
were, however, seen by the provisional government to be a 'deadly threat,'
and were defeated in the streets by armed force. True to the melodramatic
visualization, things are darkest just before dawn. The Bolshevik chance
came with the attack on the government by former Tsarist soldiers. In the
expectation they would defend the government, the Bolsheviks were provided with arms.

Bolshevik rhetoric and Bolshevik arms resolved the 'historical contradictions.' This event has been visualized as a revolution, and not only by the
CBC. The authorized knowers served as sources to authenticate the visualization initially introduced by Cameron. The USSR was 'born' with a great
deal of violence, and the violence continued over the next several decades.
No one quoted Marx's odious aphorism about violence being the midwife of
history.

Bill Cameron: The promises of 1917 were perverted and broken. The country that
was born in fire and blood went through decades more of both. And, in spite of that,
there was enough left of the old dreams of 1917 to change the way the world was
run. Not only in the Soviet Union, as the old Russian Empire had become, but
everywhere.

That is, despite the misery that came after 1917, the regime was still visualized as progressive: it 'changed the way the world was run,' not just in the
USSR, but 'everywhere.'

On 20 November 1987, *The Journal* took note of Gorbachev's book, *Perestroika: New Thinking for Our Country and the World*. David Gilmour, the
'book news' reporter, summarized the work as a 'stolid position paper from
the Kremlin,' and introduced Terence McKenna, another journalist, who
claimed to have read the book. According to McKenna, *Perestroika*, the
book, 'is really a dramatic revolutionary change in the Soviet Union.'[12] It
was worth reading and it was interesting, but it 'reads like his speeches,
which are, in fact, quite long and boring.' Boring books make poor material
for entertaining news. The only 'big surprise' was Gorbachev's sexism. He
'suggested that, perhaps, we should have a debate about returning women
to their more purely womanly mission.' Of course, Gorbachev was not
actually identified as a sexist for advocating traditional roles and behaviour
for women. Rather, his remarks were 'interesting' because there is an
'approaching serious problem of unemployment in the Soviet Union, and it
might be an indication that he's thinking of addressing that, by coaxing

women out of the work force and back into the kitchen.' One wonders how the opinions of Brian Mulroney or Michael Wilson would be described if they advocated a policy of unemployment reduction by ensuring a more womanly mission for the female citizens of Canada – not as 'new thinking,' at any rate.

On 30 November, *The National* broadcast an excerpt from an interview with the general secretary by NBC anchor Tom Brokaw. Brokaw never said anything, and the CBC used the interview as a primer for *The Journal*'s feature 'Inside the Gorbachev Revolution.' The CBC hardly ever uses foreign feeds on its own broadcasts. Accordingly, it is important to notice what was stressed. Three topics were mentioned, each of which consisted of a lead-in by the CBC anchor and a translated Gorbachev sound-bite.

Knowlton Nash: On arms control, Gorbachev said he thinks the U.S. and the Soviet Union can make headway on a 50 per cent reduction in their long-range nuclear missiles.

Gorbachev was, in fact, much more vague.

Mikhail Gorbachev [voice of translator]: There are real prospects ahead of us. We believe that it is possible to do a lot of work with this present administration, still with this administration, so as to, so, so that we could make headway on this major direction, uh, in the area of arms control.

According to Nash, Gorbachev next was asked if the firing of Boris Yeltsin was a mistake.

Mikhail Gorbachev [voice of translator]: No, there was no mistake. No. You know, uh, we will follow the path of *perestroika* firmly and consistently. We will follow the path of democracy and reforms firmly and consistently, but we will not jump over fences. We will not allow any adventurism, but we will not allow conservative, conservatism to be rampant either.

This sound-bite served to reinforce the angle already established, that Gorbachev was steering a middle course between 'adventurism' and 'conservatism.' Lastly, he was asked about his wife, Raisa.

Mikhail Gorbachev [voice of translator]: We discuss everything, including Soviet affairs at the highest level. I think, uh, I have answered your question. In total, we discuss everything.

Summarizing this sequence, the audience has been primed to see Gorbachev as a moderate man who respects women and is devoted to nuclear-
arms reduction.
   Barbara Frum immediately appeared to promote *The Journal*.

Barbara Frum: Inside the Gorbachev revolution. The Soviet economy is in decline.
Industry is lumbering and outdated. Food subsidies are breaking the state bank. The
quality of consumer products is awful, and the boss admits it.

Mikhail Gorbachev [voice of translator]: Only socialism would take it for so long. In
capitalism, we would have gone bankrupt a long time ago.

Adding to the qualities indicated earlier, Gorbachev also appeared to be
witty and open. He never was allowed to appear as tough, and was called
tough only by deviant sources.
   In his lead-in to *The Journal's* coverage, anchor Bill Cameron tied all
these qualities together.

Bill Cameron: When Mikhail Gorbachev signs the arms agreement next week, part of
his agenda will be to take some of the money his country spends on weapons and
redirect it into the economy. His plan is based on a radical restructuring of the
Soviet economy, a policy he calls *perestroika*.

Terence McKenna, the correspondent, confirmed the angle that Gorbachev
was different. He refused to brag about an economy that was 'a total mess.
And he's turning away from some key elements of Marxist-Leninist theory.'
McKenna did not indicate immediately or explicitly what those key elements were. He turned instead to Gorbachev and visualized him 'as campaigning like a Western politician, pleading with Soviet citizens to support
his policy. Commiserating with them about a sorry state of Soviet production. Just listen to him.' A suitable sound-bite followed. The most interesting thing about McKenna's coverage is the contrast it made with the kind of
coverage journalists conventionally give to Western politicians. No 'dialectical' or point/counterpoint model here. Gorbachev's words were taken at
face value, and evidence was produced to support those words. Accordingly,
McKenna spoke broadly of new incentives for workers, of administrative
decentralization, of great obstacles, of private enterprise in the form of
farmers' markets, and of cutting the massive state bureaucracy.

Terence McKenna: Like an ambitious Western business executive, Mikhail Gorbachev wants to attack the overstuffed bureaucracy by cutting dead wood. Firing unproductive managers, and rewarding good ones.

Perestroika, according to McKenna, amounts to 'kick-starting the economy' by 'private enterprise experiments,' the very opposite of what the kick-start means in Western economies – namely, government spending. There followed a series of interviews and stand-ups providing images of the inefficiency of the Soviet economy and of the difficulty that adjusting to *perestroika* entailed. One person, interviewed in Riga, had turned a dismal state-run restaurant into a successful cooperative. He insisted that his achievement did not constitute a restoration of capitalism.

Anatole Povars [voice of translator]: Remember we do not set the prices, all prices are fixed by the state, and all restaurants must charge the same amount, so there is no resemblance to capitalism.

Even more important than market prices for a genuine restructuring of the Soviet economy would be the existence of private property and the rule of law, both of which are required for markets to exist as anything other than 'experiments.'
    In the first week of December, Joe Schlesinger reported from Washington on 'the run-up to next week's summit.' He provided a highly ambivalent message. On the one hand, it was all just public relations: the Russians were 'playing the good guys,' and Reagan was making 'a gesture to his erstwhile allies.' But, on the other, the Soviets really *were* the good guys and the Americans, if not the bad guys, were the inflexible guys or the slow guys. He began by emphasizing superficial things.

Joe Schlesinger: So the Russians are in town, playing the good guys whose feelings have been hurt by American suspicions. As for Reagan's complaint about Soviet ABM violations, it's a gesture to his erstwhile allies which says, 'See, guys, I can still be tough with those Commies.' So, for the moment anyway, Reagan's main battle may not be with the Russians. It's likely to be with his oldest and closest friends.

In the hopes of making a 'counterstrike' in the battle for U.S. public opinion, President Reagan 'gave a rare television interview to four U.S. anchor men.' Reagan was 'optimistic' not only with respect to the INF Treaty, but also with respect to reducing strategic nuclear weapons as well.

Joe Schlesinger: But he squashed one idea of easing tensions, a proposal that, if the

Soviet Union should set a date for pulling its forces out of Afghanistan, the United States would reciprocate by stopping arms shipments to the rebels there.

If the Americans were of the opinion that the supply of arms, and Stingers in particular, to the mujahedeen was to some degree responsible for the defeat and retreat of the Soviet armed forces, there was no way in the world they would agree to the Soviet's *quid pro quo*. Moreover, the senior CBC correspondent in the United States must have known this.

In his wrap-up, Schlesinger summarized the CBC visualization of the summit. It was a two-man show between a young, reformist Russian and an old, suspicious conservative. Accordingly

in the image contest that's been going on here, Gorbachev has been clearly gaining on Reagan. In one poll in which Americans were asked to judge the performance of the leaders, 35 per cent said that Reagan was performing fully, while only 20 per cent thought that Gorbachev was falling down on the job. Joe Schlesinger, CBC News, Washington.

Schlesinger's alleged poll was scientifically meaningless. The point of the numbers was to indicate quantitatively that Gorby was whipping Ronnie, the great communicator, even in the 'image contest.'

The lead story on *Sunday Report*, 6 December, concerned the meetings that were to take place the following week. Coverage opened with an account of a protest in Washington against Soviet emigration policies. The correspondent, Terry Milewski, began by emphasizing organization, not the ostensible purpose of the demonstration.

Terry Milewski: It was carefully planned. Taking place before Mikhail Gorbachev gets here so as not to compete in the headlines with his arrival, and to avoid disruption of the summit or embarrassing Ronald Reagan. The point of it all was simple. To insist that all refuseniks, not just a token few, be released from the Soviet Union.

Two sound-bites, from well-known spokesmen for the Jewish community, followed, and an additional visualization cue: 'The rally was peaceful and even polite, endorsed by the Reagan administration and a must for presidential candidates.' Then came a clip of George Bush: 'Let's not hear any more claims about protecting state security or about the United States organizing a brain drain. Mr Gorbachev, let these people go.' Let them go. In case the first visualization cue – namely that this demonstration was a highly organized domestic U.S. political event – was missed, Milewski then

pointed out that such rallies were 'highly unusual': 'It's a semi-official demonstration. Not a protest against the government, but sanctioned by the
government in order to put pressure on Gorbachev.'

The second story built on the lead story: there was 'a protest rally in
Moscow today with a similar theme to the one here.' The only difference
was that Moscow's was broken up by 'hundreds of burly men calling themselves "peace demonstrators," but they were widely believed to be plain-
clothes Soviet police.' Equivalent coverage, not verbal cues, suggested the
meaning of these parallel events. It was enough to suggest they were equivalent.

Later in the newscast, at story position eight, the anchor, Peter Mansbridge, indicated the schedule of meetings between the two leaders and the
purpose of their meeting – namely, to agree to reduce intermediate-range
nuclear weapons:

Peter Mansbridge: Most people accept the notion that, when it comes to nuclear
weapons, the fewer the better. But over the years, many Americans have come to
count on nuclear missiles not only to protect them, but to provide them with a livelihood.

In order to find such people, who may be visualized as benefiting from
nuclear weapons, the CBC sent Joe Schlesinger to a small town in Missouri
near a missile base, which was itself visualized as a hole next to a turkey
farm. Schlesinger interviewed children who indicated they were afraid of
the base, but knowledgeable about, and proud of it. Two adults were interviewed, one of whom underlined a fatalistic, and so irresponsible, view:
'Ground-zero's everywhere. And should a, should a war occur, no one in the
world can escape it, and we'll just go quicker possibly, and that may be a
blessing.' The other, the town mayor, allowed as the missile base was
needed to protect the United States: 'So I don't feel bad about it. I wouldn't,
I wouldn't lose a minute's sleep over it.' Schlesinger summarized the first
half of the story with an almost predictable cliché: 'The town has not only
learned to live with the bomb, it would have a hard time living without it.
Eighty per cent of its business comes from the base.'

Because this town, near a missile base in Missouri, had been visualized as
owing its prosperity to the existence of weapons that threaten everyone else
in the world, the summit could be visualized as threatening that prosperity.
The possibility of reducing nuclear weapons, which 'most people' accept as
a good thing, was not, in this visualization, accepted by these people in Missouri. 'Most people,' unlike the man interviewed, do 'feel bad' about

nuclear weapons and do (or ought to) lose sleep over them. Only self-interest and misguided patriotism enabled this man to get a good night's sleep. These Missourians were, therefore, visualized as deviant.

The second half of the story underlined the visualization of the first half. If the summit threatens the prosperity of the town, it ought to be 'big news here, [but] it isn't,' Schlesinger said.

And there is a reason. The exciting news here is that Knob Noster will be getting *more* nuclear weapons. The base here has been chosen as the home of the newest American strategic weapon, the B2 Stealth Bomber.

Mayor: I feel real excited about that.

Joe Schlesinger: The town is expected to double in size. A new motel is already going up. In two years, this cow pasture will be filled with housing. At the Ace Hardware Store, they're spending $750,000 to triple their floor space. Store owner Larry Brian is betting in effect that there won't be an arms cut that would effect Knob Noster.

Larry Brian: I just don't feel like it, it'll happen. No, I'm not a bit scared about it.

It is unclear whether Larry Brian was 'scared' of an arms race, and the visualized threat it expressed, or of the adverse effects of an 'arms cut.' One might summarize the visualization of the town populace, and thereby all misguided U.S. patriots who think nuclear weapons help protect their country, as people who are making a living by threatening the rest of humanity. Knob Noster, Missouri, was America's version of Darra, Pakistan, a town that prospered by the manufacture of weapons. In both instances, the merchants of death opposed the Soviet Union.

Schlesinger emphasized this final visualization with a cut-back to the schoolchildren.

Joe Schlesinger: But in Mrs Stubb's class, some children are worried about the future of the missiles.

Boy: You know, my dad, he, you know, he's an important part because he helps make 'em, and you know, every time he comes home from work he talks about making 'em, and you know, that's part of my life because you know, he's talked about that ever since, you know, I remember. And so if, if they cut out all the missiles, my dad would be out of work and so, you know, we'll just be ...

Joe Schlesinger: As the people of Knob Noster have learned to live with the bomb, so have many other Americans. Millions in one way or another make their living from nuclear weapons. And millions of others see them not just as means in defence of the West, but also the symbol of nationalist strength and pride. And that's what makes so many Americans different from most of the rest of us.

With this final visualization of the deviant Americans, Schlesinger returned to the Mansbridge image of 'most people' who 'accept the notion that when it comes to nuclear weapons, the fewer the better.' Americans, however, don't; and that's what makes so many of them different from most of the rest of us.

This appeal to anti-Americanism was, no doubt, the purpose of the entire exercise. Certainly, neither the real purpose of the missile base – namely, to help provide the strategic defence of North America – nor the real purpose of the INF talks or of the summit ever featured in Schlesinger's report. There was no discussion of deterrence, apart from the words of the town mayor, and he was visualized as deviant in the extreme, nor of the role of the ICBMs at Knob Noster in ensuring the credibility of deterrence. No distinction was made between strategic defence of North America and the INF talks, the relationship between intermediate-range nuclear missiles and NATO strategy. All were 'nuclear weapons,' and 'most people' – which is to say, in CBC imagery, all reasonable people – accepted the notion 'the fewer the better.'

There followed immediately a report from 'halfway round the world' where Soviet citizens 'are also watching them build up to the summit.' Lest we visualize Soviet and U.S. citizens 'watching' with the same political sense of participation, Mansbridge assured his audience that 'the Soviet leader doesn't have to pay as much attention to public opinion as an American president.' Differences, therefore, do exist. But they are minor, because 'no political leader likes to be unpopular.' Politics in both countries is (whatever the differences) essentially a matter of popular leaders whose deeds are 'watched' by citizens. The audience again received the message: the Soviets are *really* just like us.

The report, by Michael McIver, continued the visualization by beginning with an account of the weather. It was cold:

but it's never cold enough to stop Moscovites from indulging their passion for ice cream. Or cold enough to stop them from standing in line, especially to buy a rare delicacy like oranges. They're expensive, but that doesn't seem to matter. Nearby, the first sign of a coming holiday. An outdoor vendor doing a brisk business selling Christmas cards. Moscovites going about their daily business. Although doing so in winter can be tough, even treacherous. Mothers are forced to struggle. The elderly, too, walk with extra care. Mind you, as in Canada, ice can be fun too, especially if you're a kid. But just mention the summit and many people will stop whatever they're doing and discuss it.

The context, cold weather, established the link with Canada: 'ice can be fun too.' The Soviets were preparing for Christmas, just as Canadians were. But it could never be too cold for ice cream or for talk about the summit. One woman said she hoped it will go well; McIver added that 'many think that, over time, further, even total disarmament is possible.' As for the American president's allegations of human-rights violations, 'most Muscovites say he should mind his own business.'

Michael McIver: And then a plea from a World War II veteran who was there when Soviet and American forces linked up at the Elbe River.

Veteran [voice of translator]: I must say that when that victory was achieved and we met with the Americans, we all talked about only one thing. That this would be the last war for both of us, and I want to die knowing the Second World War was the last one.

Michael McIver: Moscovites are clearly hoping that the Washington meetings will ease tensions, reduce arms, and lessen the risk of war between the superpowers.

The visualizations of hopeful and peace-loving Moscovites provided a stark contrast with the Americans making money from nuclear-weapons production. The problem of human rights in the USSR was no one's business but the Soviets.

For a U.S. assessment of Mikhail Gorbachev, the CBC found a professor of political science who explained that the absence of Italian restaurants in Moscow was a consequence of Russian xenophobia. This xenophobia was being overcome by 'the generation which wanted blue jeans when it was young, which wanted rock and roll, jazz, Western film. The twenty-year olds of the 1950s are now the fifty-year-olds. And they're in power today.' Mansbridge then asked if the professor was sure that the Soviet rockers of the Eisenhower era were really in power. He was.

Absolutely no question. The West has properly paid great attention to Raisa Gorbachev, because what Raisa Gorbachev is, is precisely a symbol. That when, when Mikhail was young, he was that kind of young, Western person who chose a young

Western girl, a Western-oriented girl, a modern girl, as, as, as his wife! And that, he puts her on television! She dresses the way she does! It's a powerful symbol of just what he is and what he's going to do to Russia.

There remained only the Canadian response. Now, Canada, Mansbridge explained, 'is not a nuclear power. But that doesn't mean a nuclear threat is remote. If missiles ever do fly between the United States and the Soviet Union, many would fly right over Canada. So Canadians have plenty to say about nuclear weapons in general, and this week's summit in particular.'

To find out what Canadians had to say, Claude Adams interviewed some world-weary students in Toronto. One of them explained that 'they' could still ruin the world and that he, at least, would not sleep properly until there were no nuclear weapons. Two other students gave their observations.

Student #2: We have no idea whether this is a first step or, or the last step.

Student #3: They're going to do, take out one small evil and leave the large evil there.

Adams visualized an explanation for their 'bleak view.' They were, he said, 'a generation raised with the bomb, living in a country that has little influence at the nuclear bargaining table.' Canadian lack of influence had, apparently, turned these students into 'pessimists' and 'cynics.'

Not all who were interviewed, however, were cynical pessimists. One student uttered 11 words: 'an agreement is an agreement. An agreement is a step forward.' An student expert on strategic matters was permitted 18 words to indicate there may be 'momentum' in the negotiations. These two were contradicted by 190 words explaining that 'tons and tons of cruise missiles' were excluded, that U.S. foreign policy was a 'sham,' that conventional wars lead to nuclear wars and, of course:

Student #4: We have to live with nuclear weapons. It's a scary thought, and we're never going to be able to get rid of them no matter what the superpowers negotiate.

Claude Adams: And no matter what Reagan and Gorbachev sign, these students are convinced the bomb is here to stay.

The pattern of visualization continued over the next few days.

The American president and the Soviet general secretary signed the INF Treaty on 8 December 1987. Joe Schlesinger led off *The National* with remarks on how strange it was to hear the Soviet anthem played on the White House lawn and for Ronald Reagan to welcome Mikhail Gorbachev, 'the leader of what the American president still likes to call the evil empire.' Schlesinger then summarized the day's events.

Joe Schlesinger: Reagan did a bit of boasting.

President Ronald Reagan: I first proposed what would come to be called the zero-option. It was a simple proposal, one might say, disarmingly simple.

Joe Schlesinger: Gorbachev responded with a call for a little modesty.

Mikhail Gorbachev [voice of translator]: It's probably still too early to bestow laurels upon each other.

The differences remaining between the two countries were visualized in the closing statements of the two leaders:

President Ronald Reagan: Let us remember that genuine international confidence and security are inconceivable without open societies with freedom of information, freedom of conscience, the right to publish, and the right to travel.

Mikhail Gorbachev [voice of translator]: ... people want to live in a world in which American and Soviet spacecraft would come together for dockings and joint voyages, not for Star Wars.

The Americans, and, in particular, the Strategic Defense Initiative, were, in the CBC visualization, the major obstacle to even greater agreements, and eventually 'world peace.' In terms of the dialectic of deviance, it was clearly visualized that the United States and NATO were at fault, and the USSR was peace-loving and progressive. No attempt was ever made to visualize the Strategic Defense Initiative as what had led to the Soviet presence in the U.S. capital, nor was the foreign policy of the Reagan administration or NATO strategy ever visualized as having contributed to the Soviet desire to negotiate the INF Treaty.[14]

Meantime, back in the USSR, according to Mansbridge, 'the summit's getting saturation coverage in the media, and Soviet citizens seem fascinated by it all.' In London, Patrick Brown visualized the British response.

Patrick Brown: Anti-nuclear campaigners broke out with champagne tonight, feeling their years of marching and demonstrating deserves some of the credit for today's agreement, but vowing to keep on campaigning for a nuclear-free world.

A representative of the disarmament movement indicated there was still much to be done. As evidence of how much, video sequences of cruise-missile launchers were shown leaving Greenham Common, and interviews with protesters followed:

Member of Women's Peace Camp: If they're saying to the world that they've got rid of the cruise missiles and they're still taking them out on the roads. They're still exercising with them. Then they can still use them.

Brown's wrap-up provided a summary visualization: most people 'accepted' the agreement, but 'outside the peace movement there have been fears that Western Europe will become more vulnerable if the nuclear umbrella is folded up further.' In other words, there were now two sets of deviants. The right deviants were those who saw the INF Treaty as a partial dismantling of the NATO strategy that had brought a generation of stability to Europe. On the other side were the left deviants in the peace movement. And, in the middle, were 'most people.' According to the CBC visualization, 'most people' were prepared to accept the Washington agreement and especially the 'warm atmosphere' that accompanied it, which, in turn, 'has gone some way towards allaying those fears.'

Unfortunately, it was not only the fearful European allies in NATO that stood in the way of warm feelings towards the USSR. Even in Washington, there remained that regrettable concern for Soviet human-rights violations.

Peter Mansbridge: For hundreds of protesters, the feeling towards the Soviet Union is very chilly. There are demonstrations every day. Serious ones, against the Soviet record on human rights. Against Soviet foreign policy.

These 'serious' demonstrations, which might have altered the CBC visualization of the summit, did not count as news. They were overshadowed by others, demonstrations 'that don't seem to have too much to do with the superpowers at all.' Terry Milewski, the correspondent covering these 'other' demonstrations, visualized them all in his opening words.

Terry Milewski: If you've got a cause, you're selling it in Washington, now. The hopes aroused by this summit have brought an invasion of causes to a city which sees demonstrations all the time. But never, ever, anything like this cacophony, almost all of it directed against the Soviets.

The first anti-Soviet cause for which a sound-bite was offered was a clip of an agitated demonstrator.

Man on street – demonstrator: A Hare Krishna woman became subject of a very severe persecution.

The imagery of Hare Krishna no doubt primed the audience to dismiss the 'causes' of the remaining 'other' demonstrators.

Terry Milewski: They have come from all over the globe to pray, shout, and plead their cases. Exiles from the Russian Caucasus, Sikhs from the Punjab, you name it.

There were even Afghans, for whom

the summit is not just a photo opportunity. It's a matter of life and death, carrying posters of relatives they say were maimed by Russian troops. They demand attention, and they get it. They get it, because when the two most powerful men on earth meet, it is an absolutely massive media event.

For such a media event, both U.S. and Soviet spokesmen were hard at work, trying 'to put a favourable spin on the news.' One such 'polished spokesman' was Vladimir Posner, who was immediately introduced to give a 46-word sound-bite on *glasnost*, followed by 6 words from a Jewish protester: 'It proves how false *glasnost* is.' Milewski then summarized the whole collection of 'other' demonstrations: 'for every Soviet spokesman, there's a protest calling him a liar.' It is perhaps fitting that Milewski, having been primed by a Hare Krishna devotee, ended his report by emphasizing the extent of Soviet success at this 'massive media event.' He characterized it as a 'charm offensive.'

Terry Milewski: The Soviet charm offensive has made a powerful impact in Washington. Raisa Gorbachev fascinates the media. Her clothes, her hair, her smile. But the Gorbachev magnetism has also attracted those who say that *glasnost* has not worked for them.

Lest the audience be left with a negative image of the USSR by mention of those for whom *glasnost* has not 'worked' (notwithstanding their association with the severely persecuted Hare Krishna woman), Barbara Frum immediately appeared to remind the audience of an upcoming story on *The Journal*:

Barbara Frum: Tonight, we meet the people whose lives will be directly affected by today's treaty. Gillian Findlay visits the towns where America's weapons are made.

If Joe Schlesinger's angle worked the night before, it might work again.

Before presenting that story, an elaborate stage was set. Barbara Frum had an extensive conversation with Stephen Cohen, of Princeton University; Brent Scowcroft, a former national security adviser under President Reagan; and Oleg Bykov, identified only as a professor accompanying the Soviet delegation. Frum began by extolling Gorbachev's ability at 'communication.'

Barbara Frum: It's been Ronald Reagan who's been called the great communicator, but today it was Mikhail Gorbachev who was using the airwaves to great advantage. Everywhere he appeared, he carried the same message. This treaty is just the beginning. This could be the start of a new era of peace. Nowhere was the new style of the Soviet leader more apparent than at this afternoon's extraordinary meeting with American intellectuals and celebrities. With me now are two Americans who were there.

In previous programs, as we have seen, Cohen had proved himself to be capable of highly imaginative visualizations of the significance of Gorbachev's 'reforms.' It was altogether fitting that Frum pose him the first question: 'Are expectations being raised too high?'

Stephen Cohen, Princeton: Well, they may be raised too high. But the. What we can say is that this is a gigantic stride, a gigantic step. But it is only the first step. And it is a long long journey, even to approach this vision that both Reagan and Gorbachev have held out, which is a radical reduction in nuclear weapons.

By Cohen's standards, given such an inviting question, this was a modest and restrained answer. Frum gave him another, stronger cue.

Barbara Frum: But the flavour, the flavour of that session that you were both at today, at the Soviet embassy, have you ever seen that before?

Frum had already indicated that the day was without precedent and contained the possibility of a new era in human history; how could Cohen decently disagree even if he wanted to? He didn't.

Frum then turned to Scowcroft.

Barbara Frum: It's a whole new ball game, isn't it, General Scowcroft?

He agreed, too. Frum then turned to Bykov, and asked him to explain why Gorbachev seemed to be so impatient. First, he signed the INF Treaty, and now, she said, he is talking about conventional-force levels, chemical weapons, strategic weapons. Why the big hurry?

Oleg Bykov: Well, time is of essence, because the clock is running, not only on the Soviet Union, and not only on the United States for this matter, but on entire mankind. And a new beginning, with the INF Treaty, today signed at the White House by the General Secretary Gorbachev and President Reagan, really is a new and genuine beginning. It has to be sustained. The momentum is there.

Bykov's initial response was to repeat the core of Gorbachev's contribution to Marxism – *novoye myshleniye*, new thinking. As indicated in the previous section, 'new thinking' amounts to a denial of the traditional Marxist-Leninist categories of class struggle, international proletarian solidarity, and imperialism. A less kind way of putting it would be to say that 'new thinking' is the final act of revisionism and a public confession that Marxism-Leninism is nonsense. In ideological terms, it was as if Gorbachev had received, ten years late, Solzhenitsyn's *Letter to the Soviet Leaders*, which pointed out that Marxism-Leninism 'has long ceased to be helpful to us here at home, as it was in the 'twenties and 'thirties.'[14] In fact, both Solzhenitsyn and Bykov were saying that the official ideology was a sham, a lie, and everyone knew it, especially the Politburo. Frum, however, failed to apprehend that Gorbachev and Bykov had repudiated the perverse faith of their fathers.

She turned instead to the image of 'momentum,' which was visualized, not as an inapt metaphor to describe the conduct of foreign policy, but as a concrete description of reality.

Barbara Frum: When I met you for the first time, earlier today, you suggested that your side is afraid of losing momentum. Now, why?

Oleg Bykov: Well, this is something which I think is one difficulty, and a danger to lose the momentum. Because, however important in itself, the INF Treaty is only a good start. It's an opener, if you will.

Barbara Frum: But are you afraid that something is going to happen in this administration? Or that there's going to be another tiff between the two sides that's going slow this down?

Oleg Bykov: No, what I mean is the momentum has to be sustained. And, indeed, it has to be enhanced in every way, and not simply doing more of the same, but doing more and better. And the obvious candidate, of course, is the strategic armaments.

Of course, scrapping strategic nuclear weapons, especially in Europe, has been the perennial long-range Soviet objective. This had been pointed out to Frum several times on earlier shows. Rather than question it and raise the unseemly facts of conventional Soviet superiority, Frum turned to the ever-ebullient Cohen.

Barbara Frum: Professor Cohen, the INF Treaty took six years, seven years? They're talking now about cutting the nuclear arsenals in half in seven months. Is that doable?

Stephen Cohen: It's doable. Yeah, if there's a will, there's a way.

Cohen had learned again to take a hint and went back to the 'momentum' question.

Stephen Cohen: But you, you're, we lost sight of one thing. The reason that the momentum is important, is that there's opposition, powerful opposition, to this process in the United States. And though the professor might not acknowledge it fully, there's even some opposition of this type of process in the Soviet Union. So we need a lot of leadership. We've got a presidential election coming up in the United States. There are a lot of factors gonna play a role. That's why momentum is important.

Scowcroft, who had had actual experience in negotiating with the Soviets, was more cautious.

Brent Scowcroft: I think too much momentum is dangerous. What I'm seeing now is a repetition, even more extreme than in 1972, when there was a great sense of euphoria, when the new relationship between the two sides was oversold, and the reaction that set in has been, was very serious and took a long time to get over. This is not simply a case of misunderstanding between the two sides. There are real issues between us, and if we imagine them away, we could be moving toward a let-down later on.

Frum then discussed the verification procedures involved in the INF Treaty and returned to the question of a 'let-down.'

Barbara Frum: I heard, uh, Mr Shultz, the secretary of state, say just before he went into the White House dinner tonight that Mr Gorbachev's plan to get rid of all weapons by the end of the century is totally unrealistic, that, uh, the world is gonna be based on mutual deterrence for a long time to come. Is that fair to say?

A cue for Cohen. Maybe we can't 'get rid of 'em all,' he said,

but there's two things we can do. We can stop building them. That's the key, to stop building 'em. For that we need a test-ban freeze. You can't test, you can't build. The second thing is, we can reduce what we got, very significantly. That's achievable.

Cohen was restoring the earlier visualization that 'most people' believed that the fewer nuclear weapons, the better. Scowcroft had to restore some sense of reality.

Brent Scowcroft: I think, the major issue between us, and the major thing we ought to work toward, is not counting numbers of nuclear weapons, but reduce the chances of conflict between us. That is the important thing. It's not how many weapons we have, it's whether or not we are likely to go to war with each other.

Frum immediately changed the subject to something more congenial than complex and unpleasant reality – namely, imaginative speculation.

Barbara Frum: I'm coming to the end here. Professor Bykov, for years the United States said, we can't really do anything significant with the Soviets. Look at all their leaders. We have to wait for the new face on the Soviet side. Clearly President Reagan is no longer at the height of his powers. Do you think you can do these things you want to do with this administration?

Bykov pointed out the obvious, that they *were* dealing with the Reagan administration. By implication, they would deal with Reagan's successor in the same way. The Americans then said they were not so sure. The topic had gone nowhere, but by avoiding the real problems of NATO/WTO balance, the imagery of progress, a new era, and so forth, could be sustained.

Frum turned again to Cohen to recharge the discussion

Barbara Frum: Stephen Cohen, we sit here at the end of a day of surging expectations. I mean, we all watched. You, too, in that room, and one had a feeling of, maybe this is a new era, is it? Is it, really? Or is it just show business? Political show business?

Stephen Cohen: I don't have surging expectations, myself. I study the Soviet Union. And I will tell you, it's a new era inside the Soviet Union. Whether that's gonna lead to a new era in world affairs, I don't know. A lot depends on the United States. A lot.

Cohen's 'professionalism' intervened to deflate Frum's surging and disordered rhetoric. He spoke as one who studied the Soviet Union, and he found new things; it was now up to the United States to match those innovations. I have not the enthusiasm of a journalist, he was saying. Nevertheless, his remarks served perfectly to reinforce the strategic visualization of the CBC: the United States was the great brake to historical progress. Bykov agreed that a 'tremendous change' had taken place, and Scowcroft urged caution. By now, time was genuinely running out.

Barbara Frum: Anybody got a final sentence? Only time for one final sentence.

Stephen Cohen: Yeah, wait and see if the Americans are willing to talk with the Soviets about Gorbachev's proposal to stop testing nuclear weapons. That would be a major development. If it happens.

Cohen's overkill ignored not only Scowcroft's prudence but the earlier words of the Soviet general secretary, that it was still too early to bestow laurels. But Frum had turned the topic from the actual words and the real interests of the political leaders to the media event, the news, and its spin. Perhaps, under the circumstances, wild speculation and the use of powerful metaphors such as 'momentum' were appropriate. It surely was riveting TV and good entertainment.

This sequence was followed by an excerpt from a British 'docudrama' dealing with the previous summit in Reykjavik. The U.S. president, according to this account, 'was taken aback' by the Soviet proposals and was 'maybe out of his depth,' dealing with a general secretary 'whose style of conducting negotiation was obviously based on being a very long-term shrewd negotiator.' The contrast between the progressive Soviets and foot-dragging Americans was dramatically expressed by this fictional visualization of the two leaders.

The next step was to extend the contrast to their respective wives. Bill Cameron, the anchor, provided some gossip concerning what 'many Soviets' think about Raisa Gorbachev.

Bill Cameron: In October, former party boss Boris Yeltsin criticized her for boarding a Soviet ship that was off-limits to women. That may have cooked Yeltsin's goose.

Certainly criticizing Raisa Gorbachev was no way to win points with her husband.
He admits he talks about everything with her. And it's going to stay that way.

She was, moreover, 'a Doctor of Philosophy, a former university lecturer,'
and, to complete the visualization of the dynamic leader's consort, 'abroad
she is considered as well dressed, well informed, and as sleekly controlled as
the actress Nancy Reagan.' Unfortunately the two women did not get
along. 'In Geneva, Mrs Reagan wanted to talk about their children; Mrs
Gorbachev wanted to talk about Marx.' The contrasting visualizations were
now complete: the reluctant Americans, out of their depth, facing a shrewd
negotiator on a roll; the wives were equally well turned out, always an
important consideration for TV. But Nancy was old-fashioned: she wanted
to talk about the kids. She was also merely an actress. Raisa, in contrast, was
a new woman. What could be more chic than chatting about Marx while
taking a stroll by Lake Geneva? And Raisa was real. She had a PhD to prove
it. The stage was nearly set.

True to Postman's 'Now this ...' formula, Cameron moved on: 'Now
some comparative numbers on the U.S./USSR.' Comparative demography
revealed a higher rate of population increase in the Soviet Union, reinforc-
ing the dynamic visualization. (Nothing was mentioned of the declining
rate of *Russian* birth being more than compensated for by a rapidly increas-
ing birthrate among the non-Slavic and predominantly Muslim population
of Soviet Central Asia.) The observation was also made that the Soviet
Union 'lost a lot of young people forty years ago, in the Second World
War.' (Nothing was said of 'losses' ten and twenty years before the war as a
result of the Great Terror.)[15] These sins of omission, while introducing
some obvious imbalance, are comparatively unimportant. As we saw in
chapter 1, what is not visualized is not missed. The demographic interlude
supported the visualization of a dynamic USSR; the losses of the Second
World War primed the audience for the next, superficially incongruous,
sequence on chemical weapons.

Shots of Iranian corpses accompanied Bill Cameron's visualization of
these 'efficient, cheap, easy-to-make, easy-to-hide' and very lethal weapons.
Four years earlier, the United States had proposed banning chemical and
biological weapons (CBWs) and included a treaty provision requiring site
inspection of CBW facilities. 'The Soviets wanted no part of that. They
didn't admit they had chemical weapons until this year [i.e., 1987]. But a
couple of months ago they changed their minds.' Up to this point in the
sequence, the visualization was simply a continuation of the 'momentum'
story: the Soviets were flexible, progressive, and, in the interests of banning

CBWs, able to overcome their xenophobic suspicions. From the previous sequence, the audience had been primed to understand the reasonableness of Soviet suspicions: the great loss of young people in the war.

Having gone the extra mile and put aside their legitimate fears and suspicions, the Soviets then invited the United States to send observers to witness the destruction of Soviet chemical weapons. One might have expected a consistent visualization to have indicated that Soviet progressive flexibility must meet with U.S. intransigence. But, no; the United States reciprocated and invited Soviet observers to Utah for the same purpose.

Now the problem was how to account for U.S. flexibility in a manner consistent with the visualization of the United States that has been developed to this point. The simplest answer, immediately given, was: U.S. treachery. What they destroyed in Utah, said Cameron, was 'old material. The Americans haven't made chemical weapons since 1969, and they're destroying what they have.' The Americans, therefore, were simply getting rid of obsolete weapons. Moreover, these weapons were dangerous to Americans themselves, not least of all because they were difficult to store. To overcome both these problems, 'this month the Americans will begin making binary weapons. These involved loads of two chemicals, each harmless when they're apart, deadly when they're mixed. They represent a technical escalation of the chemical weapons race. They worried the Soviets, and they should worry all nations.' Nothing was said of Soviet binary weapons; accordingly, it was possible to maintain a consistent visualization of the United States as deviant. However, Cameron, or rather his script writer or producer, attempted to suggest that the U.S. destruction of the obsolete material and 'technical escalation of the chemical weapons race' may 'explain the Soviet change of heart.' By this visualization, U.S. technological superiority is what brought the USSR into a situation where they would agree to site inspection and to CBW destruction. This visualization, however, could also be applied to the entire summit event. To repeat, it might have been said that what brought the Soviet president to Washington was not his youth, vigour, new ideas, or brilliant wife, but SDI, which Gorbachev mentioned at least as often as *glasnost*. This alternative visualization, however, was never explicated. Nor was attention drawn to the fact that the Soviets continued CBW production after the Americans had quit.

The next sequence, by Cameron, reiterated the contrast between the two countries, this time in terms of 'taste.' The Soviets, he said, 'love movies' and constitute the largest movie-going audience in the world. 'And they read other people's books. In one recent year, they translated and published five times as many titles as the Americans did.' The visualization was intended to indicate the elevated literary taste of Soviet citizens, but anyone who has read Soviet literature could think of an obvious and contrasting reason why the Soviets do so much translating. Finally, Cameron ended with a humorous contrast: 'statistical research indicates the existence of a vast sheep gap. This could explain everything or nothing at all.' Barbara Frum then reappeared with a prelude to the final act of the evening.

Barbara Frum: When we return: there's widespread optimism after today's agreement. But there are Americans who fear their paycheques could be the first casualty of this arms treaty.

Frum's lead-in repeated the visualization of the 'other' protests. The bizarre was represented now not by Hare Krishnas, but by U.S. Buddhists. In addition, a mixed collection of Afghan, Estonian, and Ukrainian nationalists filled the 'showcase for demonstrators.' And then, 'in the corners of power, a more effective protest. American Conservatives worry that the United States is reducing its military strength.' According to Bill Cameron, ten million Americans have jobs 'linked to the war machine.' Gillian Findlay was sent to Amarillo, Texas, 'a community that's hooked on bombs,' for a report.

Outside Amarillo, visualized now as 'Texas through and through,' lies the U.S. Department of Energy's Pantex facility, 'the Western world's largest producer of nuclear weapons.'[16] For many years 'it was Amarillo's best-kept secret,' and even today it looks innocent enough: it 'could pass for a dairy. But deep inside this complex, workers put together every nuclear weapon in Ronald Reagan's arsenal.' The juxtaposition of seeming innocence – a building that looks like a dairy – with profound and personalized malignancy – Ronald Reagan's nuclear arsenal – was continued in the next visualization. Pantex represented *either* 'enough fire power to eventually destroy the earth' *or* '$12.77 an hour,' which, we are assured, is a good wage for factory workers in Texas. The implicit question posed by this visualization: What sort of person would accept $12.77 an hour in order to help destroy the earth? What sort of political organization recruits such people? The answer: deviants working within a deviant system.

The Pantex workers 'need a higher security rating than the normal factory worker,' but 'they see nothing abnormal about the product they make.' Findlay probably did not wish to imply principally that 'normal factory workers' required security clearance, but that these workers, who did require security clearance, should be visualized as having the attitudes of normal factory workers who happened to be well paid. In the first interview, a long-time worker declared he was proud to help in the defence of his country. The head of security at Pantex was interviewed next. According to Findlay, 'for him, making nuclear bombs is no different from making widgets.' What the individual said was that the production of nuclear weapons served deterrence:

Head of security – Pantex: I don't see one of those as it comes off the line, so to speak, as the killer of people and the destruction of property. Because, I don't think it will ever be used either. But I do think, if it wasn't comin' off that line, somebody'd use one on me.

Findlay then picked up the phrase 'comin' off that line' (pronounced 'laan' in Texan) and refocused her visualization. 'And if it wasn't coming off that line, this city would grind to a halt.' She then provided statistics and interviews to substantiate the contribution Pantex made to the economy of 'a part of the country still reeling from the slump in oil and wheat prices.' The first question was therefore answered: people in Amarillo will take $12.77 an hour to help destroy the earth because of a depressed local economy; indirectly, they did so because of capitalism and its cycle of crises.

The indirect reason was the next matter to be visualized in Findlay's report. Amarillo's economy would be worse off without Pantex, 'and so would hundreds of other U.S. communities that have been fed by the arms race.' Statistics followed, and then a personal visualization: 'But no president has pumped more military money into the Amarillos of America than Ronald Reagan.' A Republican congressman from Amarillo provided a sound-bite, declaring the gratitude of the American people to President Reagan for strengthening national defence, and Findlay linked his observation to the views of unnamed 'conservative economists who claim high military spending is essential for defence. And for business.' These views were soundly rebutted by William Arkin, identified as a 'nuclear analyst.'[17] According to him, the U.S. economy is 'a mess' that has been caused 'by America's addiction to military bucks.' As evidence, Findlay mentioned the stock-market correction 'Black Monday.' This 'agonizing symptom of America's illness' was also a reason for hope. According to a 'Wall Street defence analyst,' arms control, such as was contemplated by the INF Treaty, might become a substitute for defence spending. The visualization, if not the logic, is clear: the capitalist U.S. economy is in a mess because of defence spending, which can be reduced by arms-control treaties, which will restore the economy to health.

A final visualization tied together the kind of deviant people who work in

128 Sins of Omission

places such as Pantex with the larger concern for capitalism and its erratic, messy, and dangerous economy.

Gillian Findlay: In Amarillo, as in America, support for Pantex and the bomb is more than just a question of jobs. People here pride themselves on their patriotism. They're pro-conservative, anti-communist, and staunch believers in peace through deterrence. They're also extremely religious. And here, in the heart of America's Bible Belt, any discussion about nuclear war ultimately includes God.

Not everyone who talks about God has to be a Bible Belt fanatic. To present such an image would show lack of 'balance.' So the voice of reason made an appearance in the person of the Roman Catholic bishop. He once called upon Pantex workers to find other jobs and since then 'has been seen as odd man out, even by his parishioners.' The bishop said he had been to the USSR, and that he had received letters from parishioners working at Pantex who explained the need for deterrence. 'My reply to that,' he said, 'was that you don't defeat an idea with a bomb.' The bishop, therefore, was visualized as a man of ideas the soundness of which would defeat the less sound ideas of the communists. But, if anything ought to be clear from Gorbachev's 'new thinking' (to say nothing of subsequent events), it is precisely the unsoundness of Marxism. There is, in reality, no question of 'defeating' the unsound ideas held by communists, because they have abandoned the central opinions of Marx all by themselves. The reason for U.S. opposition to the Soviet Union had little to do with their unsound 'ideas' anyway, and rather more to do with their actions and capabilities. These latter two considerations involved notional 'bombs,' not 'ideas.'

However that may be, Findlay presented the bishop's statement as the image of reason. In contrast to what might, with charity, be called his touchingly naïve faith, she presented the faith of another and more exuberant preacher. This sequence began with a sound-bite: 'The word of God declares very distinctly, and very clearly, that this earth will be purged by nuclear war.' Findlay established the context of this remark: Amarillo was mostly fundamentalist, and many fundamentalists agreed with the sentiments just uttered. More important, this anticipation of a nuclear apocalypse was visualized as part of U.S. patriotism. 'By building bombs,' Findlay said, these fundamentalists say 'they're keeping America strong long enough to save more souls, souls that God will raise up when the nuclear holocaust comes.' And for this reason, they have a great distrust of Gorbachev.

Man on the street #1: I don't trust 'em, and I never will. As long as they's a Communist Party, I never will. I don't wanna have any dealing with 'em. I don't wanna let 'em into America.

Man on the street #2: You know, it's, uh, a lot of garbage, I think, as far as Russia is concerned. I don't think they really mean what they're sayin'. I, I feel like that, uh, actions speak louder than words. Poland and Afghanistan is, uh, two good examples, as far as I'm concerned.

Man on the street #3: ... 'cause I wouldn't want my kids to grow up in a communistic state.

Gillian Findlay: Would you rather have them perish in a nuclear holocaust?

Man on the street #3: Yes, 'cause I know they'd be in heaven.

In her wrap-up, Findlay brought together all the elements of her visualization. The people of Amarillo make their living 'from the weapons of war.' As the 'rituals of peace' unfolded across the country, the visualization of Amarillo indicated it all 'may be misleading. Amarillo, perhaps more so than the rest of America, is addicted to her bombs. Here in the Texas panhandle, being strong still means being the biggest nuclear gunslinger on the globe.' What the rituals of peace signified, according to this version of events, was an opportunity for Ronald Reagan to gain 'his place in history.' Behind those rituals, however, suspicion of the Soviet Union, the irrationalities of fundamentalist Christian eschatology, and the patriotism of Texas gunslingers combined to produce an ideological false consciousness that was dangerous to 'peace.' Findlay's visualization went considerably beyond that of Joe Schlesinger in characterizing American deviance.

On 'Day Two of the Superpower Summit,' December 9, 1987, the lead item featured Joe Schlesinger's report on the day's activities. On Afghanistan, a Gorbachev sound-bite indicated the Soviets had been ready to withdraw for some time.

Joe Schlesinger: But Reagan wants a precise date for the withdrawal, and Gorbachev wants a commitment that the United States will no longer supply the Afghan rebels with arms.

The 'but' with which Schlesinger began his report indicated that the U.S. president was asking for something unreasonable. Again, the Americans were the deviants, the Soviets normal. No reason was given why the Americans wanted a 'precise date' rather than a vague promise. The 'and Gorbachev' suggested that, even if Reagan was unreasonable, at least the Soviet leader was not: how could he leave Afghanistan if the Americans kept supplying the 'rebels' with arms? Schlesinger's format once again illustrated the doctrine of moral equivalence presented in the guise of balance. On the one hand, there is the U.S. demand, which is unreasonable anyway, and, on the other, the Soviet one.

Schlesinger continued:

Gorbachev also criticized the American demands for human-rights reform in the Soviet Union.

Mikhail Gorbachev [voice of translator]: What moral right does America have to assume the pose of a teacher? Who has given it the right to teach us moral lessons? I told the president yesterday, 'Mr President, you are not the prosecutor and I am not the accused.'

According to this visualization, the Americans were doubly at fault: for presuming to instruct the Soviets at all, and for being so tasteless as to bring up the issue in the first place. This question was touched upon explicitly later in the program.

In the remainder of his report, Schlesinger indicated that Soviet spokesmen were jolly fellows; the other minor agreements were reported, and the state dinner at the Soviet embassy was described as 'upbeat.' According to this visualization, the 'momentum' remained with the USSR.

In his introduction to the next report, Peter Mansbridge explained why. 'The Soviets,' he said, 'have been working hard here to get their point of view across, not just on arms control, but on a whole series of changes in Soviet society.' Michael McIver went on to present an account of Gorbachev's 'strong performances before influential people.' According to McIver's account, it was a great success.

Michael McIver: And a lot of people like what they hear.

Man: Most Americans like what you say, and many others believe what you say. I'm one of them.

American 'media experts' agreed that the Soviets had orchestrated a 'superb sales campaign.' If this is so, one wonders why these 'professionals' and 'investigative journalists' did not expose the Soviet hidden agenda or, indeed, inquire further about what the Soviets were 'selling.' Instead, there followed another report on Raisa Gorbachev, her tour of the White House, and further gossip about her relationship with Nancy Reagan.

On *The Journal*, Barbara Frum talked with Gennady Gerasimov, a Soviet delegate, 'familiar with the Soviet leader's agenda' and 'one of the most visible Soviets in Washington.'[18] Gerasimov assured her that the talks were going 'much better' than the talks had gone at Reykjavik. The INF Treaty was a prelude to a treaty that would reduce strategic forces as well. Frum then asked about congressional reaction in light of Soviet human-rights and emigration policies, and in light of Afghanistan. The issue was alluded to in the Gorbachev sound-bite objecting to the United States as a teacher of morals. In the jargon of visualizing negotiations, this is called 'linkage.'

Gennady Gerasimov: Well, I don't know. It's just a question of linkage again, all over again. These things are separate. Of course, for overall improvement of our relations, we must discuss everything, including bilateral relations, including human rights. And human rights is, by the way, a two-way street. But, uh, I think that ratification is there, it will be there. The signs are ...

Barbara Frum: You're saying that there would be linkage.

Gennady Gerasimov: We can argue endlessly, until we have this moment of ratification. And the president said that the treaty is going to sail through the Senate. So, what you are asking me is their problem. I'm, I can answer about our own problem. You see, not many, not all our people think that, uh, it, that we can trust America completely. We had a opinion poll, and just about 45 per cent of those who were asked said that they do not trust America. Then maybe they're going to cheat on this treaty. So it's possible that, uh, we have some discussion, serious one, on this treaty, when it is going to be ratified by Supreme Soviet.

By this visualization, the Soviets were not merely morally equivalent to the United States, but faced with equivalent policy and institutional problems. On policy, 'human rights ... is a two-way street.' If there have been Soviet human-rights abuses, so have there been American ones. Institutionally, the Supreme Soviet was compared with the U.S. Congress: both were filled with people who distrusted the other side. The Soviets even had an opinion poll to monitor the feelings of their citizens, just as did the Americans. The interview with Gerasimov was also part of the sequence or strategy of visualizations that aimed at showing the Soviets were like 'us' or like 'most people.' In the conceptual language we have been using, they were very normal indeed.

The interview ended with Frum asking Gerasimov whether Gorbachev was feeling 'that this trip has been a triumph for himself.' Gerasimov allowed that the president was pleased and content because the discussions had been business-like, constructive, and useful. No more normal an answer could be given.

To discuss 'Summit Fever' from the U.S. perspective, Frum next conversed with Richard Perle, identified as 'a former assistant secretary of defense, always described as a hard-liner who's been associated with the early anti-Soviet line at the White House,' and with Paul Warnke, who 'headed the American delegation at the SALT II talks.' He was *not* identified as a 'soft-liner' from President Carter's day. Perle's response to this 'fever' was to stress that there was a proper relationship between the United States and the Soviet Union.

Richard Perle: And that relationship encompasses a willingness to negotiate, where we can achieve agreements that are equitable, that are fair to both sides, that are verifiable. Agreements that are going to make the stability of the relationship between us stronger. But not all agreements are of that nature.

For his part, Warnke was delighted at what had been achieved.

Paul Warnke: I congratulate Richard Perle, and his colleagues, in reaching an agreement that's almost as good as those that we'd reached, during the Carter administration.

Frum then asked Perle what would change his mind about the Soviets and he replied: changes in their behaviour.

Barbara Frum: He's talking, of course, Paul Warnke, about linkage, about not giving any concession on arms control until there's some matching movement on, let's say, emigration, or Afghanistan, or some of these other issues. Do you favour that kind of policy, as well?

Paul Warnke: There is no way in the world that you're going to give concessions on arms control in order to influence Soviet behaviour some place else. Arms control has to stand on its own merits. It's either good for us, it's good for our security, or it's not. You can't tie the two together. So as a consequence, no. Supposing that all of a sudden Mr Gorbachev said, I'm gonna adopt the American Bill of Rights and you give me a 50 per cent advantage in strategic arms. That'd be totally absurd. The two have got to be separated.

According to Frum's visualization, 'linkage' meant being a 'hard-liner,' a deviant among deviants. Warnke pushed the linkage argument to an absurd conclusion, which, in turn, implied that Perle's position was absurd. He was made to look even more deviant because Frum had just described him as 'the favourite guest' of Nancy Reagan. Gorbachev himself 'made a point of clinking his glass against yours, right after his toast of peace and prosperity in the world. He wants to change your mind. He knows you're influential.'

Warnke had just said that arms control and Soviet adoption of an acceptable human-rights policy had to be 'decoupled.' Frum then underlined Perle's deviance with the question 'Why do you make the connection then?' Perle had not, of course, made the connection in the first place. His reply attempted to make clear his real position.

Richard Perle: Well, I, I, I, in fact, agree with what Paul has said. Arms-control agreements ought to be evaluated on their merits and approved or disapproved on their merits. But I do think that, in the long run, if we are to compose a truly cooperative relationship with the Soviet Union, it is going to take some change in that society in the direction of a much more open place. It is Andrei Sakharov who has identified the relationship between openness, between public participation in policy decisions, and the long-term evolution of relations between East and West. Human rights has to be a part of that, because it is the involvement of the broad public in political decisions and gives us some continuity and some confidence.

This clear statement was then nullified by Frum's quick response. 'Sorry. Excuse me. Mr Warnke ... ' She then asked Warnke why Gorbachev was in such a hurry. The damage to Perle had been done, and so Frum returned the visualization to the 'momentum' theme. Warnke gave his reply, but it was somewhat at odds with the end result of the 'momentum' theme – namely, the abolition of nuclear weapons, visualized now as 'a true relaxation of tensions.'
In the next sequence, Frum emphasized this larger theme.

Barbara Frum: Last quick point, if I could. The president himself has now set, as his own objective, a nuclear-free world; you're telling him that's categorically wrong-headed. You seem to think we're going to have nuclear weapons with us a long time. The world doesn't want to hear that any more. They want to believe that there can be a true relaxation of tensions.

Richard Perle: You can have a true relaxation of tensions without eliminating nuclear weapons. And I think you'd have terrible tension if we made the mistake of believing we had eliminated nuclear weapons, because ...

Paul Warnke: There's no way it can be done. Not in my lifetime. Not in Dick's. Not even in yours.

Frum had said that nuclear disarmament meant a 'true relaxation of tensions' and the two Americans were disputing that visualization. Whatever the differences between the 'hard-liner,' Perle, and Warnke, they were both, as Americans, deviant. This was emphasized in the next exchange. 'But,' said Frum incredulously, 'you [Perle] seem to be making a case that they [nuclear weapons] can be useful in relaxing, relaxing tensions.' And how, by implication, could anyone but a deviant hold such a perverse, wrong-headed, downright wicked view? Perle replied by introducing evidence.

Richard Perle: We've had forty years of peace, the longest period of this century. Nuclear weapons have introduced real sobriety into the relationship. Risks are not taken that might be taken otherwise.

Against mere raw evidence, however, slick visualizations cleverly produced will always triumph. This time Frum introduced the elusive symbol 'public sentiment,' which invariably supported 'a true relaxation of tensions.'

Barbara Frum: But look at that public sentiment out there for a nuclear-free world. Where is that going to go? Those people are not going to want to be disappointed.

Richard Perle: Well, they're going to be disappointed.

Paul Warnke: Yes, they are.

Perle again tried to suggest that Frum's visualization was in error, and Warnke agreed.

Richard Perle: But I don't believe it's [public sentiment for a nuclear-free world; i.e., Frum's visualization] that deep and that salient a motivation. They want to know that there's some security.

Paul Warnke: The objective is to avoid nuclear war, and *some* cuts would increase the risk of nuclear war. What we have to have is the absolutely assured retaliatory deterrent, no first-strike capability on either side.

Barbara Frum: And when there's another crisis? There's always another crisis. They push. You push back. Then what happens? Has that changed?

Richard Perle: We've been through crises before, and I rather suspect

Paul Warnke: And no nuclear war.

Richard Perle: And no nuclear war, and we've been through the kinds of crises that in the past would have meant a terrible conventional war. And that is the, uh, peaceful aspect of nuclear weapons.

A great deal of evidence had been introduced that contradicted Frum's visualization of a true relaxation of tensions through nuclear disarmament. For whatever reason, Frum brought the discussion to an abrupt conclusion.

The final sequence on *The Journal* dealt with images of the USSR in the U.S. media. 'Russians,' Bill Cameron, the anchor, said in his lead-in, 'are still shown in a very peculiar way. Kevin Tibbles reports on the distorted images.' The first set of 'distorted images' was used for comic purposes.

Kevin Tibbles: Getting a good laugh by exaggerating what is different about the other guy is easy humour. It always works. Yakov Smirnoff knows that. This Soviet emigré had become one of America's hottest comedians. He's even played the White House.

Yakov Smirnov: The reason the Americans laugh at the Soviet jokes is because they have enough knowledge of the certain stereotypes, and that's enough to make people laugh. What Americans think of Russia, well, is: everybody is a ballet dancer in Russia, and, uh, everybody lives in Siberia, it's very cold, and the KGB listens to every conversation.

The basis for Smirnov's jokes was then visualized by Tibbles as a serious lack of information. Exaggerated concern about the KGB was less significant than not knowing 'what the average Soviet does with his spare time, or eats for dinner.' It's true, of course, that the Soviets have 'also gone to great pains to ensure the outside world isn't looking in. But American culture hasn't done much to unlock that mystery,' which seems to suggest that the task of 'American culture' is to dissipate into a wised-up cosmopolitanism rather than to defend its own particularity, patriotism, and 'way of life.' By contrast, one can easily conceive of the CBC's view of American culture that did try to unlock the mystery of Soviet culture as being visualized in terms of intrusive arrogance, the sort of cultural imperialism so familiar from CBC visualizations of Canada–U.S. relations. In any event, we have already been primed to acknowledge Soviet suspicions as legitimate. The Americans, who have no such reasons to be suspicious, have made matters worse by exaggerating differences. Two 'expert knowers,' a former film critic and a 'Washington-based writer,' confirmed Tibbles's account. He then made the 'distorted images' more precise: the Russians were imagined by Americans to be benign and romantic, but the Soviets were hostile and a threat.

Kevin Tibbles: This is an image that has helped numerous Hollywood producers pay the bills. The romantic Russian. Noble, cultured, somewhat larger than life. Mikhail Baryshnikov has had an easy time of it seducing the Americans on, and off, the screen.

The romanticism extended to the Russian landscape, 'a perfect setting for love, American-style.' The Soviets, however, have always been suspect: 'no image of the Soviets is stronger than the great threat the Soviets posed to everything America stands for.' This was especially true 'during the Red Scare of the fifties.' Cartoons, for example, started appearing in the mass media. 'It was a frightening image of the Soviet threat posed to humanity, Christianity, and ultimately to America.' Cartoons also supplied useful visuals to ridicule U.S. concerns. One of the authorized knowers confirmed the groundlessness of fearing the Bolsheviks.

Jonathan Halperin: We've been led to believe, because of certain parts of Soviet and communist ideology, that they are quote/unquote godless communists. And that has been played up as a threat.

The problem of communist atheism is, in reality, not simply one of ideological perversity but of active persecution of Christians and Jews and Muslims. Common sense, but not the CBC version of normalcy, might reasonably view that behaviour as a threat.

Tibbles then turned to another, equally 'ridiculous' image – the communist as gangster. A former publisher of *Look*, a U.S. magazine, provided a sound-bite.

William Atwood: Stereotype was that they were slaves, and you better get a big chain gang. It was a, it was brutal. Jailers, and, uh, and, uh, one big slave-labour camp.

Tibbles comment was, in the aftermath of Solzhenitsyn, to say nothing of two generations of scholarship devoted to the study of Soviet governing practices, something of a surprise.

Kevin Tibbles: Fortunately, for the people who wrote the headlines, the Soviets always helped keep the threat alive.

Halperin provided his own equally weird reading of this misperception.

Jonathan Halperin: You're starting from a historical reality and then you run with that for whatever it's worth. And that's where you really do it disservice. The Hollywood people or other people that perpetuate those kinds of stereotypes. It's really manipulating people, in the worst sort of way.

The great offender, in Halperin's view, was *Red Dawn*, a 1984 movie about U.S. resistance to a Soviet invasion.

Tibbles pushed the theme of invasion by Soviet paratroopers into the theme of invasion by aliens from outer space.

Kevin Tibbles: The idea of the Soviets kicking down America's door has been stretched a long way. In the film *The Invasion of the Body Snatchers*, they're the alien invaders.

Nora Sayre, film critic:[19] The Martians are the strongest metaphor for the Russians, because they're the invaders who are either going to obliterate our entire culture, or they're going to take us over by enslaving our minds and even inhabiting our bodies, so that you can't tell which they ah, who they are. They look just like the rest of us.

The imagery worked both ways: since it was silly to fear Martians and body-snatchers, it must be silly to fear Communists. Accordingly, the next theme was that of paranoid 'competition' between the Soviet Union and the United States in space, in hockey, and in *Rocky IV*, a movie in which, eventually, Sylvester Stalone beats up a steroid-enhanced mountain of communist thuggery in a boxing match.

The wrap-up said nothing about the accuracy or inaccuracy of these simplified images, or about the real sources of conflict between the Soviet Union and the West. Instead, it suggested that a solution to 'distorted images' was better communication.

Jonathan Halperin: Much easier to portray the ten-foot-tall threat and the nice child reading poetry than it is to show that the ten-foot-tall threat is maybe the father of the child that's reading the poetry. And that those two things co-exist in Soviet society. And that they make up the complexity and the richness that is Soviet society.

Such a visualization may or may not be persuasive. Either way, it is based on nothing: not on fact, not on common sense, not on even a limited under-

138 Sins of Omission

standing of the sources and significance of political conflict or of political interests.

Tibbles ended on a note positive in its imagery if not in its logic.

Kevin Tibbles: Just like smiling Uncle Joe Stalin in '43, now it's Mikhail Gorbachev's turn to be romanced on the cover of *Life*. Soviet First Lady, Raisa Gorbachev, has a cover of her very own, and as far as New York fashion is concerned, the best-dressed capitalist should look like the romantic Russian. Even when the American public may be ripe for more realistic look at the Soviets, Hollywood ladles out *Ruskies*, a film about a runaway Russian sailor befriended by the boys next door. It's not threatening, like *Red Dawn* or *The Iron Curtain*, but it's just as unbelievable. Mischa sports a California tan and a Walkman.

If *Ruskies* is just as inaccurate and distorted as *Red Dawn*, and a smiling Stalin as inaccurate as a well-dressed Raisa, in what does accuracy consist? The assumption seems to be that the American public is 'ripe for a more realistic look at the Soviets.' The most generous thing to be said of Tibbles's report is that he didn't provide it. So what, then, was the point?

Considered by itself, it was simply fragmentary. About all that emerged was a sense that what Americans knew of the Soviet Union was somehow distorted. Considered in terms of a larger strategy of visualization, however, Tibbles's report served the perfectly intelligible purpose of priming the audience in such a way that they would be open to the new imagery that the CBC was undertaking to provide.

The last day of the summit, 10 December 1987, continued the visualizations of the preceding days, but emphasized as well the imbalance of extensive public relations with modest achievements. In his report, Joe Schlesinger introduced a clip of the U.S. president with the words 'tonight, Reagan addressed the American people on television and spoke of his ideological agenda.' What President Reagan said was this:

We've dealt not just with arms control issues, but also with fundamental problems such as Soviet expansionism, human-rights violations, as well as our own moral opposition to the ideology that justifies such practices. In this way, we have put Soviet/American relations on a far more candid and far more realistic footing.

Schlesinger's wrap-up again emphasized the 'ideological agenda.'

For three days the two leaders talked about cooperation instead of confrontation. Tonight, with Mikhail Gorbachev's plane barely in the air, Ronald Reagan was back talking about the Nicaraguan Contras' freedom fighters again. And boasting how he stood up to the Russians on Star Wars. The summit is over. Now comes the political selling job.

Michael McIver, the CBC Moscow correspondent, provided his assessment of the Soviet leader's 'final word on the summit.' The event was called a press conference, and, the anchor, Peter Mansbridge, explained they anticipated 'a chance for a little give-and-take.' Instead, the journalists received 'an opening statement that lasted over an hour, a lengthy lecture on Soviet attitudes, and the Soviet view of the summit.' McIver's first remark concerning the marathon speech, which incidentally illustrated the incompatibility of Gorbachev's residual primary orality with the requirements of secondary orality, was that the general secretary 'never seems to get tired.' McIver summarized Gorbachev's assessment of the 'progress' achieved with the talks, and introduced a sound-bite:

Michael McIver: Then, he made a pledge.

Mikhail Gorbachev [voice of translator]: ... we want no unilateral advantages for ourselves. We are prepared to move along all the directions in the process of reducing arms, but so that at each stage there should be a balance.

There was no visualization of any ideological agenda for Gorbachev.

Michael McIver: And Gorbachev said he discovered here that ordinary Americans, like ordinary Soviets, want an end to the superpower confrontation. And it's time the politicians listened to them.

Mikhail Gorbachev [voice of translator]: You know, I said to the president and his colleagues, 'Do you not think that the politicians of our two countries are lagging behind the mood of the peoples of our ... of their peoples?'

In his wrap-up, McIver stressed the success of the Soviet leader's visit:

He signed an historic arms deal. But, he accomplished much more than that. Through his charm and candour, he's managed to convince many Americans that the Russian bear is not all growls and snarls, and that's bound to have a positive impact on superpower relations.

A night earlier, McIver's colleague, Tibbles, had explained at great length the different imaginative resonances created by the adjectives 'Soviet' and 'Russian.' By reverting to the traditional, and doubtless 'distorted' image of a *Russian* threat, McIver may have cast doubt on the validity of Tibbles's carefully articulated distinction. However, it is doubtful that anyone noticed. The cliché of the Russian bear is much more familiar than the distinction Tibbles was trying to make. For every Canadian who speaks of a Canada–Soviet hockey series there must be a hundred who speak of a Canada–Russia series. McIver's message regarding the Russian bear that no longer growls and snarls was that they were like 'us.' They were normal and we should trust them.

Mansbridge provided his own wrap-up to the entire sequence: 'it's been a remarkable few days in Washington.' He stressed the continuity of the story, that more remarkable things lay ahead in Moscow, and handed the anchor's chair over to Knowlton Nash in Toronto. Nash promised 'more on the summit later, on *The Journal*.'

During *The Journal*, Barbara Frum interviewed a former U.S. negotiator at SALT I. This authorized knower allowed that there had been movement, but a number of problems remained.

Raymond Garthoff: I would say that the possibility of reaching such a, an agreement, ah, during this next year, ah, was raised from below fifty-fifty, last week, to better than fifty-fifty tonight.

Barbara Frum: I'm glad you used the phrase 'fifty-fifty,' because that's what they've been saying all week. They want to slash their arsenals in half. Have you had a chance yet, to absorb enough of the details to see if that's going to satisfy American defence critics, who think that that's too extreme, and won't be strategically safe?

The meaning of the phrase 'fifty-fifty' when used by Frum was not what Garthoff had in mind at all. The poor man was confused. He failed or refused to take up the last question and visualize the opponents of the agreement for her; instead he spoke of the likelihood of continued technical debate 'But, none the less, it will be a substantial reduction if agreement is reached. And I think, um ...' Garthoff was not doing what Frum anticipated; she intervened and changed the topic.

Barbara Frum: You know, everyone, always wants to know, who's the architect of this deal? And who gave way? Is that an agreement that, that makes sense to both sides? Or has somebody given way to the other?

Raymond Garthoff: Well, I don't think there will be an agreement or should be, unless it does make sense to both sides. Unless both sides feel that their interests are served by it. On the ... yes ... it's, ah, the most ...

For Garthoff, the conduct of foreign policy involved negotiation to obtain an agreement where the interests of all parties are served. For Frum, it was more like melodrama with heroes and goats, winners and losers, trivia that made for good entertainment.

Frum then turned to 'two veteran journalists' more adept at the techniques of visualization. Bill Cameron, co-anchor, interviewed a specialist in Soviet trivia (there are 13,000 female beekeepers in the Soviet Union), Gus Hall, a leader of the CPUSA, and provided yet another series of comparisons between the United States and the Soviet Union in terms of book, meat, cigarette, and alcohol consumption. The observation was also made that Soviets like to suntan standing up, and Americans lying down. Further discussions of these weighty themes by the journalists followed.

During *The National*, Gorbachev had 127 words quoted, and Reagan 83. He was mentioned twice as often as Reagan. The following day, on *The National*, Joe Schlesinger continued to explore the angle that Reagan would have difficulty 'selling' the results of the Summit to Congress, particularly to those suspicious 'conservatives.' The somewhat incongruous 'ideological agenda' was also reinforced. Notwithstanding all the goodwill and public relations, 'the United States today went ahead with a test of its new Trident II missile that it has postponed so as not to disturb the summit. And that, in a way, was perhaps a sign that the superpowers were back to business as usual.'

'Business as usual' meant a resumption of the pre-summit process of priming and agenda-setting for the CBC as well.

9   LITTLE ANTS IN MOSCOW

There were fewer stories about the 1988 summit than about the December meetings in Washington. Prior to late May 1988, we recorded only three stories. On 21 February, Sue Simpson reported on a meeting between the U.S. secretary of state and the Soviet foreign minister. Eduard Shevardnadze indicated that the Soviets wished to be more active in the Middle East. The Americans, however, had set certain conditions.

Sue Simpson: Washington wants Moscow to establish diplomatic relations with Israel and to allow more Jews to emigrate. During the morning session, Shultz raised human rights. Later, the American secretary of state met privately and unofficially with Soviet human-rights activist Andrei Sakharov. Shultz also talked with less-well-known dissidents. The American secretary of state promised continued support for them.

Even in a routine meeting where little was accomplished that could be made public, the United States was visualized as blocking Soviet foreign initiatives and meddling in internal Soviet affairs.

On 5 April, Barbara Frum conversed with a British journalist who had been granted an audience in Moscow with Kim Philby, the British traitor. In her preview on *The National*, Frum began the priming by describing him as 'the model for the best spy novel,' a 'mole deep inside the heart of British Intelligence' who has 'inspired the writings of John le Carré and Len Deighton.' Only after having visualized Philby as a larger-than-life fictional inspiration did she mention that this man was a traitor, not a character in a spy story. But even then her rhetoric indicated fiction.

Barbara Frum: It's all too true. Too true for the Western agents he betrayed. Too true for British Intelligence whose operations he ruined.

Paul Griffin continued the visualization of this 'too true' story: Philby was a mystery man. Before Frum's conversation took place, however, more props were wheeled on stage: Anne McMillan presented 'the Philby file.'

The 'file' opened with McMillan's version of the strategic CBC visualization.[20]

Anne McMillan: It's a classic spy story. A tale of double-dealing, treachery, and a dramatic escape.

Man [film]: The dicks are watching me.

She then went on to say that the film clip was 'not fiction' but a 'dramatization of a true story.' Like Frum's 'too true,' the 'dramatization' was meant to indicate the deeper reality of treason. This deeper reality was indicated by McMillan's biography of Philby. He was 'a highly placed official in MI6, the British Secret Service, but he was also a Soviet spy.' Philby happened to come by these two somewhat incompatible positions when he was 'an idealistic undergraduate' at Cambridge and became a 'convert to communism.' The passive voice was used to describe the rest of his career as well: idealism led to communism; he was asked to become a traitor, told to appear as a 'conservative,' and so 'his life as a double agent had started.' This sanitized account of the process of Philby's recruitment and of his job description was followed by a single example of what he actually did when he attained a position where he could seriously betray his country: several Albanians were killed. An Albanian life may be equal in the eyes of God to that of an Englishman or a Canadian, but it is very hard for Canadian audiences to visualize concretely what an Albanian might be. Who, after all, really cares about a few dead Albanians? Were they like Albinos?

The point of such an elaborate introduction was to emphasize even more the unreal nature of Philby's treason. In the world of the CBC, we are primed with the knowledge that no real treason takes place, only exciting stories get dramatized. And only remote Albanians get murdered.

So Philby, the former idealist and whistle-blower on Albanians, carried on, and anonymous 'other lives' were lost. These 'others,' who could have been more vividly visualized as Canadians, Americans, or Britons, were not mentioned further. Instead, she turned to the dramatic bits of his life.

Anne McMillan: In 1945, Philby came dangerously close to being unmasked by Igor Gouzenko, one of the most important Soviet spies ever to defect. Gouzenko turned himself over to Canadian authorities in Ottawa, bringing with him the names of Soviet agents involved in a Canadian spy ring.

Philby escaped this dangerously close shave with justice and went on to Washington where he was British liaison officer with the U.S. Central Intelligence Agency. 'Now,' McMillan said, 'he could provide the Soviets with American secrets as well as British.' Lucky him! But nothing lasts forever.

Anne McMillan: Eventually Philby's double life began to catch up with him. This movie shows how his warning allowed two double agents to escape to Moscow.

McMillan's emphasis on double-dealing, double life, and double agents is, so to speak, disinformation and double-talk. Philby, Maclean, and Burgess were not double agents; they were traitors. They were British intelligence officials who betrayed their country to a foreign, and, by and large, unfriendly power. Double-dealing is a term from the gaming room; it is a highly inappropriate euphemism for treason. Whether any or all of the British traitors had a double or a triple or a mega-multiple life is beside the point so far as politics is concerned. Nevertheless, introducing such considerations and doing so by using actors to play the part of Philby in a 'dramatization of a true story,' which in plain language is to use a slick fake, did enable the audience more easily to sympathize with these people. Poor Philby! A Cambridge idealist who had to lead a double life.

After Maclean and Burgess escaped, Philby was a prime suspect. 'An investigation,' said McMillan, 'failed to prove his guilt.' Yet he was dismissed and MI6 landed him a job as a journalist for *The Observer*, working in Beirut. 'But over the years, evidence that he was working for the Soviets mounted. In 1963, he disappeared from Beirut, turning up months later in Moscow. Philby has until recently lived in relative obscurity.' The CBC has convicted others – the U.S. Marine colonel Oliver North, for example – on a lot less evidence than this. The very word *treason* was never used during this entire sequence. The word *traitor* used but once: Philby was 'Britain's most famous traitor,' a locution that could be extended to include Britain's most famous mathematician, department store, or race horse.

So, the famous, and even notorious, Philby 'turned up' one fine day in Moscow and lived in obscurity until October 1987, when 'he made a rare appearance in a television program about unrest in the Baltic Republic of Latvia. He claimed that British Intelligence has used Latvian exiles to stir up demands for independence.' The item to which McMillan referred was broadcast on 18 November 1987. Knowlton Nash reported on 'the notorious British double-agent':

Moscow's English mole in British Intelligence had a cup of tea in front of him when he tried to discredit dissident nationalists in Latvia ... Philby is speaking out now to blame Western spies for stirring up unrest in Latvia. Today, at a counter-rally, thousands of Latvians did what Philby wanted. They pledged support to Moscow.

Nothing further was said, and nothing serious was said about Latvian politics. In the spring, this October or November story was recalled: the last prop was in place. Frum's performance could begin. McMillan's wrap-up was also an introduction to Frum.

Anne McMillan: This month in an interview with Phillip Knightley for London's *Sunday Times*, Britain's most famous traitor has broken his twenty-five year silence to talk about his life as a Soviet agent. For *The Journal*, I'm Anne McMillan in London.

Barbara Frum: That British journalist who spent six days interviewing Philby in Moscow, Phillip Knightley, is in our London studio. Mr Knightley, you've been circling this quarry for twenty years. How did it feel when you were finally summoned to meet the notorious Kim Philby?

Phillip Knightley: Well, it was a great moment. Ah, not only a great moment in the sense that my perseverance was paid off. If there's any lesson for a young journalist, it is never give up. I mean, don't take anyone's no's being a final no. But it was also like a scene out of John le Carré or Len Deighton.

The major item in this story was not the tea-drinking traitor, but the *journalist* who circled the quarry for twenty years, who never gave up, who never took 'no' for a final answer. It was, he said, just like a spy thriller. Earlier, Philby's *life* was called an inspiration for le Carré and Deighton; now just meeting the man evoked these great masters of spy fiction. Mere fact and dull political judgments expressed by the terms 'traitor' and 'treason' have no place in this kind of exciting entertainment.

Knightley described his arrival at Philby's apartment, courtesy of the KGB:

and then suddenly the door opened and there was the master spy himself. Absolutely charming. 'My dear fellow,' he said. 'How good to see you after all this time. Please come through, what would you like to drink?' And it was just beyond believable. It was such an exciting moment.

And Frum, all agog, was captivated. It was all so fascinating, of course,

but you must have been suspicious about his timing. Why do you think after putting you off for all those years in letters, he finally said yes?

Knightley, invited to speculate *ad libitum*, did not decline. First, Philby wanted to scotch rumours that the KGB had cut off his funds and that he was ill. But he also wanted to 'revitalize maybe, ah, his reputation' and maybe

just to show that, ah, *perestroika* works, and *glasnost* works. And maybe it is to plant some disinformation that may cause the mischief that he was quite famous for ah, in Western intelligence agencies.

Now, if the last 'reason' was even remotely accurate, Knightley and Frum were self-consciously abetting Philby in his 'mischief.' Of course, no one thought to elaborate on how putting the words of a British traitor in a British newspaper showed that *perestroika* and *glasnost* 'works,' whatever that verb might indicate.

Frum moved on, probing deeper, looking for gossip and significant trivia.

Barbara Frum: Paint us a word picture please, how he lived, how he looks, how he moves, how he talks. Um, I know he's got another wife. That was one of the most fascinating details. He's been married so many times and had so many women besides that, on the side.

Knightley replied, lightly, that Philby deceived women, ha, ha, by never telling them about his work. He went on:

Ah, word picture. Well he lives in great comfort. He has a very substantial apartment in Moscow, two apartments knocked into one. It used to belong to a very high official in the Ministry of Foreign Affairs. It's nicely decorated; it's full of furniture that he gathered during his world travels, all brought to him from his last ah, house in Beirut courtesy of the KGB. His library, ten or twelve thousand books. He has a nice study, um, he doesn't work very hard but he has quite rewarding work. They send ah, the work to him. He doesn't have to go into the KGB headquarters. In fact, he said he's only been there twice during the whole time he's been in Moscow.

The word picture now complete, she asked Knightley what the hours of interviewing added to what was already known. Knightley replied that the most interesting new thing he turned up was that Philby had had his doubts about whether he had chosen the right side. This little existential twist served to excuse Philby's otherwise ugly private life.

And it was only after, I mean those periods of doubt that's so deep and disillusionment was such that he was on an almost suicidal alcoholic binge that seemed to go on for years and years. It was only meeting his new wife and being ah, rehabilitated by the KGB and given work again to do that ah, sort of pulled him through. And, of course, now, he says that he's, he's found in Gorbachev, the leader that justified those years of faith.

Not only did the interview with Philby help show that *perestroika* and *glasnost* worked, but that the very being of Gorbachev completed the KGB rehab program that dried out Philby, the poor, drunken womanizer and former idealist.

There remained the nasty part to get over: Philby was, after all, a traitor who was responsible for the deaths of a large number of people. Frum put it as briefly, it not as delicately, as possible.

Barbara Frum: What about the betrayal of his country, of his friends and associates?

Phillip Knightley: Well, he's not worried about his betrayal of this country, because he gave up, I think, on Britain after the disillusionment in the 'thirties. Ah, he is worried and feels rather regretful of his personal betrayals. He said that he regretted having to betray friends. He regretted having to ah, lie to them, deceive them. But he said he felt it was all in the greater good. And because he is ah, above all, a political person and the political side of his life takes precedence over his personal life. Now that may be a sad thing to say, but that's the way he feels.

And, of course, if he *really* felt that way, nothing further can be said that might question, say, his motives or British intelligence, or Soviet recruitment of 'idealistic' young men of a certain class and personal predisposition. Moreover, both Knightley and Frum accepted without comment the fact that Philby 'gave up' on Britain in the 1930s, after being 'disillusioned' in some unspecified way. Nothing, of course, was said about the Soviet Union in the 1930s, and no comment was made about the sort of person who was 'not worried' about treason. Such silences are significant. If it did not occur to Frum and Knightley to raise such topics, even for speculation, perhaps it was because they or their script writers did not find them newsworthy, which has the curious implication that treason, for some people, is a kind of normalcy and patriotism is deviant. Here, for example, the treatment of Colonel North, to say nothing of the mayors of Amarillo or Knob Noster, provides a suitable counterpoint. A question remains, however: how normal would Philby's treason have seemed or how romantic and exciting would it have been visualized had the enemy to whom he betrayed state secrets been the national rather than the international socialists?

Frum then touched on the Canadian theme, Gouzenko.[21] Philby had said to Knightley that Gouzenko's defection was a disaster for the KGB and Frum asked: why? Apart from exposing Soviet spies in Canada, Knightley replied, Gouzenko's greatest damage was technical: he provided a great deal of information about Soviet codes. Whether Gouzenko knew about Philby was unclear and Philby did not make it clear. Nor did he say much about any other traitors. All of this very obscure non-information was visualized in highly melodramatic imagery: code names for traitors, moles, 'fifth men,' taking secrets to the grave, and so on.

Frum then cut off the dark talk of spies. Now this:

Barbara Frum: Let's move along now to the time when ah, he is given a chance to escape from Beirut to Moscow. Um, the whole question about how embarrassed British Intelligence was that they kept this man, what, seven or nine years or twelve years past the time they first had suspicions of him? What a laugh he must have had on British Intelligence.

Phillip Knightley: Well he did. I suppose he did. Yes, they re ... rehabilitated him in 1955, '56 to '63, another seven or eight years worked for British Intelligence. They not only rehabilitated him, they re-employed him. So the embarrassment when evidence finally came through that he was, without a doubt, and had been all along, a serving officer in the KGB was such that they frightened him into going rather than have the embarrassment of bringing him back to Britain for a highly publicized trial and ah, a court case.

According to this visualization, getting a laugh on the stuffy old Brits is the real significance of his 'escape' to Moscow. Instead of the embarrassment of a British trial, Philby was frightened away to Moscow. There were other options: perhaps his political masters ordered him to Moscow? Perhaps the British could have hired James Bond to shoot him? Perhaps he was told to leave by yet another mole?

Frum had gone to great lengths to make treason sound like exciting fun, on the one hand, and a kind of whimsical game of spy fiction, on the other. Now she made the leap into self-conscious double talk.

Barbara Frum: To end, are you being criticized for glamorizing the old spy yet again?

Phillip Knightley: I'm afraid so. Yet, um, I tried to anticipate that criticism by saying that anything that a traitor such as Philby said, that would cast the slightest light on his motives, in the way he operated, ah, would be invaluable news to help us learn something from the whole affair. Ah, and I think that ah, what I did was a normal ordinary piece of journalism. Fortunately for me, my persistence in wanting to see Philby has paid off. But I see it as nothing more than an ordinary sort of story, which should be published.

If a man has been described as a master spy and adept at making mischief for Western intelligence, any journalist who deals with him must either be remarkably stupid or remarkably confident in his or her own intellectual powers and in his or her ability to detect disinformation and 'mischief.' No doubt Knightley, and perhaps Frum, would consider the latter description more accurate. Unfortunately, it is impossible for outsiders to judge whether their self-confidence was justified. In any event, overconfidence is often indistinguishable from stupidity.

Late in May 1988, pre-summit fever hit the CBC. On 24 May, *The Journal* rebroadcast a 'look at America's celluloid Soviets,' prepared by Kevin Tibbles. It had been aired 'before the last superpower summit, and it seems fitting to rebroadcast his report now.' Tibbles's earlier report served to prime audiences for the CBC's visualization by showing them a series of what were called 'distorted images.' They were conflicting images, to be sure. Whether distorted or not depends on how adequately they presented reality, and that topic was never considered. The one failing of the earlier broadcast was that it was shown *during* coverage of the summit, on 9 December. This time it was put where it would do the most good, before coverage began. The implicit purpose of an otherwise incoherent report, we recall, was to provide the following message: 'you people in the audience know nothing; what you think you know is confused and contradictory. Stay tuned and we'll straighten you out.' The assumption behind the rebroadcast was equally simple: if it worked in December, it would work again in May. That's what made it fit to be rebroadcast.

Coverage began for real, so to speak, on 27 May. Four out of the six days came within our sample. The INF Treaty had been ratified by the U.S. Senate, and President Reagan would sign it into law that very day. Unfortunately, general rejoicing could not yet be authorized. The Americans were getting picky again; this time it was about the old problem of human rights. Knowlton Nash was visibly disappointed.

Knowlton Nash: In a speech today, Reagan made it clear that, besides arms control, he plans to put another issue on the summit agenda, human rights. He called on the Soviets to release all political prisoners and to allow free emigration and religious tolerance. The Soviets immediately called Reagan's speech condescending and out of date. They say it could cause a lot of problems. Joe Schlesinger has more on the ideas that Reagan and other Americans are taking to the Soviets.

Schlesinger stated that Reagan had 'sent a tough message to Mikhail Gorbachev.' Apart from releasing political and religious prisoners, Reagan called for 'the dismantling of all barriers between Eastern and Western Europe. But Reagan praised the Soviet leader too, for easing some restrictions, and he was optimistic about their talks next week.' Schlesinger was less optimistic. He did not say that it would be foolish to think the USSR would change its policies on human rights, which would introduce a new and negative angle from which to visualize the USSR. Instead, he provided a visualization that no 'breakthroughs' were expected. A State Department official provided a plausible sound-bite, and Schlesinger took up the theme of breakthrough: a Cajun cook was able to open a restaurant in Moscow; according to Schlesinger this 'breakthrough of sorts' took place:

when the summit came along, and the recalcitrant Russians all of a sudden said, 'Come, but hurry,' five New Orleans chefs rushed in with fourteen tons of catfish and burgers and shrimps and, of course, hot sauce. And: success.

There was no hint by Schlesinger that this move by the Soviet authorities might have been a piece of public relations. It was, he said, a 'ten-day experiment,' the success of which would depend not upon Soviet administrative whim or deliberate policy, but on whether 'the Russians take a liking to Louisiana alligator sausage [and] Creole gumbo.' Schlesinger was asking his audience to accept the visualization that the success of a Cajun restaurant in the Soviet Union depended on the market, just like in North Bay or Halifax. After all, we know that the Soviets now eat pizza.

Joe Schlesinger: Pizza is already in. The chain that brought in this mobile pizzeria as an experiment has won a contract to build twenty-five pizza joints in Moscow. In a speech today, President Reagan was most pessimistic about the prospect of reconciling the differences between the capitalist and communist economies. Pat the pizza man has no such doubts.

According to Pat, the Soviets 'need fast food desperately,' and he was pleased to meet the need. The problem was Reagan.

Joe Schlesinger: This is an awkward stage for the Americans in their relationship with the Soviet Union. Ronald Reagan is torn between calling the Russians names and calling Mikhail Gorbachev his friend. And a few of the enterprisers he admires most, people like the Cajun cook and the pizza man, they're ahead of him, and ahead of the doctrinaire communists too, doing what capitalists do best, trying to make a buck. Joe Schlesinger, CBC News, Moscow.

Schlesinger's accounts were consistent in so far as Ronald Reagan could do very little that merited the approval of the senior CBC correspondent. Reagan was said to be pessimistic about the possibility of reconciling capitalism and the communist economy: Schlesinger also indicated that this pessimism was unwarranted because of the success of Pat the pizza man and the Cajun cooks. But one could just as easily visualize the success of these two 'capitalists' as proof that Reagan was right. First, these two enterprises were both burdened with the significant euphemism 'experimental.' Whatever that term meant, it implied that the capitalists were there only so long as it suited the Soviets. Second, it was not stated whether or not the 'bucks' that these capitalists made would be dollars or rubles, or, therefore, whether they could be repatriated as profits. It was not even indicated whether the Pepsi solution was possible, and pizzas or alligator sausage could be bartered for Ladas or vodka. Third, it was highly irresponsible to visualize Reagan's concern over Soviet human-rights violations as 'calling the Russians names.' If the Soviets thought that U.S. concern for human rights, including the right to emigrate, was purely a matter of public relations, then the consequences would be felt, not by the Joe Schlesingers of the media world, but by people living under Soviet power. And finally, if the capitalists were 'making a buck,' in the sense that that phrase would normally be understood by his audience, it is certainly true that they would be 'ahead of the doctrinaire communists,' because they would be actualizing economic liberties. But, in fact, they were part of an 'experiment' run by 'doctrinaire communists.' (Are there any other kinds?) However, if the pizza man and the Cajun cooks were able truly to make a buck, they would not be 'ahead' of the U.S. president; they would be carrying out his policies and proving that capitalism can displace communist 'planning' any day of the week for the simple reason that it and the market deliver the goods, and communism doesn't. They would, in short, be proving Reagan right on the irreconcilability of capitalism and communism. As usual, however, Schlesinger was not focally concerned with economics, with Moscow pizza joints or anything similar, but with criticizing the U.S. president.

Schlesinger's report was the lead item. The second story, by Don Murray, was also on the USSR. Nash provided the introduction: Gorbachev had just published some details on his 'reforms.' Murray allowed as they were proposals, not laws. The emphasis, however, was not on the difficulties in reforming the Soviet Union but on the excitement and debate that the proposals aroused. The only ones for whom these 'reforms' posed a problem were the left deviationists who, for some unexplained reason, wanted to establish their own political party.

Don Murray: But Mikhail Gorbachev has made it clear he won't tolerate any other party but his. The meeting [to establish another party] was broken up by the police. Sergei Gregorian, a dissident editor linked to the democratic union, was arrested. He now says the road to change, to democracy, will be very slow. Everyone in the West, he says, must realize that lives in the bureaucracy are actually threatened by these changes. No one can predict, not even Gorbachev, what will happen.

Murray concluded his visualization by celebrating all this verbal activity as if it had the same significance in the USSR as it would have in a liberal democracy.

And so in the Kremlin, in newspaper offices, in the streets, the debate is fully engaged. It's remarkable for its exuberance. And for the diversity of opinions expressed. But what's most remarkable is that, just three years ago, it all seemed quite unthinkable. Don Murray, CBC News, Moscow.

The next day, 28 May, Schlesinger was back to report on Soviet ratification of the INF Treaty. As did Murray, he adopted the utterly abstract and unreal assumption that Soviet and U.S. ratification procedures were fundamentally alike.

Joe Schlesinger: The Praesidium of the Supreme Soviet, debating the ratification of the INF Treaty. The Soviet/American agreement to destroy their medium-range nuclear weapons. It took the U.S. Senate two weeks of bitter debate before ratifying it yesterday. Today it took their Soviet counterparts less than two hours to rubber stamp it. President Andrei Gromyko called for the vote. It was unanimous.

Thanks to this act of statesmanship by the Praesidium, the two leaders would have something to celebrate, 'even if they don't agree on anything at all in the next five days.' Schlesinger adopted the persona of a serious man who didn't expect much.

It would, of course, be a media event, but to such a serious analyst of international affairs as Joe Schlesinger, this aspect of the summit was of little interest. His report of President Reagan's appearance on Soviet television was, therefore, suitably ironic.

Joe Schlesinger: Reagan was full of praise for Gorbachev. He also ran into some sharp questions. The interviewer noted that the president had often quoted Lenin. Our experts, he said, have carefully studied this and not found anything similar to your quotations in Lenin's work. Have you ever read Lenin's writings?

President Ronald Reagan: Oh my. I don't think I could recall and specify here and there. But, I wasn't making anything up.

One wonders what to make of this 'hard question.' Schlesinger and the Soviet journalists and any other modestly competent observer of the U.S. president is aware of the role of speech writers. No one has ever claimed that Ronald Reagan was a serious student of Lenin, or that his quoting of

Lenin had more than rhetorical significance. One wonders what Schlesinger was trying to convey to Canadian audiences with the news that the U.S. president couldn't recall where his officials found their Lenin quotations or that Soviet researchers were mystified by it all.

Schlesinger himself provided a clue in his wrap-up.

Joe Schlesinger: Nothing substantial may happen once Ronald Reagan gets here. But something important is happening when an American president can go on Soviet television, pleading for religious freedom, and when this particular American president, the quintessential anti-communist, admits that he has changed his mind about the nature of the Soviet leadership. Joe Schlesinger, CBC News, Moscow.

The 'hard question' was entirely unrelated to the substantive event, the appearance of Ronald Reagan on Soviet TV, delivering a plea for religious freedom. So why was it mentioned? If we recall that the messages diffused by television need not be logically connected, that meaning is conveyed by a series of images and not by a common-sense coherence, consistency took the form of negative visualization of the U.S. president and positive visualization of all things Soviet. Consistency does, however, go into the production side, in the selection of images, not their content.

It did not matter what the content of the question asked by Soviet journalists was: the important message was that Reagan could not answer a 'hard question.' The negative visualization was continued in the wrap-up: 'nothing substantial may happen once Ronald Reagan gets here.' What had happened was 'important,' and it was seen to be entirely a result of Soviet action: first, Reagan was invited to go on Soviet TV, and, second, the nature of Soviet leadership had changed so that even the 'quintessential anti-communist' had to 'admit' he had 'changed his mind.' The Soviets were flexible enough even to allow Reagan to make a plea for religious freedom; Reagan's 'anti-communism' had, up to now, prevented him from seeing the truth, but not even he had to 'admit' he had been wrong about the USSR.

Other visualizations were, of course, possible. Emphasis might have been placed on the fact that it took an American to speak out on religious liberty, and that no Soviet leader ever had done so. To indicate, as President Reagan did, that Gorbachev was different from his predecessors hardly impugns his opposition to communism as a political movement. To use the term 'quintessential anti-communist' in the first place was simply to adopt a fashionable ideological phrase of the contemporary American left.

Sheldon Turcott introduced the next story, delivered by Don Murray. It was concerned with the attitudes of Moscovites to the impending visit.

Inside the Kremlin things were well ordered and orchestrated. Outside, in the city, matters were more confused.

Sheldon Turcott: But Moscovites do seem keen to receive Ronald Reagan, the man who has fed his career vilifying communism. The CBC's Don Murray reports on the many moods of pre-Reagan Moscow.

According to this visualization, their confusion, their 'many moods,' was a result of a conflict between their good-natured desire to be hospitable and the fact that they were being hospitable to 'the man who has fed his career vilifying communism.' Reagan, the vilifier, was placing a strain on Moscow's good graces. But the Soviets met the challenge and, once again, walked that extra mile.

Don Murray: Musicians for peace. Students for summits. It is in Moscow sufficient excuse for a rock concert these days. Heavy metal on the stage, the paraphernalia of peace and diplomacy in the crowd.

They were a peculiar set of rockers, however, because they were polite, animated by politics, and, apparently, by tourism and capitalism as well.

The fourth superpower summit in three years, like the concert, is an occasion for polite enthusiasm. There's more than polite interest, however, in the benefits such summits might bring. We should know each other's countries better, he says. We ought to be able to hop on a 747 and go and see the U.S. At the Riske Market, where private sellers are crowding out state shops, business in bikinis is brisk, and thoughts of Ronald Reagan are kind.

The only dissenter Murray found was a black-market dealer in Chiclets: everyone else was enthusiastic about the summit. In contrast to the suspicious, hostile, and deviant Christian fundamentalists of Amarillo, Texas, 'the reaction to Reagan and his impending arrival here is above all relaxed. The American president generates very little controversy here now, and even less fear.' The students at Moscow University were especially eager to talk with the president. One was quoted as saying she wanted to learn why Reagan had changed his mind. We already know: the forces of progress proved irresistible, even to the great vilifier and quintessential anti-communist. In Murray's wrap-up, the friendliness of Moscow was cosmic:

And so bathed in spring warmth and benevolent expectation, Moscow waits for Ronald Reagan. Don Murray, CBC News, Moscow.

On 31 May, Peter Mansbridge opened *The National*.

Peter Mansbridge: Good evening. It was another amazing day in Moscow, filled with images of change and optimism. Ronald Reagan walking under the Kremlin wall, his arm around Mikhail Gorbachev. The gesture of friendship almost unthinkable until now. And there were other dramatic signs of the improved relations between the superpowers as the summit continues.

Schlesinger reported on the discussion between Reagan and the students at Moscow University. He was there, said Schlesinger, not to 'knock communism,' but 'to sell the Soviet students on the virtues of American democracy.'

President Ronald Reagan: Go to any American town, to take just an example, and you'll see dozens of churches, representing many different beliefs. Go into any union hall where the members know their right to strike is protected by law.

Joe Schlesinger: It was vintage Reagan. He compared the precariousness of the *perestroika* reform with the dangers faced by Butch Cassidy and the Sundance Kid when they were trapped between a posse and a cliff and then he added reassuringly.

President Ronald Reagan: By the way, both Butch and Sundance made it.

Reagan was then shown to be supportive of Gorbachev and of *perestroika*. According to Schlesinger, Reagan blamed the bureaucracy, not Gorbachev, for the restrictions on emigration.

Joe Schlesinger: Part of the reason for the changed tone, Reagan has been discussing *perestroika* with Gorbachev. This morning, the two men went into overtime while Gorbachev explained his reforms. As for the main issue here, a treaty to cut strategic nuclear missiles, Gorbachev was optimistic.

The initiative remained with Gorbachev. He had educated Reagan about *perestroika*, and maybe even 'the big one' – namely, that a reduction in strategic missiles was possible. The obstacle remained Reagan.

Joe Schlesinger: Before the warming up of Ronald Reagan to the world's chief communist, he gave no sign of being ready to drop the main obstacle to such a treaty, his Star Wars plan. Joe Schlesinger, CBC News, Moscow.

Don Murray provided a report on the walk around Red Square by the two leaders. Even here, nearly all the points were made by Gorbachev. He 'didn't miss a beat,' he 'grabbed the initiative,' he made a 'well-placed jab aimed with a most disarming smile,' he was 'clearly pleased with his performance in the superpower media duet.' And as for Reagan, 'the man who'd spent a political career denouncing Lenin's legacy' was heard to 'murmur' that the monuments of Red Square were 'wonderful, magnificent, even more spectacular than I've been told.' He retracted his 'evil empire' quip and showed himself, as Gorbachev said, with a laugh, to be 'a cautious man.' He closed with a 'message of avuncular harmony,' the one positive visualization the CBC allowed.

Barbara Frum then appeared.

Barbara Frum: From the halls of learning to the streets of the city, summit fever grips Moscow. Tonight on *The Journal*.

Her more subdued introduction to the program promised to cover three topics, Reagan's visit to Moscow University, how the Soviet capital was coping with 'media siege, and the impact of *glasnost* on Soviet foreign policy.'

The visit to the university was visualized as a contest.

Barbara Frum: Reagan scored points for charm and warmth. But some of the students scored points with sophisticated questions.

Four questions were shown being asked. First, would the Americans help find Soviet soldiers missing in Afghanistan? (They would.) Second, would the strategic weapons treaty be signed by Reagan? (No; it would probably be signed by his successor.) Third, how have young people changed since Reagan was a student? And fourth, what about the refuseniks?

President Ronald Reagan: We are people made up of every religion, nationality and race of the world, and the result is that, when people in our country think someone is being mistreated or treated unjustly, ah, in another country, these are people, who still feel that kinship to that country because that is their heritage. Your generation is living in one of the most exciting hopeful times in Soviet history. We do not know what the conclusion of this will be, of this journey. But we're hopeful that the promise of reform will be fulfilled. In this Moscow spring, this May 1988, we may be allowed that hope.

This fairly creditable performance was preceded by Susan Reisler's introduction and by Barbara Frum's postscript.

Reisler's introduction may serve as an example of balance CBC-style. It consisted of seven sentences.

Susan Reisler: [1] Moscow State University is one of seven very similar architectural achievements that Joseph Stalin bequeathed this country. [2] They call them Stalin's seven sisters and this one is the largest. [3] Mikhail Gorbachev graduated from the law faculty and many of his inner circle colleagues went to school here. [4] Normally 28,000 students move in and out of the building. [5] But the school was virtually closed for the Reagan lecture. [6] A university official said it was the U.S. Secret Service who had requested it. [7] American officials apparently also asked that the eight hundred students and faculty invited to attend the speech be knowledgeable about Soviet/American relations and know English.

The first two sentences described the setting. We learned the nickname for Stalin's 'architectural achievement,' a studiously neutral term for a group of monumental buildings of questionable charm. This restraint regarding socialist realism obscured their significance as architectural statements. Third, it was Gorbachev's *alma mater*; and, fourth, it is a busy place. By these statements we are primed to accept Moscow University as a typical big-city locale and the training ground for the Soviet leadership.

There followed an ominous 'but.' But the school was closed; and the Americans were responsible; *and* they made other demands. In terms of the dialectical point/counterpoint formula, the first four sentences indicated normalcy or, as in the case of Stalinist architecture, defused any negative response by indicating that these huge ugly buildings were called (with affection?) Stalin's seven sisters. The last three sentences signified deviance.

In her postscript, Barbara Frum asked two people, whom she identified as Soviet journalism students, to discuss Reagan's talk. Why did the first student, Albina Cardanova, want to go? To see what he looked like. And what did she conclude? That he was charming. Why did the second one go?

Igor Sharushkin – student: I wanted to see him as a good politician I knew him as a good politician, and he really is so. And um, I wanted to see an actor, Hollywood actor, also. And I've seen an actor on the scene. He spoke, spoke about a lot of things, but at the same time, he spoke about nothing. I think so, it's my personal opinion. His speech was like, like water. It was very, very beautiful, if it's possible so to say. And ah, in general he didn't say anything ah, new.

And, as for Reagan's talk of freedom, Sharushkin replied,

I think that we have different um, understanding of the term of 'freedom.' For example, ah, for me it's, it's very difficult to understand how, how can person go to, to simple shop and to buy a garment or machine gun. And ah, in the States and some other Western countries, it's, it's a common thing.

Asked if she understood Reagan's references, Cardanova said she disagreed with him about Nicaragua and Afghanistan. Sharushkin replied to the same question by saying that 'he didn't give any good answer.' And what about human rights, of which Reagan has made such an issue?

Albina Cardanova: I think that our problems we shall decide ourselves in our country. And we don't need help, I think. And for such power as ours it's possible to, to resolve this problem by ourselves. But ah, I'll, I said here that Mr President wasn't a teacher for us today. And ah, I liked that he just chose it that way of not teaching us but, but speaking about our problems, maybe like a friend, that way.

Sharushkin and Cardanova, if they were, in fact, journalism students, were also adept at making their own points in the guise of answering Frum's questions. Of course, nothing was said about how these two were recruited. They just happened to be 'with us from Moscow.'
    The next item was to provide two 'veteran correspondents' an opportunity to assess the 'mood' of Moscow's 'Summit Fever.' Frum provided a hymn to *glasnost* as her introduction. Moscow was a journalist's paradise.

Glasnost has given the thousands of foreign reporters who have come to Moscow unprecedented access to the city and its people. And the city is buzzing with openness.

It was also a triumph for public relations:

The city has been painted and paved in readiness for the television cameras. A public relations firm was hired to put American disk jockeys live on Soviet radio. It also arranged to manufacture ten thousand Official Summit T-shirts, to be sold by Tass as souvenirs.

The two veteran correspondents, Martin Walker of *The Guardian* and Vladimir Brodetsky of *The Moscow News*, were asked what they made of it all. Walker replied that the most surprising thing is that there have been no spats between Nancy Reagan and Raisa Gorbachev. Ronnie was 'jealous' that Gorbie stole the show in December.

Martin Walker: If Gorbachev could impress the American intellectuals for the series of meetings in the Soviet embassy in Washington, then President Reagan will meet the Soviet intellectuals and charm the pants off them, which is what he did today.

After Walker's remark, Brodetsky had to respond. Frum asked him about human rights and Reagan's tastelessness about bringing up a topic that any autocracy would find embarrassing. Brodetsky's response showed him a master.

Vladimir Brodetsky: Ah, you know last night Reagan met with some selected citizens of Soviet Union and a couple of fouls, foul ... getting ... our very prominent figure, public figure, delivered a commentary on our Moscow TV and to Moscow TV show. The meeting between Reagan and to those citizens, it was just impossible to imagine ah, a couple of years ago, even on the *perestroika* years. Ah, and we had no idea how to run such a story three or four years ago. It means that not so many citizens were surprised that Reagan, Reagan administration is dealing with our human-rights stories, issue actually. Ah, it means that ah, we're going to discuss this matter with the Americans or with the Europeans, any time, on our ground. And also on their ground.

Frum, not surprisingly, looked puzzled. She nodded as if she understood something. Now this ... What about Yeltsin? The great scandal was that Yeltsin had stated on Western television that the 'right deviationist,' Ligachev, and not he, should have been fired. Walker aired gossip about Politburo intrigue, and Frum directed a question at the Soviet editor.

Barbara Frum: Do you agree with that, Mr Brodetsky? Is that ah, what you're saying?

Vladimir Brodetsky: I cannot but agree.

Since it was not clear what Brodetsky was or was not agreeing to, she asked him to elaborate.

Barbara Frum: You will cover that story will you and what will you say?

Vladimir Brodetsky: You know we should note the last time ... today, but I do remember that this, I do understand that ah, this interview helped me to say to all people that this, story should be covered in the paper. Otherwise the policy to have openness or *glasnost* will not work.

Brodetsky was not about to say anything intelligible about conflicts in the Politburo. He, unlike Walker, had more than his visa to lose.

A final theme these two veteran correspondents were asked to consider was whether there was any 'turning back,' by which Frum meant a reversal of Gorbachev's 'reforms.' Martin said there could be, and that Gorbachev needed a 'foreign-policy success' to help him domestically. What did Mr Brodetsky think? Whatever it was, he was not letting on.

Vladamir Brodetsky: Well, the struggle's rather serious. A struggle is going go on in the party committees. But we believe that people who believe in *perestroika* sooner or later will leave. And the next, the coming, the party conference will show who is going to be on the up, on the top.

After the veteran correspondents provided the CBC with trivia, gossip, and a splendid demonstration of the art of keeping your head down, Frum turned to the intellectuals for the big picture. This time, opposite the familiar Stephen Cohen, was Richard Pipes, a Harvard historian and former National Security Council member. Frum asked Pipes the first question, secure in the knowledge that Cohen would disagree.

Barbara Frum: Gentlemen, I want to hear your views on what you think is happening here. There is some sense of euphoria, perhaps helped by the beautiful late spring weather, Mr Pipes, that the great superpower rivalry is coming to an end. Is it?

Richard Pipes: Oh heavens, no. Ah, I, I think ah, a summit like this is largely of symbolic value, and it has a certain value in terms of putting people's anxieties at ease but the fundamental problems have not disappeared at all.

Cohen, in contrast, said that there was a new Gorbachev foreign policy, 'which is committed to ending the Cold War as we've known it, which means the Cold War with the arms race. That is the policy of this leadership.' There would be future rivalry, Cohen said, but there was also an opportunity 'to reconstruct our relationship as rivals in a way that does not include an arms race. That's I think what's at stake here.' Did Pipes share Cohen's vision? Unfortunately not. There was no evidence for it.

Richard Pipes: The problem is that there's no indication of attenuation of the Soviet arms build-up so far, as far as I know. And there's good reason for this because the Soviet is a superpower only thanks to its military prowess. Therefore I think it's very unlikely that we're going to see, really, a major shift in Soviet foreign policy. I do believe that what's going on inside the Soviet Union is a very genuine change. Whether this will be reflected in foreign policy remains to be seen.

Cohen thought it could be seen already: there was the INF Treaty, on-site verification, the Afghanistan withdrawal, and the hope of asymmetrical conventional reductions.

These are significantly new proposals, which have already in some cases become actions. I don't understand how Professor Pipes can say he sees no change at all in Soviet foreign policy over the last three years.

No doubt Professor Pipes had a response that would have accounted for the events indicated by Cohen without characterizing it as a major shift in foreign policy. He did not have an opportunity to present an alternative to Cohen's authorized version.

Frum interjected here:

Barbara Frum: Okay. But, Stephen Cohen, just before I return to Professor Pipes, develop your thought a bit further.

Cohen was off and running: Gorbachev had wanted to end the arms race for fifteen years and now he was in power. 'That's not a breathing spell, that's a new kind of a relationship. Now much depends on what the United States does.' Cohen was, in short, able to present once again his entire vision of Soviet domestic and foreign policy. Once again 'much depends on what the United States does.' Rather than allow Pipes to make whatever points he might, Frum introduced a new topic.

Barbara Frum: Let me invite each of you to pick your favourite point of friction around the world. I don't know if it's the Angola war, the Vietnamese in Kampuchea backed by the Soviets; if it's the Gulf War. Where do you see Soviets changing their behaviours, Stephen Cohen?

Stephen Cohen: Look, Barbara, let me make my point again.

And he did, ending up with a standard statement, CBC–approved, of the doctrine of the moral equivalence of the United States and the USSR: 'Both sides must stop shipping this monstrous level of weapons into the Third World. We are both shipping weapons all over the Third World, and doing nothing but escalating the lethal nature of local civil war. That could stop.'

On the surface, Cohen was a bad source in so far as he refused to respond to the questions posed, and instead provided his own. One might think that people who do that would not usually be invited back. But Cohen had become a regular. The obvious reason seems to be that he was an authorized knower who *seemed* to be something of a loose cannon on *The Journal's* quarterdeck, but who, in fact, always came up with the sought-for response – namely, that the United States ought to be nicer to the Soviets, who are doing all they can to be nice.

Cohen ended his visualization with the statement that both sides 'could' stop sending arms beyond their borders. Frum accepted Cohen's statement and asked Pipes, 'Could that stop?' Well, of course, it *could*, in the sense that many things are possible. As Hegel once said, the Sultan could become Pope. His point was that such abstraction is what prevents thoughtful analysis of the real question, that being, in Hegel's day, why so few non-Italians ascended to the See of St Peter.

Pipes, like many others whom the CBC brought on as a foil to Stephen Cohen, was a commonsensical scholar, not a visionary of remote possibilities. He had been handed a heavily loaded question by Frum, the equivalent of asking if the Sultan could become Pope. He tried to answer by referring to facts.

Richard Pipes: Well, it's, it's, you know, the Soviet Union as far as I know, ah, ships roughly twice as much as we do.

Cohen would have none of that. This was TV! It was important to visualize or, failing that, to provide the play drama of a quarrel.

Stephen Cohen: That's not, that's not factually correct.

Richard Pipes: The figures I, the figures I have seen do indicate ...

Stephen Cohen: Well, the figures are wrong.

Pipes was, unfortunately for entertaining news, something of a gentleman. Rather than direct some plain words in Cohen's direction, he proposed to leave matters ambiguous.

Richard Pipes: Ah, they're certainly very major sellers of it, they make a lot of money on it. Ah, it would be good if one could stop this, but ah, will they? I don't know.

This made for bad TV. Ambiguity is not entertaining. It was time to change the subject.

Frum proposed dropping the question of arms shipments. Are the two countries going to agree on other things, such as Angola or Kampuchea?

Richard Pipes: They're making interesting shifts. Now ah, what's happening right now in Nicaragua is very interesting and it suggests how powerful Moscow's influence is over Nicaragua. The Sandinistas have now agreed to make political changes for the first time. Obviously under Moscow's pressure. If that continues, if that is done in other Soviet client states, then indeed we are seeing a new stage, but it's only the beginning. One has to wait for the results.

Pipes seemed not to understand that sensible discussion of the realities of foreign policy made bad TV. Back to Cohen.

Barbara Frum: Would you choose that example, Professor Cohen?

Stephen Cohen: I would choose Soviet/American behaviour all around the world. I think the Third World is the greatest ongoing tragedy because both sides are killing presumably hundreds of thousands of people every year for no purpose at all. The greatest danger, of course is the nuclear ...

Cohen's visions were much better. The whole world was his stage: both sides were doing mega-killing, and for no purpose. And then there's the really big danger, the bomb itself!

Pipes unfortunately remained committed to the reality of facts.

Richard Pipes: What, what exactly, where are we killing people?

Stephen Cohen: Wherever we ship weapons.

Richard Pipes: In the United States ... .

Stephen Cohen: Wherever we ship weapons we're allowing civil wars to be escalated into much more lethal warfare. Wherever we ship weapons to, and we ship weapons all over the world, just as the Soviet Union does.

Cohen got the last word, a restatement of the doctrine of moral equivalence. Time to move on.

Is each side no longer so afraid of the other's intentions? Pipes replied that, so far as the president was concerned in his explicit remarks, the question of fearing Soviet intentions was settled. So far as public opinion goes, no.

This suspicion of the Soviet Union remains very deeply imbedded amongst the large majority of people. I think something like two-thirds or more, ah, and that is not going to be very easy to eradicate. Over time it may, but in the meantime it's too very deeply embedded.

Barbara Frum: What about on the Soviet side? Equally embedded do you think, Professor Cohen?

Stephen Cohen: I think Professor Pipes is right about American opinion. I think it's less embedded on this side, for various reasons.

Cohen was not inclined to indicate those reasons. He preferred a self-indulgent anecdote concerning himself and an anonymous member of the Politburo with whom he had recently been conversing.

As a final topic, Frum proposed they 'react to the atmospherics at the summit.' More specifically, Gorbachev looked irritated when Reagan talked so much about human rights, but today things looked brighter. What's going on? Have the Soviets grown more tolerant of these lectures on human rights?

Stephen Cohen: Well, I think both sides have a goal which is to reach the START Agreement, this 50 per cent cut in strategic weapons before President Reagan is no longer President Reagan, in January of next year. Ah, both sides have put out talk about a fifth summit, which would come only if they have this treaty to sign. Behind the scenes, they're working in that direction. And nobody yet knows how far they've gone.

Pipes agreed on the importance of START, but added that President Reagan really did believe in the 'sermons' he delivered on human rights.

Richard Pipes: Ah, the president is carried away by his usual romanticism. He, he really does believe that democracy is on the march. He believes in freedom. He believes in religion. And I am not sure that what he does is really a calculative strategy. I think he's giving vent to his true romantic beliefs.

The image of a romantic Reagan altered all the visualizations the CBC had made of the U.S. president. It was time to go.

Barbara Frum: At that point, I'm going to ... I thank you both.

Richard Pipes: Thank you.

Stephen Cohen: Bye-bye.

Well, it wasn't quite time to go. Susan Reisler appeared for a final word and a preview for tomorrow's show.

Susan Reisler: Barbara, the thaw in Soviet/American relations has meant something very special to the thousands of journalists who have been covering this summit. There's pizza, Pepsi, and Baskin Robbins ice cream on the streets of Moscow for the first time. That's just one of the signs of improved trade relations between the two countries, and tomorrow I'll have a report and we'll have guests who will address the still very controversial issue of trade normalization.

Before discussing the last day of the spring summit, 1 June, and that 'still very controversial issue' previewed by Reisler, let us consider the visualizations on *The National*.

Peter Mansbridge opened the show: Reagan and Gorbachev were talking about success, but in fact their meetings 'were perhaps bigger on symbols than on substance. No real breakthroughs and the two men still disagree on issues such as arms control and human rights.' Don Murray continued this visualization of 'a summit of small achievements.' Gorbachev was pleased with the INF Treaty and saw it as evidence of new, civilized politics.

Don Murray: Half an hour later he met the media. It was a Gorbachev summit summary such as the world has come to know. Exuberant, verbose, frank, assertive. For almost two hours, the words, the information, the opinions spilled out. He paused only long enough to redirect traffic.

There followed a clip of Gorbachev ordering Soviet officials to change places with some Western journalists whose simultaneous-translation earphones didn't work. Then 'it quickly became clear that Gorbachev was frustrated, annoyed with Reagan's emphasis on human rights here this week.' So far as Gorbachev was concerned, all this talk about human rights was 'propaganda gambits' and 'spectacles,' not 'real politics.' According to Murray, Gorbachev's 'frustration ran much deeper.' His 'litany' of complaints was long, and it centred on 'American indifference or opposition.'

Don Murray: And then, tearing up the diplomatic rule book, he told of his efforts to get Reagan to sign a document with him renouncing military force and embracing peaceful coexistence. It was a scathing sketch of a president overruled by his own adviser.

According to Gorbachev, Reagan said he 'liked' the text of a joint statement on 'peaceful coexistence,' a phrase much favoured by Khrushchev, but 'not everybody likes it,' so Reagan changed his mind. This act by Reagan caused Gorbachev much 'frustration.'

In Khrushchev's understanding, which was shared by the Americans, 'peaceful coexistence' referred to a temporary state of affairs during which capitalism and imperialism had the upper hand. It was necessary for the forces of historical progress, incarnate in the CPSU and led by the Politburo, to call a halt to the export of revolution, whether at the point of a bayonet or by the less lethal means of agitation and propaganda. The U.S. position regarding arms negotiation has been, in public and in private, that agreements would be successful only when the interests of all parties to them were served. Nothing would be gained by agreeing to meaningless formulas or language that had one meaning to a communist and another to a non-communist. Gorbachev's frustration was understandable; expressing it by 'tearing up the diplomatic rule book' was in reality an example of a 'propaganda gambit' and 'spectacle.' The CBC presented it as an example of his 'exuberant, verbose, frank, assertive' character.

Joe Schlesinger continued the theme that Gorbachev had been frustrated by Reagan's opposition to progress in general, and his 'reneging' on the 'peaceful coexistence' text. Accordingly, Reagan was 'on the defensive,' being forced to 'explain his change of heart on the Soviet Union being the evil empire,' and 'rejecting accusations' that he was in a hurry to sign the START Treaty before leaving office. Schlesinger then characterized the summit as having been 'dominated' by Gorbachev. In Red Square, 'the old crowd pleaser' was 'upstaged by the Kremlin commissar,' putting the lie to his boast that he would 'outshine' Gorbachev. Mostly, said Schlesinger, he was a 'mute bystander.' He dozed off at the Bolshoi Ballet and thereby 'reinforced reports that he seemed lethargic, even sick.' This provided the theme for Schlesinger's final visualization.

Joe Schlesinger: Reagan has charmed many Russians. And he has offended many others. None, though, could fail but notice the strong contrast between their energetic leader and the aging and fading American. It's a strong message, that as far as Ronald Reagan has gone in abandoning his 'evil empire' ideas, if the Russians expect another great breakthrough they will have to wait for the next president of the United States. Joe Schlesinger, CBC News, Moscow.

In sum, the reason there was no 'breakthrough' was because of Reagan; he was an old man, tired and fading fast.

Peter Mansbridge then provided a bit of gossip, complete with sound-bites, on Nancy and Raisa, who still weren't getting on. This was followed by gossip about Yeltsin and a report by David Halton on a demonstration in favour of another political party made possible by the presence of Reagan and the Western media.

Barbara Frum then appeared with a preview of things coming up on *The Journal*.

Barbara Frum: The summit spirit. The Soviets can't seem to get enough. Gorbachev wants a bigger arms pact from Reagan. And Soviet consumers want Big Macs from America.

Man: We don't mind to get high technology and to get pizza and McDonald's.

Barbara Frum: Can Americans handle those go-go Soviets? Coming up on *The Journal*.

Frum began by showing some highlights from *The National*: Reagan saying he was against deadlines and showing caution, Gorbachev moving reporters into seats vacated by Soviet officials. 'In any language, Gorbachev takes charge,' she said. In contrast, there was Reagan.

Barbara Frum: For the past three days, Ronald Reagan has annoyed his Soviet host by stressing the human-rights issue. Today, the president softened his stand, blaming bureaucratic red tape for the inability of thousands of so-called refuseniks to leave the Soviet Union. And then, late today, there was a dramatic new chapter in the story.

Twenty-eight Jewish families had been granted exist visas. Frum interviewed one of the lucky and happy recipients.

Then came Susan Reisler's report on the 'controversial issue' promised the night before – namely, trade normalization. The first to appear was George Cohon, the president of McDonald's Canada, praising the 'burger diplomacy' made possible by *glasnost*. The president of Pepsi agreed. Again, only Reagan was slowing things down.

Susan Reisler: Increased trade between the superpowers is not Ronald Reagan's priority in Moscow. He's working on his man-of-peace image. But it is a priority for Mikhail Gorbachev. At the Washington Summit last December, the Soviet leader took several hours to meet with an élite group of American chief executives. He shared his vision of a revived Soviet economy and invited them to join in the restructuring.

Reisler pointed out that Soviet manufacturing was inefficient and shoddy, and that Western technology could improve matters. Roger Robinson, identified as a former White House adviser, threw a damper on this happy vision. Pepsi and pizza was one thing, major high-tech operations another.

Roger Robinson: But we have to be particularly, particularly careful during this period of expansion that this doesn't flow over into strategic areas of the trade relationship that can harm Western security interests.

There were problems, Reisler concluded: the major source of movement towards normalizing business remained Gorbachev. Nothing was said about any economic necessities pushing Gorbachev and the Soviet economy in that direction. It was simply more evidence of Soviet progressive actions and Western foot-dragging.

Frum then engaged two expert authorized knowers who favoured increased trade. Viktor Spanderian, an economist and deputy director of the USA/Canada Studies Institute in Moscow, said that good political relations will flow from good economic relations. Jerry Hough, an American author of a book on the subject, agreed, and stressed the symbolic importance of McDonald's as a representative of Western market forces. What about high-tech? Well, Hough said, if the United States doesn't supply it, the Europeans or the Japanese will. Frum then asked Spanderian: 'You're going to get this one way or another, aren't you?'

Viktor Spanderian: No, no, I don't think we're going to play one against the other. It's not our idea. You see, we wanted to be more deeply incorporated in the, into the international division of labour, but not to, to, to make some tricks or something like this. And I should like to stress that the, that the high-tech, exchange in high-tech, is not the street that, not one-way street. You see ah, if you take the ah, *Time* magazine off the printer circle for May, you can find a list of the Soviet invention which have use in the United States. For instance, even in, in the, SDI. In strategic initiative ah, you are using some of devices which, which were invented in Soviet Union. So I would like to stress that we don't want to have one-way trade. We want a good relations, we are ready to receive your high-tech and we are ready to exchange for our high-tech.

Hough replied that it was sometimes hard to draw the line between pizza technology and cruise-missile technology. Spandarian said they had no interest in missile technology but that American 'paranoia' prevented them from buying blue-jean technology from Levi-Strauss because it 'used some automation.'

What about linkage? Hough said, go for half a loaf. Economic change will bring changes in human rights in its wake. In this context, linkage was equivalent to the Marxist doctrine of economic base and political and ideological superstructure. Here Hough seemed to be a better Marxist than Spanderian was. The problem with his Marxism was that the implication contradicted Marx's one-way vision of history. Instead of capitalism undermining itself, and ushering in the socialist revolution, it was undermining socialism and ushering in human rights. Spanderian was, perhaps, prudent in not thinking through the implications of increased trade. Or rather, he was prudent in not using Marxist categories to express his thoughts.

The next topic Frum discussed was, she said, 'the real purpose of this summit' – namely, 'to get an actual reduction in strategic arms.' However, she went on,

that effort appears stalled. And as the summit ended today, Mikhail Gorbachev was quick to blame the American side. He said he's willing to talk about reducing Soviet superiority in troops and tanks in Europe. Ronald Reagan, he said, would not deal seriously on that issue.

To discuss the question, two expert knowers were introduced – a Soviet arms-control adviser, Yevgenyi Velikov, and Richard Perle, earlier visualized as a hard-liner, but now identified simply as a 'former U.S. assistant secretary of defence.'

Barbara Frum: Richard Perle, Mikhail Gorbachev is suggesting it is the Americans who are foot-dragging. How do you react to that?

Richard Perle: Well there's a, there's a lot of history to contradict that, of course. The agreement that was ratified today, eliminating intermediate nuclear missiles, was an American proposal, rejected by the Soviet Union side under three Soviet leaders, including by General Secretary Gorbachev himself for well over a year before he eventually decided that he could agree to that proposal. The discussion that's under way now, about 50 per cent reductions in strategic forces, also flows from American suggestions going back to 1982. So I think the record is clear we have been vigorous in making proposals. We are responsive to proposals that emanate from the Soviet side. But I would not take too seriously the kinds of comments made at a press conference after a Summit meeting when one expects the participants to launch the next round of international propaganda in support of their position.

Perle provided facts and a plausible interpretation of them. His closing remarks provided a moderate visualization of the context of Gorbachev's remarks. The Soviet leader wasn't exactly lying, but, after all, he *was* speaking to the media. Velikov said that no propaganda was involved and that the proposal to reduce conventional forces was a practical one. Frum saw it that way too.

Barbara Frum: Mr Perle, the Soviets insist they are proposing a purely defensive status for conventional arms in Europe. What would be wrong with that?

Richard Perle: Well, there's nothing wrong with it. And I hope it turns out to be a correct assessment of the nature and disposition of Soviet forces. But I think we want to concern ourselves, not so much with intentions but with capabilities. And as we look at Soviet military capability, particularly in Central Europe, we find a massive overwhelming Soviet advantage. Now, hopefully through the arms-control process, that advantage will be diminished to the point where there will be parity in Central Europe, and we're very interested in that. We have everything to gain from parity, given that we start with a situation in which the Soviets have immense advantages. But it would be a mistake on the basis of mere statements to assume that there has been the kind of change that we hope will come about when we know very well that the forces that exist today are exactly the same as the forces that existed a year ago, before there was any claim laid to a new defensive strategy.

Asked a fully loaded question about what the Soviets said, Perle responded with a statement of prudent realism. The Soviets could insist on whatever they wished; they could express splendid peace-loving intentions. None of that alters their capability, and that capability, that potential, not honeyed words, was and remains the foundation (though not the apex) of the ordinary conduct of foreign policy by virtually all but the most ideologically deformed regimes. The responsibilities of power usually induce sobriety.

Frum then asked Velikov what the Soviets were, in fact, proposing in order to achieve parity.

Mr Velikov: From point of view of parity, we proposed to ah, study carefully all the asymmetry. And to eliminate any um, superiority in field of asymmetry. Going down altogether. And after it's going down together, in all the force and ah, in parallel, to change situation with some way. Like the corridor without nuclear weapons, without heavy conventional weapons, which change the posture to purely defensive. It's one of the means to make purely defence push and ah, this is the old field of possible steps.

Whatever Velikov meant, Frum was satisfied sufficiently that she asked for no clarification. Turning back to Perle, she again presented the Soviet version. Again she was corrected by stubborn facts and a few home truths about diplomacy, strategic-arms negotiations, and the media.

Barbara Frum: Mr Perle, Secretary Gorbachev said that when he asked the Americans to share data in order to start moving in that direction today, he got another 'no.'

Richard Perle: Well look, let's be serious about how these negotiations are conducted. You don't at the summit level, say, 'Let's share data' and get answer that says, 'Sure, let's share data.' We've been talking about data for fourteen years in Vienna, and we've been unable to resolve the data issue. And I think that's a dead place as a place to start. The place to start, and it would be in the interests of the Soviet Union and the United States and ah, Europe, both East and West, is for the Soviet Union to do the obvious thing and begin to diminish its enormous advantage in tanks and artillery and attack helicopters and attack aircraft, and all of the other weapons that make up that very sizeable superiority, which has caused us, on the Western side, to rely, unfortunately, on nuclear weapons. I, I'm rather optimistic and I, I think Professor Velikov means what he says, when he says the Soviet Union is interested in exploring real agreements. But I think we're not going to get very far if we talk in generalities. The place to settle these issues is at the negotiating table and not in front of the television camera.

Back to Velikov with a new topic: Why are the Soviets in such a hurry to deal with Ronald Reagan when six months from now there will be a new president?

Mr Velikov: Because of plenty to do with the new American president. Ah, we're looking on the ah, 50 per cent reduction not as a final step, or the ah, special problem, we're looking the process of ah, deep reduction in nuclear arms, in conventional arms, stop-testing, and many other problems beside weapons. And in this process we have plenty to do with next president.

Perle agreed, at least in part, with Velikov, but added his own reasons.

Richard Perle: I think the Soviets have had a disappointed experience with Democrats. The agreements that have been signed in recent memory have been signed by
Republicans, by conservatives who know why, and are prepared, to negotiate. And I
think the Soviets are quite wise to want to conclude an agreement with the president
they know and who has evidenced that he's prepared to sign agreements with them.

Frum ended the conversation at this point and turned to Susan Reisler for
some 'closing thoughts.'
    'Susan,' she said, 'will Moscow ever be the same?' Reisler could take a
hint, but she had enough common sense to be able to distinguish an invasion of journalists from, say, Napoleon's Grand Army. She began by giving
the anticipated response:

from my point of view, it's hard to believe it'll ever be the same. But, the fact is, this
is a really large city. There are over six to eight million people living here. And
frankly, you know, you can't even tell we're here. We're like little ants. I mean, it's,
it's amazing to think that so many thousands of journalists with all their equipment
can sort of take over a city and really, we're not that noticeable to, to most of the
people who don't happen to work around the area where we're stationed.

Frum then asked her to describe the 'spirit' of the Soviet citizens she has
met.

Susan Reisler: I think they've been really pleased. They, as we've gotten to know
them more, we've been here for, you know, a couple of weeks now. They've become
more friendly, they've become curious. They're, they're you know, I mean, the biggest problem has been language.

Reisler was having a few problems with language herself, so Frum asked her
about the juiciest bit of gossip: What about Raisa and Nancy? Reisler
reported that American journalists were a bit defensive about Nancy
Reagan and a bit critical of Raisa Gorbachev. But, on the whole, 'she's really
held her own, I think, on this visit, Nancy Reagan.' It seems a shame that
Frum cut off Perle and Velikov, but she doubtless had her reasons.

We can draw a few conclusions about the CBC coverage of the USSR and of its
foreign policy, especially where that policy touches the interests of the
West. First, the CBC devoted considerable resources to coverage of the USSR

and, in particular, deployed them to cover what became one of the major peace-and-security stories of 1987. The visualization of the summit meetings was remarkably consistent: the USSR was seen as a progressive and dynamic actor, the United States as a source of resistance to peace initiatives. In the language introduced earlier, the USSR was visualized as normal, the United States as deviant.

Notwithstanding all the attention devoted to the USSR, the CBC did not attempt to cover the Soviet perspective from the inside. On the contrary, the surface meaning of Soviet accounts was overwhelmingly accepted at face value. Accounts by U.S. officials, in contrast, were severely scrutinized, and alternative visualizations were presented. This does not mean simply that the CBC presented a Soviet version of their domestic policies, of their foreign-policy difficulties, and of the summit. On the contrary, the CBC presented their own visualization, which, unlike the visualization of the United States, did not contain serious scrutiny of the Soviet self-interpretation. Audiences did *not* consistently see what either the USSR or the United States sought from the meeting. What they did see enacted the doctrine discussed earlier, that audiences do not miss what they do not see. In terms of priming and agenda setting, or more broadly, in terms of myth, the CBC advanced the vision of a progressive USSR and a dangerous United States.

This conclusion raises some additional questions. What, for example, is one to make of the message of the Philby story – namely, that treason is exciting? What is the significance of the choice of sources to confirm CBC versions of events? Or of the failure to invite those who did not share the CBC view of things to expand on their opinions? What is the significance of Joe Schlesinger's sustained criticism of President Reagan? The CBC, of course, could respond in any number of ways, from a bold denial that these conclusions have any meaning at all, to a claim that they simply signify good, entertaining, hard-hitting TV journalism.

There is, perhaps, room for an alternative interpretation. The Marxists have a term, 'objective responsibility.' It was developed by Stalinist jurisprudence into the doctrine of 'objective guilt,' but its origins lay in an ethical position developed by Max Weber, which he called 'the ethics of responsibility.'[22] He contrasted it with an 'ethics of intention' in order to disabuse ideologically disordered German students of the self-serving opinion that they could avoid facing up to the consequences of their acts by pointing to their good intentions.

Weber's point bears repeating. Human rights, we are told, annoyed and frustrated Gorbachev. Accordingly, the CBC played down and all but ignored whatever Soviet reality corresponded with Reagan's criticism. This was not responsible journalism. It did, however, serve the doctrine of the moral equivalence of the United States and the USSR. But that doctrine is false. Upholding it is also irresponsible. To use Stalinist language, CBC visualizations were 'objectively' in the service of Soviet propaganda, that human rights were well protected by Soviet law and that raising questions about internal Soviet affairs was a provocation.

The account of the defeat of the Soviet expeditionary force in Afghanistan indicated the same tendency. So, too, did the persistent refusal to comprehend that nuclear weapons in Western Europe had stabilized international politics in that part of the world during the second half of this century. If nuclear weapons had been withdrawn from Europe, the WTO forces would have had a great military advantage. It has been a persistent goal of Soviet foreign policy to remove nuclear weapons from Western Europe. Why? So that they could then reduce their own military establishment? But that is precisely the problem: they can't. Not because the WTO countries need to defend themselves against a NATO invasion, but because a large standing army was considered necessary to maintain tranquillity, or at least order, in the Soviet Empire. The recent history of Poland, the former East Germany, Czechoslovakia, Hungary, and the Baltic states – in short, the disintegration of the Soviet Union, which ended the Cold War – indicates that clearly. Ignoring these realities, and playing the fiddle for what correspondent Don Murray called the 'superpower media duet,' seems to me, at least, to have been both irresponsible and in the service of Soviet interests. Put boldly, the CBC was irresponsible because its visualizations served Soviet interests.

There is a larger problem that should be considered, or at least introduced, at this point, and that is the question of the diffusion of images that deviate significantly from reality. The image of the Soviet Union as being 'like us' is, at best, a half-truth from which nothing much of political importance follows. Are they, for instance, more 'like us' than the Peruvians or the Turks? In the CBC visualization of international relations, the ethos of reformist and progressive sentimentality is never dimmed with genuine practical insights: we *do* have different and even opposed interests, British traitors *were* responsible for the deaths of several people. Ignoring these *facts*, which are well known from other sources, cannot but undermine the credibility of the entire medium. And so long as Canadians rely so extensively on TV for information, this state of affairs carries with it some sobering implications for the maintenance of a responsible democratic citizen body.

CHAPTER FOUR

Into the Dark on Africa

South Africa has a large population of European stock, unlike other countries on that continent. Coverage of South African news is likewise distinct from that of other countries on the continent. Most obviously, South Africa receives much more extensive coverage than any other African country, and is the home base to a large number of foreign correspondents. Among many factors, the weather, the local standard of living, and the relatively familiar culture account for their presence. So far as news coverage is concerned, stories dealing with other African countries seem to be a combination of natural-disaster and crime reports; South African news seems to consist of an endless stream of moralizing. When politics is introduced at all, very little is said about either Western interests in Africa or Soviet interests.[1] The focus is, as might be expected, on more spectacular and entertaining material chiefly connected to the colourful personalities of African tyrants and kleptocrats and to the catastrophic mortality statistics that, for some reason, are associated with such persons and regimes.

10   ETHIOPIA

The first story in our sample that dealt with Ethiopia was an anchor-only bulletin by Sheldon Turcott, broadcast on 13 November 1987. A U.N. official, Michael Priestly, was quoted as saying that 'thousands of people are facing death from starvation because drought has wiped out the harvest in many areas.' Consequently, a million tons of 'food aid' was needed. Moreover, matters were so bad that the United Nations was even considering sending relief to 'the north, in spite of the risk of rebel attacks.' Some food was on the way, Turcott said, from a Mennonite group in central Alberta. It was the first 30,000 bushels of an expected 90 cars of grain. In order even to begin to make sense of this story one would like to know how many bushels fit in a grain car and how many grain cars it would take to make a ton of food aid. Is 30,000 bushels a little or a lot?

In a second story, on 22 November, Knowlton Nash promised fresh disasters. Anonymous 'officials in Addis Ababa' said another 'disastrous famine' was 'just a few weeks away.' This time the response was said to be coming, not from Alberta Mennonites, but from the European Community (EC). According to an anonymous representative of the EC, this new crisis threatened to be worse than 1984, when 'hundreds of thousands died from hunger and disease.' The European response was to mount 'special airlifts of food,' for at least two months.

Just before Christmas, the CBC ran a four-part mini-series on Ethiopia narrated by Don Murray. The 22 December report opened with a service in the Ethiopian Orthodox church in Mekele, celebrating the close of Advent. 'But to outsiders,' Murray said, 'there's something odd. The drought isn't mentioned.'

Don Murray: Money, all of it, will go to repair the church. Later, Archbishop, [or] Abuna, Fron dismisses a query as to why. The church, he says, often talks of the drought and aids the afflicted, but what more can be done?

The Abuna [voice of translator]: The drought comes from God. Only saints can stand the hunger. God is punishing his people.

Don Murray: On the devastated Plain of Eritrea, God's wrath whispers among the dead lives. Crop failure in the province is total. And fatalistic acceptance of that failure as preached by the church is widespread.

A fatalistic farmer confirmed Murray's visualization.

But it takes more than drought to cause famine in Ethiopia. According to Murray, 'man's quarrels' make the effects of the drought worse.[2] The government militia were fighting rebels or guerrillas who desired independence from Addis Ababa.

Don Murray: The central government has spent precious money and resources in a vain effort to try to contain the rebels. But, in this region, they still roam at will. And their presence all but paralyses the delivery by road of emergency food aid in this season of drought. The rebels are well armed and well equipped. And in time of drought, they too supply food to hungry Eritreans. Several thousand tons a month, brought from Sudan. They say government planes bomb their food depots. But they've also attacked a U.N. convoy bearing food to Tigre. Twenty-six trucks destroyed.

Michael Priestly, the U.N. representative who was quoted on 13 November, said that such attacks by the rebels could result in a 'major catastrophe' if they were repeated. Murray summed up his visualization:

Don Murray: In the tragic tangle of drought, division, and fatalistic submission, brutal underdevelopment is the inevitable result.

But all was not lost. He ended his report on a note of hope, shots of Ethiopians building a dam by hand, and a sound-bite by a Canadian aid worker assuring the world of his 'feeling of optimism.'

Don Murray: Feet pound the ground when no machines can be found. Feet bear the burden of construction. In a corner of this plagued country, human will measures itself against the scourges of nature and determines that it shall prevail. Don Murray, CBC News, in the Abya Valley, Tigre.

This story was followed by a report from Ottawa of a squabble between private relief agencies, who claimed that the Canadian government wasn't giving them enough money, and CIDA officials who sought to excuse themselves.

The Christmas Eve report from Mekele concerned children who had escaped the death and starvation that had killed their parents. The account of these 'last living links to their families,' these 'orphans of the famine,' was delivered with considerable emotion: 'They have suffered enough ... Her parents died. But she lived, an infant at her mother's dead breast.'

On 12 January 1988, Wendy Mesley reported on a grain shipment from Montreal to Ethiopia that had been donated by Canadian grain farmers. A more thorough report was broadcast on 15 March 1988. The correspondent, Brian Stewart, had covered the 1984 famine. In pre-broadcast promotions on earlier shows of *The Journal*, the report was given the dramatic title, 'Life after Death: Ethiopia's Struggle to Survive.' Stewart began by remarking that 1988 was not as bad as 1984.

Brian Stewart: So far, just enough relief aid is making it through to avoid horrors like that, though it's very close. Instead, we examine the crisis and raise a central question. Why does Ethiopia receive aid and food, yet so little outside help in ending these disasters? We also look at what Ethiopians themselves are doing to try and end these ghastly cycles of starvation. A struggle that is at once both desperate and also deeply stirring.

Stewart's first sound-bite was from David McDonald, a former MP and, at that time, the Canadian ambassador. McDonald said it was important that people be kept out of 'famine camps.' McDonald returned later in the show, but first Stewart personalized his visualization. In 1984, he took pictures of a dying girl, Berhan, and her father. 'But even as her grave was being dug, she pulled through.' She and her father left the 'famine camp' and

were swept up in the famine storm outside. In '84, they became part of that vast migration across the northern highland, where famine was along every road. Part of that long trudging army that resembles survivors of a nuclear holocaust. Over the years we tried repeatedly to find them, but heard they'd been forcibly resettled far to the south. And that all trace of Berhan had been lost.

Stewart asked 'Ethiopian officials' about her, and they 'sent word through villages' near Mekele.

Several days later, to our surprise, they traced her to a small village which was expecting emergency rations. They suggested, if we showed up, we just might recognize a face. It was again, Berhan, now age seven, and her father ... They had been forcibly resettled, moved by the government 800 kilometres to the south, in the 1985 panic evacuation of famine refugees, in which so many died.

Berhan's father said he walked back to Tigre with Berhan on his back, and Stewart commented:

The long march of one father and daughter, cruel irony. They were barely back in Tigre when drought again devastated the countryside.

Stewart apparently had to leave Berhan and her father in the village with some haste. 'The crisis in the northern war was building hourly along the roads,' he said, which may have meant that his escorts, government troops, decided they were no longer safe.

Stewart then switched the visualization from this ikon of Ethiopian survival to the familiar image of a slender lifeline by which Western food reached the hungry poor being threatened by 'secessionist rebels and government troops.' Suitable sound-bites from both sides followed, each blaming the other; a U.N. official and a Red Cross official agreed that things were

terrible. Stewart then declared that 'the international community is increasingly exasperated by the recklessness of these endless struggles within a desperate land,' and David McDonald obligingly indicated his exasperation at
Ethiopian recklessness. In case the message of Stewart's visualization had
been lost, he made it explicit.

Brian Stewart: Some immediate conclusions. Governments and aid groups must
exert far more pressure for a cease-fire. And a key lesson – Ethiopians cannot remain
at the mercy of eleventh-hour rescue attempts. If not this time, then the next: the
lifeline will snap and millions will die. Ethiopia simply must feed itself. And that
requires from the world massive long-term development, of irrigation, of wells, of
roads, of everything needed to boost food production.

The problem, in short, was famine, and the solution was development. Politics had not been mentioned.
    Armed with this 'conclusion,' Stewart then looked for obstacles to this
simplest of all possible solutions. A missionary assured Stewart that Ethiopians were not lazy. It followed, according to this source's logic, that 'there
is need for more help and more help for development.' Stewart saw a scandal in not helping these dignified and hard-working people to 'develop.'

Brian Stewart: A bizarre fact of our time. Ethiopia is the poorest country. It needs
the most help. It gets the least. Compared to some neighbours, only seven dollars
per capita goes to Ethiopia for development. Kenya gets four times that. So does the
Sudan. Somalia receives fifty dollars per capita, seven times what Ethiopia gets.
Ludicrous, and grossly unfair, agrees Canadian ambassador David McDonald.

He agreed warmly. So how to explain this bizarre fact?

Brian Stewart: Ethiopia's Marxist government gets some of the blame, along with its
secretive, often brutal, chairman, Mengistu Mariam. Allied to the East Bloc, it has
hurled itself into a form of 1950s Stalinism, its policies as rigid as its Stalinist government. But World Bank economists are encouraged by some plans for reform.
Official promises to pay higher prices to peasant farmers, to make the economy
more competitive, to favour small farmers over state farms. Top former officials,
now in exile, like Dawit Giorgis,[3] are sceptical.

Dawit Giorgis: They have political objectives, and therefore they want to achieve
those objectives, whatever the consequences, even if it would require millions of
people dying. They're not bothered about it. They have a political objective and

their political objective is to create a structured, regimented, and controlled society.

The policies of the government, now identified as Marxist, were at length said to be at least partly responsible for the undoubted distress of the Ethiopians. 'Balance' required that the 'scepticism' of Giorgis be answered.

Brian Stewart: But other critics, veterans of '84, feel it makes no sense to deny development help.

The 'other critics' may have been as 'sceptical' as Giorgis, but they did not voice their opposition to the government over the CBC. One of them was visualized by Stewart as 'the angel of Quoram,' a woman who led a team of French doctors in 'the famine wars.' The purpose of the sound-bite offered by Brigitte Basset was to answer the 'sceptical' remarks of Giorgis by saying that it was worthwhile to prevent people from starving. No one, least of all Giorgis, denied it. The question at issue concerned the connection between the ideological commitment of the government to Marxism and starvation. How much was a consequence of forced collectivization and other socialist policies? How much was a consequence of the conventional civil/ideological war waged between the central government and the rebels? How much was a consequence of the use of famine relief by the central government as a weapon? These are not simple questions to answer.[4] But one cannot even begin to answer them if they are never raised.

Stewart then turned to a visualization of 'development' as undertaken by the industrious Ethiopians. As with the earlier report, shots of building dams by hand and foot accompanied Stewart's praise of Ethiopian efforts and call for sustained long-term development funds, especially from Canada. The U.N. official, Michael Priestly, the Canadian minister for external relations, and David McDonald provided appropriate sound-bites. Yet, the 'bizarre facts' remained stubborn and 'extraordinary.'

Brian Stewart: The 1984 famine pictures brought unprecedented donations pouring into private non-governmental organizations, the NGOs. Much went into food, which saved enormous numbers, but all agreed this was just a stop-gap until long-term development could begin. The fanfare private groups, the NGOs, set up Partnership Africa–Canada to support African development. It got seventy-five million dollars from the government. But, on Ethiopia, it bogged down in debates over how to spend the money. And on which side of the fighting. John Weiler is chairman of Partnership Africa–Canada. We asked him how much of the seventy-five million dollars has actually gone to Ethiopia. How much? None. It does seem extraordinary, though, that Ethiopia's suffering helped spur the setting-up of Partnership Africa, and yet Ethiopia's got very little out of it.

Weiler couldn't figure it out either, and McDonald said it was not enough just to raise money. Stewart ended by remarking that 'most Canadian private groups have pulled out of Ethiopia' and that those remaining would be gone soon.

Brian Stewart: One looks at the wider picture with a sense of faded hopes. Canadian development help to the worst famine sown on earth amounts to twenty cents per Ethiopian, which even here means virtually nothing. So when we hear again that Ethiopia is in crisis, and still cannot feed itself, perhaps nothing is more surprising than our surprise.

A final story on Ethiopia was broadcast on 5 April 1988. It was a BBC report of a significant victory by Eritrean rebels over Ethiopian soldiers. The significance of the fighting was indicated as follows:

Fiona Holden: All the weapons used by the Eritreans have been captured from the Ethiopians. They proudly display their latest acquisitions. Large Soviet-built artillery guns. They say weapons like these will help them end the war. The capture of three Soviet officers is also regarded as a crucial development. The rebels hope this will force the Soviet Union to think again about backing Ethiopia. As the fighting continues, morale among the rebels is high. They believe they've reached a turning-point in the war, but the Ethiopians, with their powerful friends in the Soviet Union, show no sign of giving in to Eritrean demands for independence.

In the sequence of stories on Ethiopia, this was the second to mention politics. It originated with a foreign news agency. In contrast, the CBC's visualization of Ethiopia was summarized by Don Murray in his Christmas Eve story: drought, division, and fatalistic submission have led to brutal underdevelopment. Drought was an act of God; division was 'man's quarrel,' which made things worse; fatalism was a temporary disorder, probably caused by the church. Really, the Ethiopians were proud and hard-working; just look at all those dams they had made by hand. And Canada was doing its bit, though, of course, more needed to be done, especially in the area of long-term development. Murray's visualization was plausible, otherwise it could not have been used. The only thing that disturbed it were those troublesome sceptics and the Eritrean rebels fomenting the division of an otherwise happy society. True, Mengistu was a Stalinist, and secretive and often brutal, but that meant only that he deserved some of the blame, and he got it only from 'sceptics' such as Giorgis, who probably had an axe to grind anyway, being a 'former top official, now in exile.'

What was *not* said of Ethiopia could sustain several programs of *The Journal*. Between 1979 and 1982, after the military coup but before the famine, the government of Ethiopia collected $900 million in bilateral and multilateral aid, a large amount of money by anyone's standards.[5] And, if Ethiopia remained the poorest nation on earth, even after receiving such aid, the reason just may lie with the kind of government it enjoyed. After all, under Haile Selassie, Ethiopia fed itself most years, and consistently exported agricultural products. And Kenya, which suffered an even more severe drought than did Ethiopia, suffered no mass starvation. If Kenya received more aid per capita, the reason may be that aid was not used to support the largest standing army in Africa, more than 300,000 men.

Some of the omissions from CBC reports would make good, entertaining TV. Mengistu was described as brutal and secretive. He certainly was a colourful personality. Some reports indicated that one of his first acts as tyrant was personally to smother the frail old emperor, Haile Selassie, with a pillow. In the fall of 1987, on the thirteenth anniversary of his rule, he put on an extravagant party and elevated himself to the presidency. He gave a six-hour speech to the assembled citizens of Addis Ababa, and never mentioned famine.[6] He could easily have been visualized as an African tyrant following the model of Amin or Bokassa.[7] There are interesting policies associated with his regime that could lead to speculation on the future course of events. There are rumors, for example, that Mengistu had established a 50,000-man special forces unit and an African KGB for use elsewhere on the continent.[8] Certainly Ethiopia's neighbours must have wished the rebels of Eritrea and Tigre great success in their endeavours. The northern front-line states – Sudan, Kenya, Uganda and Somalia – would have been unlikely to welcome the advent of a victorious Ethiopian army.

Other facts, associated with internal policies, are less colourful and less entertaining, but still might be worthy of mention. Chief among them: driving 60,000 peasants from their farms, mainly in the northern provinces, and forcing about 8 million unwilling peasants onto collective farms.[9] Compared with the forced collectivization, the price-fixing, crop requisition, and extensive and enthusiastic purges of Marxist rivals were relatively minor disasters. Even when the brutality of the 'resettlement' policies was indicated, as in the story of Berhan and her family, the focus was not on the Stalinists responsible for the atrocity but on the admirable endurance of her father in giving her an 800-kilometre piggy-back ride. Nothing was said of Mengistu's soundly Stalinist policies of making use of famine and drought to attempt to crush his opposition.[10] Nothing was said of the $50 per ton 'handling fee' extorted by the government from aid donors. No coherent reason for the existence of the rebels in Eritrea or Tigre was ever given.

The significance of some facts seems to have been entirely misconstrued. It was, for example, the French organization Médicins sans frontières, to which Brigitte Basset, the angel of Quoram, belonged, that first drew attention to the consequences of resettlement – namely, 100,000 deaths – in 1985. They were immediately expelled from Ethiopia.[11] A few weeks after the broadcast by Brian Stewart on 6 April 1988, the government of Ethiopia expelled all relief workers from the northern provinces, which was at least consistent with its earlier actions.

The problem with these facts, and accounts that might be developed on the basis of them, is that they would entail considerable alteration in the visualization that the CBC developed. If the CBC were as interested in reporting as the BBC seemed to be, they would have done something more than visit government-run concentration camps. If they were capable of taking a detached view of the Soviet Union, they would see that the efforts of the inhabitants of Eritrea and Tigre had resulted in a very efficient relief agency and, at the same time, had done a great deal to diminish the resources of a Soviet client state.[12] Moreover, if there was even a modest degree of common sense to the CBC visualization of 'development,' there would be no stirring calls to increase Canadian aid to the tyrants who ruled that country and whose policies were responsible for so much misery and death.[13] It is true that, if one is interested in avoiding an increase in state-directed murders, then one must be circumspect in dealing with governments that use starvation as a technique of population management and public policy. But it is surely questionable whether the CBC has helped matters by refusing to consider the sheer murderousness of Mengistu's policies. Instead, the attempt was made to manipulate CBC audiences into feeling guilty for events far beyond their control. What else can made of Stewart's closing lines: 'nothing is more surprising than our surprise' at the continuation of famine. In his 15 March 1988 report, he raised the question: why does Ethiopia not receive aid to end the disaster? The answer seems obvious enough: such aid would consist in removing the Stalinist government that controlled the country.

It is difficult to know what to make of a news organization that is incapable of seeing tyranny and unable to apprehend the role of the state in transforming a food shortage and hunger into famine. Two explanations suggest themselves, neither of which is particularly comforting. The first is that they were incompetent in so far as they were unable to see what was before their eyes and what was, in any case, being reported by others.[14] The second is that they were concerned simply to entertain Canadians with foreign horror stories.

11   SOUTH AFRICA

There are many tyrannies in Africa. Indeed, tyranny is the most common regime in all parts of the continent – north, south, east, and west. Whether sub-Saharan or washed by the Mediterranean, whether military or civilian, Marxist or anti-Marxist, the African continent contains precious few regimes that, by Western standards, are even minimally decent. A glance at any annual report by Amnesty International indicates this unequivocally. In Africa, one may say, tyranny is normal. The reasons for this state of affairs may be disputed, but the facts are tolerably clear.

Among all these tyrannical regimes, one stands out. It is unique not because of the degree or extent of its human-rights violations, which may serve as the common standard by which tyranny may be measured, but because it is the only African tyranny ruled by individuals of European stock. That fact, and not the tyrannical nature of its government, which is shared with its neighbours, is the chief focus of news coverage in southern Africa. South Africa was normal for the African context in so far as it was a tyranny, but deviant in so far as it was a White, not a Black tyranny.

Nearly all the stories on South Africa focused on Apartheid and 'resistance' to it both inside and outside the country. The internal resistance was presented in terms of peaceful opposition to a fundamentally evil regime. External resistance focused on the question of 'sanctions.' The two were linked in a general visualization: Apartheid was the problem and sanctions were the solution. Successfully applied, sanctions would, apparently, return South Africa to normality.[15]

The first story we found, however, was an anomalous, short bulletin by Knowlton Nash, delivered on 12 June 1987.

Knowlton Nash: The South African government may have released hundreds of people detained without trial. An independent civil-rights group there says eight hundred detainees have been let go in the past two days.

Four days later, Nash provided a dramatic summary of dramatic events that had taken place eleven years earlier.

Knowlton Nash: A tragic annual ritual was enacted again in South Africa today. At least a million and a half Blacks staged a protest strike to make the eleventh anniversary of the Soweto uprising. The stay-at-home protest was to commemorate that bloody day in June when police opened fire on marching schoolchildren, killing two of them. In ensuing riots, nearly six hundred people lost their lives in one of the biggest anti-Apartheid demonstrations. One of the children killed, a twelve year-old boy named Hector Peterson, was remembered today at his graveside. A Black political leader paid a moving tribute to him.

A suitable sound-bite followed, and Nash concluded that 'today's anniversary passed off peacefully without a single incident reported by the police.'

On 9 August 1987, gold and coal miners went on strike, and this labour strife became a major focus for several stories. On 12 August, Nash provided a brief anchor-only report of a police raid on a union meeting where seventy-eight striking miners were arrested, 'not for activities related to the strike, but for conspiracy to murder.' Specifically, the arrested individuals were alleged to be planning to 'necklace' their opponents.[16] Nash then explained that necklacing meant putting a tire around a victim's neck and setting it alight. He tastefully omitted discussing the suffering of the victim that this mode of killing entails, and concluded by remarking that 'the miners' union says the arrests were part of a concerted government effort to crush the strike.' Next day, a much longer report appeared on *The Journal*, with Bill Cameron as host.

He introduced the story by linking White wealth to Black exploitation.

Bill Cameron: The wealth of South Africa was built on gold. And the cheap labour of Black workers to mine that gold. So this week's strike by the Black miners' union goes to the heart of White dominance in that country.

The strike, accordingly, was not about wages or working conditions, but had become 'a symbol of the demand for economic justice,' a topic that could be visualized more dramatically than the expression of mere trade-union mentality and the familiar demand for higher wages or better working conditions. Moreover, once an event becomes a symbol, its meaning can expand to fill the world.

Co-host Paul Griffin turned the strike into a threat to the government, visualized constantly as 'the White minority government.' He began where Cameron left off. He reviewed the day's events and again mentioned the arrest of seventy-eight miners (nothing was said of necklacing or other violence). It turned out that the National Union of Miners (NUM), and the mine owners, the Chamber of Mines, were not far apart. The NUM demanded a 30 per cent across-the-board raise. The chamber offered a 23 per cent raise for lower-paid workers and a 17 per cent raise for higher-paid ones. Colliery workers were offered raises from 15 to 23 per cent. It was necessary, therefore, to clarify what looked to be a fairly generous opening offer.

Paul Griffin: On one level, the strike is a straightforward fight over money. Black miners average $150 to $250 a month. White miners make at least $750. But, on another level, the strike is a politically volatile form of muscle flexing for South Africa's increasingly militant trade-union movement. The spectre of a large-scale withdrawal of cheap Black labour from a modern economy utterly dependent on it could mean a major crisis for the White minority government.

If that version of events were correct, the 'White minority government' would be on the side of the mine owners and active in crushing the strike in order to avert a crisis.

To confirm this visualization, the CBC contacted Cyril Ramaphosa, general secretary of the National Union of Miners. He became a regular source of vivid sound-bites. It was true, he began, that the government agreed not to intervene unless both sides requested it. But, in fact, they had been systematically arresting the leadership of the union.

Cyril Ramaphosa: They've been going around the country arresting many of our strike leaders. Yesterday they arrested seventy-eight strike committee leaders. Members, who were at a meeting, peacefully discussing the progress of the strike in their region. It would look like the government is now beginning to make all attempts to crush the strike.

There was 'no truth whatsoever' to the allegation that the men arrested were conspiring to necklace non-strikers. They were engaged in peaceful discussions, and the government 'has viciously started attacking by arresting and assaulting our leaders and members.' Whether or not the miners necklaced their opponents, it is certainly true that clashes between strikers and mine security personnel and between strikers and non-strikers resulted in fatalities.

Cameron then offered a follow-up question that seemed to suggest that Ramaphosa may have been exaggerating the cleanliness of the miners' hands.

Bill Cameron: Well, this is a very angry time, a very angry strike in South Africa. Are you telling me that there's no violence, there has been no intimidation on the line?

Ramaphosa agreed that there had indeed been violence, but it had been

initiated by mine management, and their stooges. Mine management is the one that when workers are peacefully sitting, on strike in their rooms, management has charged in with shotguns in their hands. And has been using tear-gas canisters to try and get our workers back to work. Workers have been literally forced down the mines at gunpoint.

The innocence of the miners having been established beyond question, Cameron safely turned to the topic of politics and economics.

Bill Cameron: What is your analysis? Is this strike entirely economic, or is it political as well?

Cyril Ramaphosa: The government has turned the strike into a political strike by its intervention.

Bill Cameron: So it is now political?

Cyril Ramaphosa: The government has decided that they want to crush the strike, and they are using their political operators to try and crush the strike. And obviously our members have to react to the actions that the government is taking.

Ramaphosa's last few remarks were a clearly constructed and even plausible account of what the South African government was doing. One must recognize, however, that he had no information at all on the government's plans. Cameron had evidentially caught the mood of Ramaphosa's speculations himself.

Bill Cameron: You must know that many senior White politicians must be saying to themselves, let's throw this fellow in jail and be done with it. If we call you next week. Would you be around to talk to us?

Cyril Ramaphosa: If I'm not in jail, yes, I'll be around to talk to you.[17] Ah, but they can do that any time if they want to.

Bill Cameron: Mr Ramaphosa, thanks very much. Good night.

Cyril Ramaphosa: You're welcome. Thank you.

Bill Cameron: When we return, a strange and mystical vision of harmonic conversions.

Cameron and Ramaphosa had their own strange and mystical visions. Ramaphosa 'must know' what the South African leaders 'must be saying.' Hence the plausibility of the entirely hypothetical question about Ramaphosa's availability next week. No other sources were used. On some questions, evidently, balance and objectivity can be found on only one side.

A week later, on 20 August, Nash provided an anchor-only report.

Knowlton Nash: South Africa's mine owners appear to be getting tough to try to end the strike by 300,000 Black miners. Union leaders said 6,000 of their members were fired today after they refused an ultimatum to return to work. And at one big gold mine the entire work force of 22,000 men said they'd quit if the mine owners keep threatening to fire people. The strike, now eleven days old, has crippled many of South Africa's gold and coal mines.

Reading between the lines, Nash was indicating that the miners were winning, and that, by 'getting tough,' they were making the mine owners desperate. Another week went by and the same message: the miners were hanging in there. On August 26, Peter Mansbridge reported.

Peter Mansbridge: Miners voted to stay off the job in spite of threats they'd be fired if they refused to return to work. The offer marginally improved fringe benefits, but ignored the union's demand for a 27 per cent wage hike.

If this report and earlier reports were accurate, the two sides were 3 per cent apart in terms of wage demands. Ramaphosa was back, not having been jailed after all, to emphasize the non-political nature of the strike.

Cyril Ramaphosa: The strike, which our union has been involved in in the past seventeen days, is a just struggle by thousands of mine workers for a living wage and improved working conditions.

A sound-bite from a representative of the mine owners expressed regret that the miners refused to settle for a 23 per cent raise. Next day, 27 August, Mansbridge reported that 20,000 miners had been fired 'after strikers rejected a take it or leave it offer to get back on the job. This gave the strikers fringe benefits only. But what they want is a hefty increase in pay.' The mine owners' offer of early August had now evaporated.

Three days later, on 30 August, the strike was settled. The CBC and its audience had not been prepared for this development. This clear and unequivocal defeat of the miners would have to be transmogrified by the magic of TV into a moral victory. Mansbridge broke the news quietly.

Peter Mansbridge: South Africa's coal and gold miners begin returning to work tonight, ending a three-week strike which had become the biggest, the longest, the most violent, and the most expensive in the nation's history. The miners seemed to have lost. They wanted wage increases but were faced with mass dismissals. James Robbins reports from Johannesburg.

Robbins reported that the miners had, indeed, been defeated.

James Robbins: For the leaders of the strike, today's talks were about getting miners back to work with the minimum loss of face. The union leader, Cyril Ramaphosa, knew he would make no headway on the strikers' central demand. Higher wages weren't even discussed.

The spokesman for the mine owners declared they had been firm and that the miners were capably led. Ramaphosa said the miners had not been defeated.

Cyril Ramaphosa: Our membership does not regard this as a defeat or as a loss. They see it as part and parcel of a struggle where the union is going to continue fighting the Chamber [of Mines] until we win all the demands that we seek to win.

It may be noted that the CBC did not mention at any time after the initial report of 12 August what the mine owners' offer was. Much of the visualization was as dramatic as it was abstracted from the actual context of bargaining and negotiation. Robbins ended his report with solace for the defeated.

James Robbins: Some strikers will be back at work tonight. Most, not all, the sacked men, will be re-employed. But this was not the strike to end strikes. The union hopes to be stronger next time. In Johannesburg, this is James Robbins for CBC News.

On 13 October, six weeks later, the CBC went over the entire story again on *The Journal*, ostensibly because they had some new pictures. The introduction by Frum and co-host, Paul Griffin, set the tone.

Barbara Frum: It was the longest mine strike ever in South Africa's history, though it lasted just three short weeks. In the end, the National Union of Mineworkers only gained a few concessions. The strike had taken its toll. Nine workers killed, five hundred injured, four hundred arrested. Tens of thousands had been dismissed.

Paul Griffin: With the power of the state behind them, South Africa's mining corporations managed to squash the strike. But when it was over, even they were conceding that they've underestimated the determination of the union. Recently *The Journal* obtained some exclusive footage of the strike that had been carried out of South Africa. Lynden MacIntyre has this report.

The event was visualized as high drama: the miners lost, but, by showing more determination than had been anticipated, they really won a moral victory.

MacIntyre began his report with a portrait of oppression. The work was dirty and hot and took place a mile below ground.

Lynden MacIntyre: South Africa's mines devour manpower. Men are cheaper than machines. These Black miners earn about $300 a month. If they were White, they'd earn three times that.

The gold these miners produced accounts for 60 per cent of South Africa's foreign earnings, MacIntyre said, 'but it hardly dents the systemic poverty of the men who dig it out of the rock.' One reason for the low wages of Black miners is an ample supply of Black men willing, for pay, to endure those living conditions and the pain of separation from home and family. MacIntyre indicated this basic economic fact.

Lynden MacIntyre: These people have all heard of the hardship. Yet many of them walked for days to line up for a job here. Their only baggage, blankets to fight the chilling mists of early morning. The lucky ones end up here, in South Africa, working on a one-year contract, renewable if they behave, earning wages one-tenth those of the average Canadian miner, enduring living conditions no North American worker would tolerate for an hour.

Comparing the living conditions and wages of Black South African miners with those of North American ones is dramatic but not serious. Poverty is, after all, an elastic notion. Nor did MacIntyre indicate an important and basic economic consequence – that the miners from outside the country were contributing to the economies of their homelands by repatriated wages. Instead, the focus shifted from the economic question of labour supply and demand to the constraints imposed on miners *after* they had agreed to work in South Africa.

According to MacIntyre, perhaps still looking with the eyes of a North American miner, the South Africans were seething with resentment. But,

their resentment is tightly capped by a brutal system of law enforcement. Apartheid forbids dissent. Since June last year, it even suppresses comment. Political opposition to Apartheid invites harsh responses. Security forces quickly confront any rebellion against Apartheid.

It is for this reason that the miners turned to trade-union activity as 'a vehicle for reform.' As trade-unionism was also visualized as 'a new force in the struggle against Apartheid,' one might anticipate that the strike would 'invite' a 'harsh response.' Instead, it was seen as 'a critical turning-point.' An exciting sound-bite from one of the 'leaders of the campaign against Apartheid' was supposed to confirm this.

Frank Chikane – South African Council of Churches: What has happened to the present moment is that there's been a clamp-down on all those organizations and groups. And the only way in which workers, who are actually the people who belong in the majority, to, in those organizations, express themselves through those channels that they find available. And I think what you are seeing since the beginning of the year is an indication of the trade-union power that is developing in this country.

In other words, the defeat of the strikers had become evidence of a turning-point – namely, the development of trade-union power. MacIntyre went even further in his visualizations.

Lynden MacIntyre: Like a black thunderhead on the horizon, the trade-union movement has become a force to watch in South Africa. It speaks for 712,000 workers through the Congress of South African Trade Unions, COSATU. Earlier this year the powerful Postal and Telecommunication Workers Union struck for a living wage.

MacIntyre did not indicate whether their strike for a living wage was crowned with success, but turned to the contrapuntal theme: government repression.[18] Ramaphosa offered a statement in confirmation that the government was repressive and assured MacIntyre he knew 'that the state has devious plans that they have made against us.' Perhaps one of their devious plans was the next thing MacIntyre mentioned, a 'mysterious bomb blast' that wrecked the headquarters of the trade-union organization. Other sources indicated that this bombing was probably undertaken by White political activists who opposed the government because it was too conciliatory.[19]

MacIntyre then moved on to the main event, the August miners' strike. The bomb blast turned out to be not really mysterious after all. It was

blunt warning to the two-year-old movement against flexing its muscles. But it wasn't enough to prevent labour from mobilizing its toughest challenge to the system, a walk-out in August by 300,000 members of the powerful National Union of Miners.

A dramatic narration of events followed. Short, punchy non-sentences. Vivid adjectives.

This is how it began. August 9th. Fed up with systematic exploitation, they began a mass exodus from the mines and hostels. It's a drastic action. Once off the job, they had no legal right to be in the country. They strike anyway. The world is startled by their solidarity. It's the largest legal strike in South Africa's history. In their protest, they turn their backs on a hard-won livelihood.

The companies tried to confine the miners, but they could not. The miners 'head defiantly for home.' The ones who stayed were just as heroic. They set up their own security officers.

They're determined to prevent any incident by their own people, or by provocateurs. That might give the government an excuse to intervene. It's a critical moment in the struggle against Apartheid. Union men check carefully to prevent violence. An innocent-looking bottle could contain the ingredients for a fire bomb. They take no chances.

'Spirited' but responsible demonstrations were shown.

The placards carefully avoid the rhetoric of the liberation struggle. This must appear to be an industrial action, a strike for a 30 per cent pay raise. Nothing that threatens the system itself.

The audiences already knew, however, that the strike was a turning-point in the struggle against Apartheid, and that appearances were meant to mislead. But to mislead whom?

The point of MacIntyre's visualization was not to mislead the South African government, but to turn the audience into imaginative co-conspirators with the miners.

Lynden MacIntyre: To the outside world the strike is a success. Three hundred thousand workers out. It drags into a third week. But, in their hearts, miners know this success cannot obscure the union's fundamental weakness. The strike can only last for as long as it's tolerated by a system not noted for its tolerance.

The audience was no longer part of the 'outside world.' They had become imaginative insiders, defiant but fearful of the intolerance of the system.

Lynden MacIntyre: The ubiquitous state security machine never lost control for a moment. The heat was on. At mine sites across South Africa people were being killed. Seventy-eight union officials were arrested. Forty thousand miners were fired.

One assumes that the people being killed across South Africa were being done in by the ubiquitous state security machine. There was no attempt to visualize the South African government as being in the middle of several kinds of conflicts. Always it was the centre of undirectional repression. Once having been manipulated into the position of imaginative insiders, the audience knew what to feel as well as what was about to happen.

The last sequence continued the contrast of appearance and reality.

Lynden MacIntyre: It looks like real collective bargaining. In reality, the miners are seventy-five years behind their counterparts in North America. They may join a union but they can be replaced by non-union workers as their contracts expire. They may strike, but can be fired for missing work. Strike funds are illegal. The raw power of their numbers is restrained by a strait-jacket called Apartheid. After three weeks, the inevitable.

Defeat. The miners 'ended up with a wage increase which management had implemented even before the strike had started.' MacIntyre again failed to indicate how much the miners' wages were raised. There was, however, consolation in having survived, and even a victory in having 'become wiser about their adversary.' As outside insiders, so had the audience become wiser. MacIntyre wrapped up with a paradox: everyone won, everyone lost.

Lynden MacIntyre: In a way, the miners' strike was an achievement for both sides. For the mining companies, because ultimately there was no change in the status quo.

For the miners, because they showed that they could rise united against a system which perpetuates their poverty. But if the miners' strike was a demonstration of potential union power, it was also a clear reminder of the very real power of Apartheid. That lesson has generated a new measure of bitterness in South Africa. In that sense, the miners' strike was an ominous failure, for everybody. For *The Journal*, I'm Lynden MacIntyre.

Perhaps such paradoxes are inevitable in Africa's only White tyranny. Throughout this story, it is perhaps worth noting, two spokesmen for the mine owners uttered 191 words and no government officials were heard. Six spokesmen for the miners, not including CBC staff, uttered 573 words. By and large, the miners pressed very serious charges, and the mine owners were conciliatory. One should point out as well that the CBC consistently overestimated the number of miners involved (according to the Race Relations Survey, a maximum of 220,000 miners were on strike), and underestimated the number of strikers arrested (about 50,000, according to this authority).[20] Moreover, the CBC never mentioned that only about a third of the mines of the country were struck, or that the NUM lost about 50,000 members as a result of the strike.[21]

Most of the remaining stories dealing with internal South African news emphasized the mechanisms of repression. Two exceptions both dealt with AIDS. The first was broadcast on 20 February 1988, the second on 12 April. Among White South Africans, AIDS was contracted chiefly in Europe or North America. Most people who suffered from AIDS, however, were Black, and most of these were migrant miners. They either brought it with them from their own countries or they contracted it in South Africa from prostitutes who serviced the miners or from homosexual relations in the hostels.[22]

More typical, however, was an anchor-only story by Peter Mansbridge. On 19 September 1987, he told of the fate of two convicted murderers.

Peter Mansbridge: Two South Africans have been executed in spite of international request for clemency. The two men were hanged in Pretoria early this morning. They'd been convicted of killing a Black town counsellor by necklacing. That's putting a tire that had been soaked in gasoline around his neck and setting it on fire. The executions triggered a demonstration by 3,000 students in Cape Town. It only ended when police used tear gas on the crowd.

On 1 November 1987, Peter Mansbridge indicated that opposition to the policies of Bishop Desmond Tutu existed within the Black population of South Africa. It was, however, of highly dubious legitimacy. The leader of the opposition group, Inkatha, was the Zulu chief Mangosuthu Buthelezi.

Members of his [Buthelezi's] paramilitary group Inkatha don't like Tutu and his call for sanctions. Inkatha has been locked in a vicious fight with the United Democratic Front. The Front rejects Inkatha as tribally based and power-hungry. The result has been the burning of homes and the killing of people as each side tries to recruit members.

Tutu had been identified by Mansbridge as having won the Nobel Peace Prize. Violence, therefore, must have been provoked by power-hungry para-military Zulu tribesmen. It is true that Inkatha was engaged in a prolonged conflict with the United Democratic Front (UDF), as with the African National Congress (ANC), both of which were composed chiefly of non-Zulus. Moreover, Buthelezi had given voice to anti-socialist and anti-terror-ist views, had criticized Bishop Tutu as having turned into a master of intrigue, and was opposed to sanctions because they were ineffective politi-cally and chiefly harmed Black South Africans. Later that month, Chief Buthelezi was awarded damages and costs in a lawsuit that judged as defam-atory an allegation that he was directing violence against the UDF and the ANC. In his defence, Buthelezi said he was committed to non-violence and that he was the only effective non-Marxist, non-revolutionary alternative committed to ending Apartheid.[23] The ANC remained committed to the use of violence, and a month later the UDF was banned. Buthelezi also com-plained of an ANC–directed media campaign against him. The most generous thing to be said of CBC coverage was that they simplified the anti-Apartheid politics of South Africa in a way that favoured the ANC and the UDF.

On 5 and 7 November, anchor-only stories described the release of 'sev-enty-seven-year-old Govan Mbeki,' who had been in jail, along with Nelson Mandela, for his activities, 'sabotage and plotting to overthrow the govern-ment.'

Knowlton Nash: Mbeki was hugged by friends as he stepped out of jail. From tomor-row he'll be muzzled by order of the South African government because he's an avowed believer in Marxist philosophy. But today he got special permission to say something. And he was still defiant.

Govan Mbeki: The ideas for which I went to jail and, uh, for which the ANC stand, I still embrace.

Knowlton Nash: Mbeki said he's confident that Nelson Mandela and the others jailed with him will soon be set free.

Nothing was said either of Mbeki's views on violence or of the relationship between him, the ANC, and the South African Communist Party. His profession of continued allegiance to the South African Communist Party was not mentioned.

With one exception, the sources of resistance to Apartheid were all visualized by the CBC as having been inspired by the ANC. That exception was a group of army conscripts who refused to cooperate with the government. Barbara Frum set the stage on *The Journal*.

Barbara Frum: South Africa has never needed its army as much as it does now. And yet it is now, for the first time ever, that there is organized resistance to the draft. The South African Defence Force is fighting an undeclared war on four fronts: in Namibia, in Angola, against the African National Congress, and against its own citizens in the townships and camps. The army depends heavily on its recruits from the White community.

Accordingly, co-host Bill Cameron continued, the government was worried about young men who refused to serve in this 'crucial institution.'[24]

Bill Cameron: There are fewer than six million Whites in South Africa. The army is their security against the South African Black majority. So, Whites do not criticize their army. Or they haven't until now.

One of the leaders of the End Conscription Campaign (ECC), Ivan Toms, a physician, had worked in the Black townships. After having to treat many patients who had been hurt by the army, 'he decided that the army had become an instrument of Apartheid' and began working in the ECC. He was interviewed prior to his trial for refusing to serve in the armed forces. He confirmed Cameron's account of his story and responded appropriately when asked to speculate on the future.

Barbara Frum: Doctor Toms, is this something entirely personal to you, or do you feel now that you're standing at the head of a growing movement?

Ivan Toms: I think very much this is a start of a growing movement. Ah, in the group of twenty-three, in August, you say that. We've had many, many people, uh, saying to us, if only we'd known before you stood up publicly we would have also joined you in making that statement.

Unlike the story of the unsuccessful miners' strike, this one, which was essentially a human-interest story, was not visualized as a critical turning-point or a major blow against Apartheid. The message, however, was clear: a minority within a minority could be decent. Deviance within a deviant regime could be normal in a European, not an African, sense.

One other story in our sample carried the same meaning. On 23 March 1988, the CBC carried a story about 38 Blacks living for four days with Whites in a Pretoria suburb, and of 170 Whites living for the same period in a Black township. It was, correspondent James Robbins said, 'an experiment running well ahead of the rest of South Africa.' But 'having fun together as equals is not the future most Whites want to embrace.'

Most White South Africans, according to this visualization, were behind or backward as compared to the experimental experience of fun shared by Blacks and Whites. The notion that history is a kind of world-immanent stream of meaning that flows in one direction has been encountered before. It is an image that may be widely shared among modern journalists, but it is not much help in understanding the specific and particular worlds of Zulus, English, Asians, and Afrikaaners, to say nothing of 'coloureds,' Bushmen, Xhosa, and so on in South Africa.

It is somewhat easier to understand why most South African Whites were said to support the army. As Cameron mentioned, it provided them with security. And security was valued by White South Africans, as it is by most people. The meaning of this otherwise innocuous observation was to indicate that such persons were but slightly troubled, or even untroubled, by the deeds required to ensure that security. On 24 February 1988, Peter Mansbridge introduced a story on new government regulations.

Peter Mansbridge: The South African government has decided to crush even peaceful opposition to its racist policies. Sweeping new restrictions were imposed today on anti-Apartheid groups across the country. As of today, there's just about nothing they can legally do to protest against the government. James Robbins reports.

Robins indicated that the new 'crackdown' had produced shock and paralysis. Anti-Apartheid organizations had, according to the government, not been banned.

They just need permission from the Minister of Law and Order to do anything more than keep their books up to date or fight for their rights in court.

A forty-five-word sound-bite from the Law and Order minister indicated that the rules were intended to curb revolutionaries and bring peace through negotiation.[25] For a reaction from those affected, Robbins first interviewed the 'most famous student' at 'Johannesburg's largest multi-racial university,' Winnie Mandela, the wife of Nelson Mandela, the jailed ANC leader. She 'seemed stunned by the scale of the bannings.'

Winnie Mandela: It is a state of emergency. It has effectively driven out the international media from reporting the truth about this country. It has literally reduced the country to a police state.

Desmond Tutu – Archbishop of Johannesburg: White South Africans must realize that they are at a crossroads. If they don't stop this government soon, and there's not much hope that they will, we're heading for war.

Robbins returned, apparently in the interest of balance, to reiterate the government's account of the purpose of the new rules – namely, to 'contribute to a climate of stability, peaceful coexistence, and good neighbourliness among all population groups. The organizations being acted against had encouraged civil disobedience and rebellion.' However, he immediately added that the real purpose lay elsewhere.

James Robbins: That message is partly directed at the White voters in two crucial by-elections. They, not the Black majority, are today's political power, shifting to the right, away from negotiations. In Johannesburg, this is James Robbins for CBC News.

Robbins did not account for this shift to the 'right' or address why such a 'right-wing' even existed. Nor was there any coverage of what might be termed religiously-based integration groups (apart from Bishop Tutu), even though these groups have achieved a good deal to promote harmony at least between middle-class Black and White South Africans. But, then again, no one who had to rely on the CBC for information on South Africa would have the faintest notion that a Black South African middle-class existed.

On 12 March, a BBC report was broadcast. Ian Hannomansingh provided the introduction.

Ian Hannomansingh: The South African government just won't let up on anyone who tried to fight its racist policies. Last month it banned political activities by eighteen groups committed to ending Apartheid. Today, it banned a new organization set up to take their place. But the leader of the new group, Archbishop Desmond Tutu, says he's not going to let the government order stand in his way. Graham Leach of the BBC reports.

Leach indicated that Tutu's group was banned because they advocated revolution and promoted the aims of the ANC. Tutu said nothing in his lengthy sound-bite to confirm Hannomansingh's paraphrase.

Archbishop Tutu: One hopes, I mean, that the world is now aware that we are dealing with a government that is totalitarian in everything but name. And when we said long ago that, uh, they were following policies that were as evil and as immoral as Nazism, uh, people thought we were being melodramatic. But now, I mean, it's becoming absolutely clear that, uh, they will stop at nothing.

The purpose of Hannomansingh's words was simply to suggest the inequality of the struggle. The imagery of David and Goliath might be appropriate, except that David won, used violence, and trusted in God.

The next day, 13 March, Robbins reported on a meeting held in Bishop Tutu's cathedral in Cape Town.

James Robbins: Political priest preaching revolution, is the government's view. Yesterday, the Law and Order minister threatened further bans. Today's increased defiance may have been peaceful, but it makes harsher direct restrictions on the church seem more likely. In Cape Town, this is James Robbins for CBC News.

Nine days later, Robbins reported again. The Anglican hierarchy was discussing what should be done to counter President Botha's 'threats of unspecified action against Archbishop Tutu. The two men had a stand-up row last week. The president demanded to know if the archbishop stood for Christianity or the ANC and communism. Today, the bishop accused President Botha of taking to himself the right to define what is spiritual.' A dramatic but unrelated sound-bite followed.

Bishop Bruce Evans: The government, in imposing the restrictions, is driving this beloved country closer to civil war.

Robbins then reported on a second action by the government, this time against Roman Catholics.

James Robbins: The Catholic bishops are the victims of the government's latest ban, closing their newspaper, *The New Nation*, for three months. The weekly sold over

50,000 copies, mostly to Blacks. The government never liked its anti-Apartheid campaigning and accused the paper of promoting violent revolution. The editor, Zwelakhe Sisulu, has been detained without trial for sixteen months.

As evidence of their subversive intentions, Robbins provided the following illustration.

James Robbins: Among stories specifically attacked was this one, the government says the word *raids*, describing troops knocking on doors demanding rent withheld in township boycotts, is wrong. 'Raids' should read 'security action.'

The implication was that a concern for punctilious word usage was trivial and therefore an indication of the pervasiveness of the evil of the 'White minority government.' In fact, *The New Nation* was owned by the Catholic Bishops' Publishing Company, which is distinct from the Catholic hierarchy in South Africa. It certainly opposes government policies, reports extensively on the ANC, and regularly uses Marxist rhetoric and iconography.

On 10 June 1988, the State of Emergency was extended for a year. No one was surprised, though journalists and Bishop Tutu provided verbal objections. South Africa, like other tyrannies, is characterized by the extensive use of violence, both by the government and by citizens. On 22 May, for example, Peter Mansbridge provided the following story.

Peter Mansbridge: A weekend of violence in South Africa has left nine people dead, including a member of Parliament. Peter Jacobs was a member of the mixed-race, or coloured body, of Parliament. The other two bodies are reserved for Indians and Whites. Blacks are excluded. Indians and people of mixed race who run for the segregated Parliament are regarded as 'sell-outs' by Black militants. Jacobs was shot as he drove home from church.

It was not clear that Jacobs had been shot by 'Black militants,' but such persons would seem to have an interest in following the standard revolutionary tactic of murdering those whom they perceive to be collaborators or moderates. In his wrap-up to the 10 June story on the extension of the emergency regulations, Robbins acknowledged that, under the state of emergency, violence had in fact declined.

James Robbins: But the government points to the undoubted fact that violent protest in the townships has largely disappeared as justification for the emergency. The army and police have established tight control and ministers insist the emergency has not suppressed genuine, widespread discontent but rather averted revolution, championed by only a few. In Johannesburg, this is James Robbins for CBC News.'

The 'but' with which he began indicated the government version was deviant. If it were removed, the larger question, which concerned the great difficulty of instituting a just regime in South Africa, would have been indicated.

South Africa has received considerable attention from foreign governments, multilateral organizations, and a wide range of private individuals as well. In mid-March 1988, six Black South Africans were scheduled to hang for complicity in the murder of a Black township councillor. 'Today,' said Peter Mansbridge, 'their lawyers asked for international support. And they got it.' Foreign leaders asked for 'clemency.' The accused received a stay of execution, 'because a witness admitted he lied about their involvement in a murder. No evidence has ever been presented that any of the six had a direct role in the victim's death. Before the postponement was announced, a car bomb, went off in a nearby town killing three people.' The bombs killed three South African Blacks, Robbins said, and 'many others suffered terrible injuries. The ANC said from their headquarters in Zambia, it was possible its members had set off the bomb to protest against the imminent hangings. In Pretoria, South Africa, this is James Robbins for CBC News.'

Other stories concerned with foreigners interested in opposing Apartheid were more exciting and glamorous than the story of the 'Sharpeville Six.' Whether they had any consequences for the course of events is difficult to say. On 6 November 1987, *The Journal* reviewed Richard Attenborough's *Cry Freedom*, a film said to be based on the lives of Steve Biko, a Black leader and opponent of the South African government, and of Donald Woods, a White journalist critical of the government because of their complicity in Biko's death or murder. On 10 June, Knowlton Nash introduced a story about a London rock concert held to honour Nelson Mandela. Patrick Brown, the London correspondent, had some difficulty taking it seriously.

Patrick Brown: The full galaxy of stars won't assemble until tomorrow, but a solar system or two showed up this morning to rehearse and be photographed. Daryl Hannah, star of the movie *Wall Street*, was there with her attendant planets.

Brown no doubt was more accustomed to visualizing politics than the disbelief of a gentleman called Meatloaf.

Meatloaf: The more aware of the situation that I've become, the more I say to myself, I can't believe this, you know. And it's, it's a devastating thing. And, and, it's, and, it's gotta end.

Brown next interviewed a Conservative MP who said that the monies raised would end up in the hands of the ANC. The organizers denied it, as did Oliver Tambo, the leader of the ANC. Brown tried to steer a middle course and hit upon the following formula.

Patrick Brown: What the musicians are giving the anti-Apartheid movement is more valuable than financial support anyway. A message beamed at the hundreds of millions of homes around the world. Patrick Brown, CBC News, London.

Later, on *The Journal*, Anne McMillan proved she was more in touch with the magical world of persons such as Meatloaf. She listed several individuals and groups who were significant in the world of popular music. She knew that Mandela 'has come to symbolize the struggle against Apartheid.'

Anne McMillan: Performers at tomorrow's concert will call for no less than his unconditional release. The first band to volunteer to appear at the concert was supergroup Simple Minds. Lead singer Jim Curb believes world protest is the key to freeing Nelson Mandela.

Jim Curb: I think it's important to spread his name around. Around the world.

Anne McMillan: I spoke to Curb between rehearsals in his London hotel. He's written a song about Mandela especially for tomorrow's concert.

Jim Curb: It's just a very simple call for his freedom. Actually it's a very, ah, although it's kind of haunting mood to it, it's a very kind of optimistic song because it actually talks about him being, being free.

Most of the attention directed by foreigners towards South Africa was mediated by governments, not rock 'n roll. Several stories dealt with Canada's relationship to South Africa and to its neighbours, the 'Front-Line States' – Angola, Botswana, Mozambique, Tanzania, Zambia, and Zimbabwe.

On 10 August 1987, the CBC carried a brief report on Joe Clark's visit to South Africa, the Ivory Coast, Zambia, and Mozambique. Clark was said both to have anticipated 'a good discussion' and not to have expected much 'to come from out of his meetings in South Africa.' A week later, he was interviewed on the results of his trip. Paul Griffin gave the introduction.

Paul Griffin: Joe Clark is back in Ottawa tonight. Canada's External Affairs Minister hasn't got much to show for his quick tour of southern Africa. No concessions from South Africa, no words of hope from the leaders of Zambia, Mozambique, and Ivory Coast. If Clark was expecting a breakthrough before the Commonwealth Summit in Vancouver, he didn't get one.

Griffin's script writer must have known that Clark had no expectations of a 'breakthrough.' By suggesting that he might have expected such a thing, the audience was primed to anticipate failure and excuses.

Bill Cameron conducted the interview. His first question was whether Clark had any indication that the South Africans 'were prepared to budge one inch off their stated position.' The question did not indicate what the 'stated position' of South Africa was or what the topic was that they were said to have a stated position on. It simply indicated that it was unlikely they would 'budge one inch' on anything. Clark replied that 'progress' was still distant, but discussions of the same questions with the ANC and with the South African foreign minister 'indicated some areas of common agreement, that if there were a will to negotiate, it could provide some basis for negotiation.'

Bill Cameron: Do you have any sense that there is a will to negotiate?

Joe Clark: I don't think there is a will yet. But, ah, neither side has rejected negotiations. Neither side has closed the door. Ah, both sides take the position that a negotiated solution is far better than a violent one.

Cameron doubted that 'a Black man sitting in the middle of Soweto' would think that the government was 'against a violent solution.' Clark replied that the same could be said by critics of the ANC.

Talking about the ANC, Cameron continued, what are they like?

Bill Cameron: People here have one or two images available of the ANC. The first is that they are simply thugs. The second is that they are martyrs of the Black revolution and something close to saints. What is your sense of these people? Are they a legitimate government-in-waiting?

Saints or martyrs? Clark had to explain that the question of such 'images' is not part of the reality of politics or of Canadian foreign policy, or of the ANC.

204 Sins of Omission

Joe Clark: The real problem of reputation that they have, I think, doesn't have to do with saintliness or martyrdom. It has to do with whether or not, and how closely, they are controlled by the Communist Party. And certainly when we were in South Africa the accusation that was being made frequently was that they are a Communist-controlled organization. I see no evidence of that. I don't believe that's the case. There are undoubtedly Communists in the ANC, but there are also a lot of other people, I would say a majority, in terms of influence, who simply want to resolve on a basis of equality the situation in their home country of South Africa.

The CBC scarcely ever used the c-word to characterize governments outside the Soviet bloc. Clark had raised a tabooed topic, the possibility that the ANC might be directed by or influenced by Communists. He said he saw no evidence that the Communists controlled the ANC, but what would count as evidence? It was true that Communists belonged to the ANC. It was not unknown for Communists in organizations such as the ANC to be less than completely candid about their political affiliations. No such follow-up questions seem ever to be asked on the CBC.[26]

Indeed, Cameron immediately changed the subject.

Bill Cameron: You see no short-term possibility of real movement on this South African side. What does Canada do now? What can we do?

Clark had *not* said what Cameron said he had. Clark had, in fact, said something quite different – that *neither* side had a will to negotiate. Clark ignored this misrepresentation and explained Canada's position – namely, that it was against Apartheid and interested in promoting negotiations.

Joe Clark: I've no confidence that the negotiating process will work. It may not. Indeed, there is a lot of evidence to suggest it won't. But it is not dead. And so long as it is alive, it is worth our trying to find ways to bring the parties together. Because if they don't come together, then we are just going to have a terrible violence that will take its toll in death and bloodshed on both sides. And it will be terribly destabilizing to the whole subcontinent.

Clark ended the interview in response to Cameron's query about the October Commonwealth meeting and the question of sanctions.

Joe Clark: In my meetings with the ANC, they did not raise the question of sanctions. They were more interested at that stage in looking at possibilities of negotiations. Now, they did that knowing that Canada had a clear position on sanctions from which we were not going to back away. Ah, but I think that we should recognize that there are a variety of means, including sanctions, but also including other things, that might help us maintain pressure against Apartheid.

Sanctions, however, sound dramatic and vivid. Negotiations do not. It is not surprising that the topic tended to recur in interviews.

Late in August, Oliver Tambo, president of the ANC, arrived in Toronto. According to Peter Mansbridge, 'the ANC wants Canada to break diplomatic relations with South Africa' (26 Aug. 1987). Mansbridge did not indicate that such a request was unlikely to be seriously entertained, let alone granted. Balance was ostensibly provided by a summary of the South African response.

Peter Mansbridge: South Africa criticized Canada's decision to welcome the ANC leader. The African National Congress is banned in South Africa because it often uses violence in its attempts to bring about change. The ANC says it's the legitimate voice of the country's Black majority.

This short item – which did, however, contain a Tambo sound-bite – illustrated well the agenda the CBC helped to set. The ANC made a demand that was visualized to the audience as a serious possibility. Canada should consider breaking diplomatic relations with the South African government: Why not? After all, Cameron had asked Joe Clark: 'Are they [the ANC] a legitimate government-in-waiting?' Cameron and the CBC had, therefore, entertained the possibility that they were. Otherwise, why ask the question? Mansbridge had just indicated that the ANC called itself 'the legitimate voice of the country's Black majority.' Why not cut our diplomatic ties with South Africa and extend recognition to the ANC as a government-in-exile? Who could oppose 'majority rule'? Nothing was said of Communists in the ANC, of its ties to Moscow, or of its doctrine euphemistically termed 'armed struggle.'

On 28 August, Tambo met with the prime minister and with Joe Clark. In his introduction, Mansbridge mentioned Tambo's request 'to step up economic sanctions against South Africa.' He also noted Mulroney's response, which criticized the use of violence by the ANC. David Halton, the correspondent, emphasized that the meeting was the first between 'the veteran ANC president' and 'a major Western leader.' A Mulroney sound-bite followed.

Prime Minister Brian Mulroney: I have, uh, indicated the position of the Government of Canada in regard to our clear, uh, hope for the evolution of a democratic society without the use of violence.

David Halton: Joe Clark, also at the meeting, hinted that the cooler approach to the ANC reflects concern that some of its members are Communists.

Joe Clark: ... the accusations that the ANC is a violent Marxist organization don't make our job any easier. Uh, and I think it is important that, uh, the prime minister had the opportunity to make that case as clearly and as eloquently as he did to, uh, to Mr Tambo.

As for Tambo, Halton said, he 'still regards Canada as a major ally against Apartheid. But in a news conference later, he was clearly dismayed by the Canadian concern over Marxists in the ANC.'

Oliver Tambo: We are not going to start in 19 ... at, at, at the seventy-fifth anniversary of the ANC, to begin to conduct a witch hunt.

David Halton: Tambo also said the ANC's armed struggle against South Africa is legitimate. He claimed that there've only been sixteen victims of ANC violence over the past two years, compared with more than two thousand Blacks killed by South African police and troops. According to Tambo, Mulroney shouldn't be opposed to the ANC's resort to force.

Oliver Tambo: We would ask the Canadians not to swallow this propaganda. It is propaganda. Because, if you want to talk about violence, what violence exceeds that of Apartheid, i-in, i-in all Africa?

The position of the ANC in the CBC's visualization was as clear as Tambo's question was rhetorical. It might become, if it was not yet, the legitimate government of South Africa. Its violence was, in any case, justified. And, as for Marxists and Communists and 'armed struggle,' that is, terror, the less said the better. It's all propaganda anyway. Most informed observers outside the CBC would agree with Joe Clark's view that the relationship between the ANC and the SACP was intimate.

In September, Clark and the British foreign secretary, Sir Geoffrey Howe, discussed the effectiveness of economic sanctions. Howe argued that there was no case for additional sanctions, and 'surprisingly,' David Halton said, 'Canada now appears to agree with Howe's view.'

David Halton: Howe diplomatically avoided commenting on Canada's apparently changed position on sanctions. But, he did make one point.

Sir Geoffrey Howe: So far as sanctions are concerned, the harsh truth is that experience over the last twelve months, ah, hasn't encouraged the view that they've been effective or that they've even changed the right direction. Um, so we have to look for other ways of doing it.

Clark and the Department of External Affairs seemed to have been convinced by evidence that remained invisible to the CBC.

The logic of sanctions was twofold. The high-minded version was that economic excommunication would cause White South Africans to feel the pinch, and, placing economic well-being ahead of racism, they would cause their government to change so as to avert a bloody revolution and, as Clark said, avoid destabilizing the entire region. For the more bloody-minded, the Marxist slogan 'accentuate the contradictions' was more apt. The logic here was to increase the impoverishment of Black South Africans to the point where they would have 'nothing to lose but their chains,' at which point they would arise, throw off the fatally weakened White oppressors, and inaugurate the rule of racial equality. Even laying aside the messianic nonsense of a revolutionary transfiguration, one might feel somewhat anxious about inflicting poverty on other people for any reason. This twinge of common sense can be overridden with the excuse that South Africa's Black leaders were themselves demanding increased sanctions. For this to be persuasive, two other things must remain undone. First, never ask whether these Black leaders were themselves messianically disordered. Second, never find out what the consequences of sanctions have been to date. One must also overlook the unambiguous evidence of *every* public-opinion poll, that South Africans, whether White or non-White, overwhelmingly oppose increased sanctions.[27] Of course, this inconvenient fact can always be explained away in terms of 'false consciousness' or something similar.

Joe Clark had, in diplomatic language to be sure, indicated that the ANC is tinged, if not infected, with messianic fantasies. It is clear that the CBC has not undertaken a scrutiny of these pneumopathologies. Indeed, one wonders if the CBC is aware that they exist. Even so, it *was* possible for the CBC to examine the effectiveness of sanctions in terms of their actual and short-term consequences. The immediate result of the 1986 American Comprehensive Anti-Apartheid Act, for example, seemed to be to ensure an additional term for President P.W. Botha. It also provided him with a substantial opposition on the 'right,' and weakened the only moderate, liberal organization in South Africa, the Progressive Federal Party. Following the 1987 election, it was replaced as the Official Opposition in the House of Assembly by the Conservative Party, which was adamant in its rejection of the 'power-sharing' overtures by the National Party.

A second and equally obvious result of sanctions was to undervalue systematically the local branches of multinational companies. Disinvestment pressures in the home countries of these companies encouraged them to leave South Africa, thereby depressing their market value. The result was to create a considerable number of South African millionaires who were able to purchase perfectly good companies at fire-sale prices. Third, the first thing that the new owners did was to remove the so-called social-responsibility programs imposed by foreign head offices. The promise of sanctions, in short, has been defeated by the results. Moreover, Pacific rim, Israeli, and even Soviet-bloc trade has filled much of the gap left when Western trade declined. And finally, there is the aforementioned evidence of public-opinion polls among Black South Africans that indicates that only about 25 per cent of respondents favoured sanctions if sanctions meant personal hardship. Even Cyril Ramaphosa's highly politicized miners realized that they and not their leaders would be harmed by sanctions. For this reason, Ramaphosa proposed a 'conscientisation campaign' to convince them of the desirability of sacrificing their jobs for a greater goal. None of this evidence, which might have raised doubts about the usefulness of sanctions, was ever introduced or acknowledged by any CBC visualization.

On 12 October 1987, *The National* and *The Journal* both considered the Commonwealth Conference. Nash and correspondent Halton both indicated that a 'clash' was imminent: British prime minister Margaret Thatcher, the prime deviant, versus the rest. Mulroney was now visualized as being on the side of 'key Commonwealth leaders' such as Robert Mugabe and Kenneth Kaunda. In earlier reports, Canada was said to have agreed with Sir Geoffrey Howe on the ineffectiveness of sanctions; Clark had said, in effect, that Canada had agreed with the Black tyrants who ruled the states surrounding South Africa only in order to sustain the process by which negotiations might begin. Canada's support, therefore, was diplomatic and highly conditional. There was, in fact, a real story at the Commonwealth Conference, and it involved a real conflict between candid common sense (Mrs Thatcher), the necessity of compromise (Canada), and the position of the 'key Commonwealth leaders' or front-line tyrants.

On *The Journal*, Barbara Frum held a baroque conversation with the secretary general of the Commonwealth, Sir Shridath Ramphal.

Barbara Frum: Secretary General, I want to know first what kind of a week you're heading for in Vancouver. Could there be a real clash, and even a productive outcome, or should everybody have just mailed in what they were going to do in the first place?

Sir Shridath Ramphal: No, I think it's, it's shaping up to be a very productive conference. I said to the assembled press a little while ago that I thought that Vancouver '87 was gonna be a little like love, a many-splendoured thing, certainly a many-sided thing. And I think, a very productive conference.

Barbara Frum: Would you please explain to me how, if Margaret Thatcher's coming to stand tough, and say 'no' to whatever you're demanding?

Sir Shridath Ramphal: Well, we might have to agree to disagree. I think it's very likely that on some aspects of the South Africa issue, particularly the area of economic sanctions, that, uh, we may not have Mrs. Thatcher with us, as before. But I think the solidarity of the Commonwealth in relation to the sanctions issue, uh, will hold, will be strong, and, uh, will proceed.

Ramphal assured her that South Africans were 'terribly, terribly worried' about sanctions, that talk with 'Commonwealth colleagues in the front line' is always useful, and so on. So, Frum said, pointedly and with a hint of impatience, what do you think Canada should do?

Sir Shridath Ramphal: Well, I don't like to think of it in terms of, Canada. I, I think the Commonwealth countries, generally, need to discuss and want to discuss, what are the areas in which the front-line countries see themselves as having supplementation of security. It's very important that we listen to the front-line states, hear what they say are the areas of security need.

Barbara Frum: Secretary General, thank you so much for talking to us tonight, and we'll watch the conference with great interest.

Next day, the conference followed the script: Mulroney said that sanctions should be increased; Thatcher declared that nothing could be gained by publicizing differences; the Indian prime minister, Rajiv Gandhi, promised a 'blood bath' if sanctions were not employed. No sound-bites from the neighbouring tyrants were heard.

12   MOZAMBIQUE

The CBC's version of recent events in Mozambique may serve as a postscript to their coverage of South Africa. Virtually all observers are of the opinion that Mozambique is a very unhappy place. Several years of drought have combined with rule by brutal and inept Marxists, and with an equally brutal but less inept rebellion (backed by South Africa) against the government, to produce a country in ruin.[28]

On 1 July 1987, *The Journal* offered a brief report. Paul Griffin spoke most of the voice-over narrative. The video portion showed malnourished residents of a refugee or concentration camp.

Paul Griffin: The guerrillas have destroyed transportation links, farms, and most of the health clinics in Mozambique. As a result, the country's economy has completely collapsed. Unlike the drought-caused famine in Ethiopia, this famine is man-made. Canadians have been rallying again to donate relief funds.

The prime minister's visit was mentioned as having indicated that Canada was about to take a 'leadership role' in relief, and a Canadian aid consortium was about to present a plan to assist the government of the country. Nothing was said of the regime or of its ideology. By this account, Mozambique was merely poor and beset with an inexplicable civil war.[29] Canada was a good guy, trying to help out.

Three weeks later, on 22 July, *The Journal* rebroadcast a longer report, 'The Siege of Mozambique.' It was preceded by an introductory account of fresh disasters.

Bill Cameron: The poorest, the hungriest, the least-educated people in Africa. They live and die in Mozambique. And now reports are filtering out about what may be one of the most gruesome massacres in the history of Southern Africa.

Co-host Sue Prestage provided details. The Mozambique government reported that rebels had killed three hundred people in a village, and that South Africa was behind the attack. There was no communication with the village, but there was Carlos Cardoso, 'director of the government-run news agency in Maputo,' who was clearly understood to be a reliable source. Cameron asked Cardoso what had happened, and was told a story of massacre, which Cameron explained as a rational application of terror. But why, he asked, did they kidnap people?

Carlos Cardoso: Well, they have to transport things when they, when they've stolen so many things from the village. They have to transport them, and this time they went further. They kidnap them, and they started shooting them on the way. And bayonetting them to death. The reports coming from Homoine of dozens and dozens of people who have been killed in the outlying bush, not inside the village. These were people who were shot or bayonetted to death after they had been kidnapped. But it's a common practice. It has never reached this level. But killing of twenty, thirty, forty people. They are so common in this country, they've almost become a daily mark of our existence. But to this level, as I said before, nothing like this had ever been reported.

It was, therefore, to find out what these events meant, to probe 'behind the abstract discussions of the effect of the Apartheid in the region, into the tragedy of murder and violence, famine and economic strangulation,' that *The Journal* would repeat 'The Siege of Mozambique.'
   Bill Cameron led off with a dramatic introduction.

Bill Cameron: This country is at war. It's a war that's never been declared. But it's very real. Mozambique is under siege. You cannot see the besieging army, the Mozambique National Resistance, the MNR, here in Maputo, not yet. But, you can see what the MNR has done. It has blown up the supply lines, attacked the roads. So gasoline in Maputo is an event. Most of the time, the pumps are empty. And when your car breaks down, it stays that way. There are no spare parts to fix it. Maputo harbour. There's no money to buy goods from abroad. Much of the little traffic here is foreign aid, rice from Japan. With luck, the rice will get to the countryside where people are starving. With bad luck, the MNR will sabotage the railroads or shoot up the trucks, and steal it. And Mozambique has never been lucky.

According to the first source interviewed, David Martin, 'journalist and consultant to the Mozambiquan government,' the bad luck began with the Portuguese.[30] The colony they left behind was a 'shambles,' an 'appalling legacy,' a 'legacy of neglect.' More bad luck followed: 'hunger and war,' Cameron said. The minister of Trade and Commerce called the 'banditism' a 'natural disaster.' Cameron had pushed the bad-luck story about as far as it could go, and turned to visualize the actual human beings who were doing all the damage.

Bill Cameron: The Mozambiquan National Resistance. At least 15,000 men, maybe more. Mozambiquans, some of them kidnapped and forced to serve. Some genuine anti-Marxists. Some alienated by the Frelimo government's tendency to push people around; armed and supplied and trained, first, by Rhodesia, now, by South Africa. Led, in part, by Portuguese colonists who want their Mozambiquan holdings back. They seem to have no platform, nothing to fight for, no ideology except a hatred for Frelimo. And they're very effective. After the MNR and the drought, there isn't much left. If you want extra rations, you line up. You pay five days' wages for a kilo of onions. A months' wages for paraffin. Two months' for shoes.

Even this catalogue of misery did not tell the audience much more than the 'bad luck' or 'natural disaster' imagery. Moreover, observers who were not in the employ of the Frelimo government, and therefore unlike David Martin, have disputed the contention that Mozambique was a 'shambles' when the Portuguese left. However that may be, the CBC still did not raise several pertinent questions: How, for example, did the Frelimo government come by its tendency to push people around? What was meant by saying both that the rebels had nothing to fight for and yet that some of them want to recover their property? Who are the 'genuine anti-Marxists'? And what makes them so effective? Being backed by South Africa? Or their hatred of Frelimo? And why would they hate Frelimo? Surely not because they don't like being 'pushed around.'

Cameron was unconcerned with such questions. He preferred, instead, to show the terrible and inexplicable damage the MNR, or Renamo, had done. David Martin, quondam journalist, officially reliable source, and current 'consultant' to Frelimo, summarized the horror and the mystery of it all.

David Martin: They had just destroyed and destroyed. They maim and mutilate people. It is always taking and destruction, no construction. Now what is different about this, this is really this point: in, in any normal war that I have ever come across and ever covered, you try to win the hearts and minds of the people, rather than destroy the hearts and minds. You do not go around mutilating people on the massive scale that's happening in Mozambique.

Bill Cameron: In a moment, Frelimo's army, the very thin front line against the MNR.

After the break, another dramatic visual and appropriate voice-over.

Bill Cameron: A Soviet-made gunship cruises above the trees south of Maputo. When the South Africans talk about Mozambique, they like to use this kind of image. Russian arms, Russian bullets, a communist base camp on their border.

So, there are Soviet helicopters, arms, and bullets in Mozambique after all! Well yes, but they don't really work, Cameron assured his audience.

Bill Cameron: This is closer to reality: a poorly equipped, badly trained, frightened, discouraged army. On a foot-patrol exercise in Inhambane, there are Soviet guns and Soviet bullets. But not enough of them to win a real battle. And more and more, when Frelimo's army meets the MNR, the MNR stands and fights. The Frelimo soldiers look fierce enough when there is no enemy in the bush. But, in the north, along the Malawi border, units like this have broken and run time after time. The Frelimo guerrillas took their country from the Portuguese. Now they must hold it in the same kind of war. And they are losing.

One may summarize the visualization of Mozambique to this point as follows: 1 / Mozambique is 'at war' or 'under siege;' 2 / the Renamo resistanceis comprised of lunatics who kill and maim for no purpose; 3 / they are 'backed' by the supremely evil government of South Africa; 4 / Frelimo once 'took' Mozambique from Portugal, and apparently also once had a 'tendency to push people around;' but no longer; 5 / now they are 'frightened and discouraged,' and 'losing' the war/siege.

Only after having provided this complex image of the Mozambique situation did the CBC introduce the audience to the fact that the government of the country was Communist, and that it had begun its existence by doing something more than push people around.

Bill Cameron: Mozambique spent the first years after independence, after 1976, in a Marxist haze, creating huge state farms that didn't work, herding tens of thousands of people from one end of the land to the other. It was rigid, pure, ideologically correct, and a disaster.

Unless one were entirely sympathetic to the aims of hazy Marxism, whatever they might be, one would draw the connection between attempting to run a country along these lines and creating resistance to such rule. Nothing was said of the growth of Renamo from about 2,000 guerrillas in 1981 to ten times that number by the date of Cameron's report. They were simply there, and backed by evil South Africa.

Marxist sympathizers excuse the atrocities of Marxist governments by calling them 'mistakes.' Stalin, for example, made many mistakes. The CBC's visualization of Mozambique also mentioned the mistakes of its government. 'Eventually,' Cameron said, Machel, the tyrant nominally in charge of Mozambique, 'realized' and 'admitted' that the rigid, pure, ideologically correct, yet hazy, Marxism, entailed disaster. 'The great ten-year plans were filed away. He began to pivot Mozambique towards the West, towards Western help and Western money.' The plans were put away, not burned; perhaps they would be brought out again later. It was certainly true that

Marxism, whether hazy or rigid, meant economic, and eventually political and military disaster. When Maputo was called Lourenço Marques, in the bad old days of Portuguese rule, it was compared with Nice or pre-war Beirut. There was profitable trade, and there were cafés and villas; the beaches attracted tourists, and the fountains along the once-elegant avenues worked. Since 1981, Mozambique has had a negative growth rate of 8 per cent a year, and people are trying to grow cassava between the palm trees along the newly named Kim Il Sung Boulevard.[31]

It is true, then, that Marxism spells economic ruin in Africa, just as in Poland or Rumania. According to the CBC, Samora Machel figured this out and, learning from his mistakes, turned to the only source in the world of help and money, the West.[32] This account is also fundamentally correct: the Soviet Union has historically been generous only with military aid to its client states. At the time the show was broadcast, for example, Machel's successor, President Joaquim Chissano,[33] still a believer in the 'scientific teachings of Marxism-Leninism,' was protected by a palace guard of 3,000 Cubans. East Germans ran his intelligence and security office, and the Soviet Union provided military advisers. Other visitors to Maputo saw them strolling about the streets, but they were invisible to the CBC's cameras. At the same time, between 1981 and 1987, the United States, under the presidency of the notorious author of the Reagan doctrine, gave the People's Republic of Mozambique $241 million in direct aid and backed another $154 million in international aid. In 1987 alone, the United States provided, free, $85 million in food. None of this was mentioned.[34]

On the one hand, if Machel's change of heart was genuine, the 'scientific Marxist-Leninists' who succeeded him would have had good reason to rejoice in his passing.[35] This interpretation was not advanced. On the other hand, if his change of heart was tactical, less uncritical observers than the CBC might have introduced considerations of economic necessity, which would have meant calling into question the ability of Marxists to run, rather than ruin, an economy. Most likely Machel, and certainly Chissano, remained committed Marxists and keen Soviet clients, notwithstanding their willingness to accept Western aid. The 'pivot' to the West was not, for instance, accompanied by a change in behaviour at the United Nations. In November 1987, Mozambique was absent, along with Rumania, the People's Republic of Cape Verde, the Seychelles (also ruled by Marxists), and South Yemen, when a vote was taken condemning the USSR for its invasion of Afghanistan (but not naming the Soviet Union as the invader). There has, in fact, been no 'pivoting.' There has been a response to military pressure and an increase in tin-cup diplomacy, a combination of voracious begging, empty promises to 'reform,' and general whining.

The CBC saw things differently. Mozambique was in mid-pivot, about to be weaned from the Soviet Union, when South Africa stepped in.

Bill Cameron: At the same time, the South Africans were squeezing Machel. They proved their military could hit Mozambique when they liked, where they liked. With an excuse or without one. In May 1983, the South African Air Force strafed two neighbourhoods in Maputo with rockets. Six people were killed, forty injured. South Africa wanted diplomatic recognition. Mozambique wanted an end to the war. South African foreign minister Pik Botha struck a deal. A non-aggression pact. South Africa would no longer support the MNR, Mozambique would no longer house the ANC guerrillas who attacked South Africa. And, on the 16th of March 1984, the leaders of the Republic of South Africa and the People's Republic of Mozambique met on their border to sign the Nkomati Accord.

The agreement was met with harsh criticism from the leaders of South Africa's other neighbours. In the event, Renamo activity did not diminish, which the CBC said was the consequence of the South African military having ignored the 'treaty.' Nothing was said of the continued support by Mozambique of the ANC.

The focus shifted to the success of Renamo in shutting down the Mozambique economy. Several dramatic video shots of railways were accompanied by voice-overs informing the audience that Mozambique was losing the economic and military war. According to David Martin, the South African strategy was 'to force the dependence of the region on South Africa's own routes by destroying Mozambiquan routes.' South Africa may have succeeded in doing so, but that did not mean that Renamo was simply a creature of South Africa. There is good evidence that Renamo was also acting on its own.

In the final sequence, Cameron focused on the drought and on the effects of terror. He even provided a primer on how such wars, which he called terrorist (not guerrilla) wars, are conducted.

Bill Cameron: The principles of terrorist war are well known. And the MNR is applying them in Mozambique. In a terrorist war, you attack the transportation links. The road and rail line. So food can't move. If there's a famine, so much the better. You go after anyone who gives people hope. The doctors, the aid workers, the priests. And, of course, in a terrorist war you use terror. When you kill someone you do your best to butcher him so horribly that his image will stand as a permanent example to the others. You steal their cattle, burn their huts. They're not much, but they're all these people have. And you do this every day, every night, across the country. Until, finally, enough people are so sick of grief, or fear, or hunger, or disease, that you win.

Cameron then told the story of a Portuguese farmer who had been killed, allegedly by Renamo. He offered a glimpse of hope for the eventual victory by the Marxists by telling about a Frelimo victory, and concluded with the recitation of lugubrious statistics.

Bill Cameron: Since 1980, at least 400,000 people have died untimely deaths in Mozambique – 100,000 in the war, another 100,000 in the famine, 200,000 because they were babies. Mozambique is a terrible place for babies. Now, a full third of the population, four million people, are homeless and hungry. In June 1987, their new leader refused once again to negotiate with the MNR, and in July the MNR came back to Inhambane.

Inhambane was the place where Frelimo had won a victory over Renamo. The picture did not look good for the government. Cameron did not look happy. What seemed to be beyond the ability of the CBC to visualize was the existence of a popular resistance to a clique of nattily dressed Marxist intellectuals, bright-eyed as gerbils. That such a resistance might mount a guerrilla war against a Marxist government was also impossible to conceive. All they could do was mount a terrorist war or engage in banditry.
    A suitable coda was broadcast on 13 December 1987.

Peter Mansbridge: Bob Geldof is back from Africa with gruesome stories of starvation and torture, there. He's the Irish rock star who raised more than $200 million for African famine relief two years ago. Geldof was home again in London today, after spending twelve days in famine-striken parts of Mozambique and Ethiopia. In Mozambique, he was especially horrified by the atrocities committed against some of the children there.

Bob Geldof: They said, 'Where are your father's friends?' And he said, 'I don't know.' So they got a blunt knife and cut off his little finger. And then they said, 'Where are your father's friends?' And he said, 'I don't know.' So, one by one they cut off his fingers with a blunt knife.

Peter Mansbridge: Geldof said the butchery and the food shortages in Mozambique were largely the fault of right-wing rebels.

Dramatic entertainment, celebrity sources, and political moralism directed against the great source of evil in the world, 'right-wing rebels.' Standing behind them was the cause of all evil in southern Africa, the government of South Africa and its doctrine of Apartheid. CBC audiences certainly know that South Africa is racist, but not that its government is but one tyranny among a continent of tyrannies.

CHAPTER FIVE

Conclusions

In the general confession, which is part of the Anglican service of Morning Prayer, may be found the words: 'We have left undone those things which we ought to have done. And we have done those things which we ought not to have done.' Mentioning sins of omission before sins of commission reminds us that such acts are most easily overlooked and forgotten. To compare noble and uplifting matters with vulgar and depressing ones, the same may be said of the television news on the CBC that we have examined.[1] In offering these few conclusions, I am mindful not only of the words of the general confession but of those of the Roman poet Horace: *Parturient montes, nascetur ridiculus mus*. Readers who have persisted through mountains of evidence may now enjoy some mousey remarks to settle the account.

We began and will conclude with the Postman hypothesis: a good TV show engages its audience. Audiences participate imaginatively in the dramatic action and accordingly are inhibited from simultaneously reflecting on the significance of what they are experiencing. This is true of all oral communications, and of many other experiences in life as well. One of the great differences that writing and literacy have made is to enable humans to consider words as things. Like frogs on a dissecting table, messages can be taken apart and examined in detail. In order to dissect the news, it must be transformed into a text and read as if it were a play or a poem. Much of this study has consisted in presenting the text and offering an analysis. Because TV shows, including the news, are put together by literate men and women who do their jobs with great skill so as to produce specific audience effects, analysing the transcriptions of TV broadcasts as texts is a legitimate procedure. In doing so, one learns not simply about what is included, but also about how much is left out in order to produce the visualizations offered to the public as news.

The importance of TV is universally acknowledged, most obviously in what we have called the agenda-setting effect. The metaphor is somewhat misleading in so far as the agenda of a meeting is usually drawn up with specific purpose by an identifiable executive or other group of individuals. There is no need for such an agenda setter when it comes to TV news, and no attempt to identify one has been made here. External and technical considerations, to say nothing of what we have called the cultural norms and conventions of journalism, are sufficient to coalesce into a strategy of news production. In short, there is no need to blame anyone or find a scapegoat. As a leading media critic of the 'cultural studies' school put it, the information entertainingly provided by TV news does not instruct audiences on 'how things are' but on 'where they fit' into the order of things.[2] The configuration of meanings produced as TV news – that is, the product – is of a specific and particular character.

Before characterizing that product, however, let us review the evidence. The USSR was viewed as a regime more or less akin to Western liberal democracies. Of course, there were differences, but not basic moral or political ones. The doctrine of moral equivalence, which is the articulate conceptual statement that the CBC operationalized in its coverage of the Soviet Union, ignored the most fundamental distinction in political life, the distinction between tyrannical and non-tyrannical forms of government. This omission led to such otherwise inexplicable curiosities as equating or balancing U.S. support for the Afghan mujahedeen with the Soviet invasion of that country. Moreover, some stories did more than bend over backwards or forwards to excuse the actions of a tyranny. Only, for example, when the Soviets were in retreat and clearly on the way out of Afghanistan did the CBC broadcast a realistic appraisal of events.

A similar perspective on the Reagan–Gorbachev summit talks was achieved by omitting mention of the achievements of the U.S. president – chiefly, a restoration of respect for U.S. foreign policy and a long period of sustained prosperity. That the former was linked to increased defence spending and to SDI, and the latter to Reagan's challenge to the welfare state, was not considered, even though there is an enormous amount of evidence and sustaining argument to that effect available for TV visualization.

African news, by nearly any standard, is not edifying. Yet the coverage of the regimes of Ethiopia and Mozambique was decidedly different from the coverage of South Africa. By casting South Africa as the villain of the continent, it was unnecessary to look to any evidence of amelioration of the tyranny of Apartheid or to any mitigation of racism. In Ethiopia and Mozambique, matters were quite different. In the northern Marxist tyranny, the drought was visualized as a natural disaster, and nothing was said of the use of starvation as a technique of population management. In the southern Marxist tyranny, the drought was man-made, by the bandits and rebels who, for reasons never made clear, were engaging in large-scale and senseless killing.

It seems to me that there is a pattern in CBC coverage of the USSR, of the Reagan–Gorbachev summits, and of the Black, Marxist, and White, non-Marxist, tyrannies of Africa. The significance of that pattern may be indicated by the following considerations. Journalists are adversarial, it is said, but they also select their adversaries. The CBC was not adversarial towards Mikhail Gorbachev, but was so towards Ronald Reagan. Why? Journalists like conflict, it is said; they know it makes for exciting news. But they treat the parties to conflict in different ways, as the CBC did in their coverage of Ethiopia and Mozambique. Why? To be more precise, what is the purpose of such visualizations? At the end of their three-volume study of the news, Ericson, Baranek, and Chan concluded:

News is *the* most available, serious, and powerful means by which we represent our social organization and aspirations. News is also one of the most available, serious, and powerful means by which each of us orders our daily life. As such, news touches everyone. It soothes some, pricks others, and wounds a few. While news is clearly 'programmed" within the economic, political, social, cultural, and technological criteria of the news-media institution, its programs can be used in myriad ways to visualize deviance, negotiate control, and represent order.[3]

Of the 'myriad ways' available to the CBC to undertake the common functions of news production, it would seem that many, perhaps most, of those ways converged in a specific message concerning progress. The Soviet Union, and especially its leader, Mr Gorbachev, embodied and symbolized progress. The United States embodied and symbolized deviance. In Africa, Soviet client-states, or states influenced by ideological fantasies once professed in the USSR, were surrogates for progress; the South African state was the embodiment and symbol of deviance. Lest this interpretation seem arbitrary, make the following mental experiment: you are a KGB or a CIA official, assigned to your country's embassy in Ottawa with the sole task of monitoring how the CBC visualized your homeland; you have closely examined the evidence presented in the preceding chapters. Do you say 'hooray' or 'boo'?

To use the borrowed Marxist terminology introduced at the end of chapter

3, it seems clear that the visualizations provided by the CBC of the Soviet Union and of their friends in Africa did, indeed, serve Soviet interests. Hence their 'objective irresponsibility.' That is, the specific content to the otherwise abstract term 'progress' was provided by the disintegrating Soviet Union. Progress by way of Soviet 'reform' or by way of anti-Apartheid agitation was, as Hall put it, 'how things fit together.' This specific and particular meaning was reinforced by more general considerations.

We argued earlier in favour of the relatively uncontroversial view that 'the media' facilitate communication among a people, especially among a large people. Moreover, TV performs the same service between peoples. In principle, 'the media' mediate, and do so without limit. In the end, as Mansfield said, 'it is for humanity itself that the media wish to facilitate communication.'[4] This is why local news is always less important than world news, even though world news is, first of all, local, and only then is transfigured by TV. An Ethiopian famine unknown to TV audiences in Prince Rupert is still a real event. In short, TV creates a virtual or imaginary world where we live in artificial contact with starving Ethiopians. TV does not communicate the real or lived traditions, religion, customs, etc., of any particular community, such as that of Ethiopia or of Prince Rupert. Those kinds of 'communications' take place as face-to-face speeches between or among community members. Indeed, these face-to-face speeches constitute the community as a community, and so are necessary to its existence. We probably should not call such speeches communication anyway, because communication is contingent, not necessary. In contrast, TV does communicate or transmit, and what it transmits is the entertainment called news.

The news, of course, is what's new. And it is very modern to want to know what's new. It is also very modern to think that 'modern' is a term of praise. This is why news production is endless and dynamic. One conclusion here, at least, seems unequivocal. The purpose served by the dynamic production of what's new is to reinforce the doctrine of progress, which is *the* self-interpretation of modern and technological society.[5] News production and technology express the essence, so to speak, of modernity, which is a movement of endless but practical self-criticism. By this vision, any practice, fashion, institution, etc., exists because it is more up-to-date than what it replaced; in keeping with its own principle of origin, this same practice or fashion or institution will be replaced, in turn, by something more modern still. This movement is said to constitute 'progress.' The CBC, like all modern media, has directed its energies towards the production of a specific configuration of opinion – namely, progressive opinion – and not towards the provision of reliable information about the world. In a modern media world there is no reliable information. It has been replaced by news. The specific mechanism by which this progressive opinion is fostered is to entertain audiences through the presentation of arresting visualizations of deviance and of deviance-being-overcome (as progress). But even the entertainment afforded by the news is not pure entertainment: it also tells us what we ought to find entertaining – namely, the latest fashions, trends, gossip, etc.: in short, what's new.

Considered as the entertaining vehicle by which the contemporary modern self-understanding is diffused, the CBC is a roaring success. Simply contemplate the size of its budget (and the inability of taxpayers or their representatives effectively to influence its disposition); just look at the extent of its facilities, its organization, and its activities. There are even Canadians who think that the CBC is what makes us not Americans, which is another thing we share with Ethiopians. And yet, its roar is as self-cancelling as the doctrine to which it gives voice. If anything is clear from recent history, it is the sheer silliness and incoherence of progressive opinion.

The argument is not complex, but it is fundamental. The common-sense meaning of modern is that it is not traditional. What is modern exists in virtue of progress beyond tradition – beyond, literally, what has been handed over or handed down. But what happens when modernity or progress, or 'the modern age,' becomes established? Of necessity, it becomes tradition, which is to say that what is modern is always about to be overcome or overtaken by what is more modern (or even by the post-modern; but we suspect that the post-modern is really just the latest version of the modern that has noticed how all previous moderns have been overtaken by the even-more-modern).[6] The conclusion to which we are drawn by these reflections is that, because what is modern always seeks to be one step ahead of itself or to be going in a certain direction, one can never understand modernity by looking towards its end or purpose in order to define it and give it coherence and form, because there is none.[7] The alternative, then, would seem to be that we look towards the beginning of modernity, to the time when progress was first set in motion and tradition was first attacked in the name of modernity.

It seems to me true to say that TV visualizations are uncongenial to an examination of the beginnings of modernity. On the contrary, the whole thrust of the media is, as we noted above, towards greater progress. In political terms, this movement translates into greater democratization, where 'democracy' means removing barriers between people in order to create, as it were, 'one world' where Ethiopians and Canadians were united in their care for one another. In short, the logic of the media in a progressive and

united, but imaginary, world, ensured that the Soviet Union, and the ideological fantasies to which it bore allegiance, would be favourably embraced.
However, the imaginary status of this media world also ensured the aforementioned silliness. As we have seen in some detail, this silliness is hidden
by the manifold sins of omission that have been indicated through the
course of this study. Considered in sum, they amount to the non-recogni-
tion of factual reality. We have just indicated the incoherence of a doctrine
that is compelled to invent the deviance of tradition in order to overcome it
as progress. The most entertaining way to present the needed visualizations
of endless progress is to invite audiences to contemplate other people's
troubles and to sympathize with them. This is why we need know nothing
about South Africa in order to feel a real (if not well-founded) compassion
for Nelson Mandela.

The invitation to sympathize, in turn, generates a twofold interpretation. The first is soft and liberal: we feel sorry for others who suffer disasters, misery, poverty, war, etc. The second is more harsh and angry: we
feel indignant that others suffer oppression. The two modes of feeling are
linked. Compassionate liberals do not get angry unless oppression is visualized as having been caused by poverty, and the angry are not concerned
with poverty unless it can be visualized as having been caused by oppression. But either way, no one cares for moderation or patience. Feelings,
not thoughts, are mobilized by the news; feelings, not duties, are liber-
ated by the news. The only exception seems to be sports. Sports news,
especially live broadcasts of games, invites us to show loyalty, not compassion, to savour the joys of superiority that come from victory, to indulge
in wilful and parochial, not compassionate and universal, feelings: we
cheer for the home team, our team, and forget about the shallow suffering and wails of those whom we properly defeat. Can anyone doubt the
news would be different if it followed the 'production values' of the
sports desk?

In this study, I have tried to indicate the errors and omissions of CBC news
coverage of a complex and controversial series of events. It is possible to
account for this result by reference to reporters' and producers' laziness and
incompetence; to pack journalism; to their psychological dispositions, ideological commitments, spiritual disorders; or to many other factors. But
what's the point? If one could establish a standard agreeable to journalists
and non-journalists – to professors of political science, for instance – and if
one found that journalists did not measure up, what then? One can hardly
expect professors of political science (who often disagree, anyway) to
become journalists and combine the roles of authorized knower and enter-

tainer. This does not mean that there is no solution to the problem of the CBC and its production of the news.

A first step, which would at least bring the problem into focus, would be to recognize that TV news is entertainment, period. This is difficult for TV journalists to accept because one of the fundamental doctrines that justifies the power and privileges of TV is the 'people's right to know,' not the 'people's right to be entertained.' That is, the people must be supplied with knowledge because it is something they ardently desire, and also because it is vaguely sensed that knowledge is required, for some reason, for democratic government. Having raised the matter of knowledge, we are invited to revise our understanding of journalism in a liberal democracy. We have argued that the old nineteenth-century notions of a market-place of ideas and of the rhetoric of print simply do not apply to the secondary orality, to say nothing of the centralized oligopoly, of TV. The fact is, TV comes from someplace, even if it aims at universalizing communication. Local influences, like local news, are subordinated to the necessities of production. Increasingly, opinions are given respectability by TV, which is to say that prejudices, or opinions lacking in respectability, will emerge only from the face-to-face exchanges between deviant or reactionary neighbours. This local speech (not communication) can give a person a very stubborn sense of direction. It doesn't look that way to TV, however. There, it looks merely deviant, which leads to the following conclusion: defence of the people's right to know means attacking prejudice, which is always local. In this way, TV draws attention to itself as a 'national' institution and invites government regulation. By seeking to destroy local prejudice (and prejudice cannot help but be local), TV opens the door to government control because that same act destroys or undermines the basis for resisting central bureaucratic authority. And, as a side-effect, combating prejudice undermines the local sources of news – namely, deviance.

A more sobering consequence follows from the agenda-setting effect. The danger here, it seems to me, is not that Canadians will come to admire tyrants who cloud their actions in lies (as tyrants invariably do), but that they will learn to disbelieve TV news in principle. The problem is not that images and stories can be adjusted to circumstance, because we know that 'credibility' requires a consistent angle. The problem, rather, is that even a consistent angle need not bear a close relationship to facts, *and everyone knows it*. This is indicated in yet another paradox or inconsistency. The people's right to know does not include the right to know the journalists' sources. The right to withhold information regarding sources is justified as necessary to supply the people with news. When it is government and not an individual that wishes to know who the sources are, the media claim the rights of sovereignty in their refusal. Where do journalists get such rights? Obviously not from the people, who may well be interested in knowing journalists' sources, and certainly have an interest in knowing them.

There is a discrepancy between the media world and the world where we ordinarily live, or the real world, that is indicated by the acknowledgment that TV creates. So we wonder: where do TV producers get their creative ideas? Journalists, according to the evidence presented by Lichter and his colleagues cited in chapter 1, are not particularly reflective. Anyone who has ever been interviewed for TV soon senses that he is in the presence of beautiful but slick and superficial individuals. Correspondents' visualizations are directed towards the question 'What will happen?' They ignore the politician's deliberative question, 'What shall we do?' and rely on others, usually intellectuals, to answer the question 'What does it mean?' For their part, media intellectuals are now sufficiently adept at expressing themselves with great sincerity, thus securing a modest place for themselves in the media world.

There are, however, two problems. The first concerns the ability of media intellectuals to get around one of the long-standing principles of classical philosophy – namely, that thinking requires (and makes possible) a certain detachment from 'worldly' affairs. If our modern-day media intellectuals are not above the fray, can audiences be unaware that they are no longer indifferent to wealth and power? But then, why should they be trusted either?

A second problem also concerns trust, and so the 'credibility,' of TV news. Facts are always contingent, and might have been otherwise. The whole web of facts can, for this reason, so easily be torn by lies. It is certainly true that facts have never been secure in the hands of political power, but neither, it seems, are they secure in the hands of media intellectuals or TV journalists. The purpose of facts is to establish reliability in an ever-changing world. This is why we so often say they are stubborn. A story emerged from the Versailles peace conference after the First World War that illustrates this problem. The French prime minister, Clémenceau, was asked by a German general what he thought that historians would make of the whole business. 'That I do not know, *mon général*. But this I do know. They will not say that Belgium invaded Germany.' And yet, not too many years later, the official history of the Soviet Union neglected to mention the contribution of the founder of the Red Army, Leon Trotsky, to the victory of the Bolsheviks in the civil war. With sufficient coercive power, even the stubbornness of facts can be obliterated for a time. And yet, humans need the reliability of facts in order to find their bearings in the world – in order to be, in the end, at home in the world. Facts can help supply that reliability so long as they are remembered by trustworthy witnesses; but the presence of trust also means that no fact cannot also be doubted. Facts are, so to speak, both stubborn and fragile. Even if political power and the power of journalism can distort, or lie, or cover up facts with layers of falsehoods, which attests to the fragility of factual truths, such powers can never replace factual truths by fictions, or even by visualizations, which attests to their stubbornness. When the media (and especially television) are more concerned with presenting entertaining visualizations than with providing reliable factual information, then it becomes exceedingly difficult, and perhaps impossible, to find our bearings in the world. It is, of course, possible to get away with single falsehoods, whether explicit lies and deliberate distortions or mere visualizations and sins of omission. Attempting to live in such a world results only in the disappearance of truth from public life. Under such circumstances we may expect people to lose their common sense, which depends on an awareness of factual reality in order to exist at all, and to place their trust in new fictions and new superstitions.

Notes

1 See George Comstock and Marilyn Fisher, *Television and Human Behavior: A Guide to the Pertinent Scientific Literature* (Santa Monica, CA: Rand Corporation 1975).

2 See Melvin L. DeFleur and Sandra Ball-Rokeach, *Theories of Mass Communications*, 4th ed. (New York: Longman 1982), for details.

3 See Harold A. Innis, *The Bias of Communication* (Toronto: University of Toronto Press 1964), and *Empire and Communication* (Toronto: University of Toronto Press 1972); Marshall McLuhan, *The Gutenberg Galaxy* (Toronto: University of Toronto Press 1962), and *Understanding Media* (New York: McGraw-Hill 1964).

4 Most accessibly in *Orality and Literacy: The Technologizing of the Word* (London: Methuen 1982)

5 Experimental evidence indicates there is no significant difference in the way audiences understand audio only as compared with audio plus video. See Richard A. Pride and Gary L. Wamsly, 'Symbol Analysis of Network Coverage of the Laos Incursion,' *Journalism Quarterly* 49 (1972), 635–40.

6 Neil Postman, *Amusing Ourselves to Death* (New York: Penguin 1985), 102

7 Richard V. Ericson, Patricia M. Baranek, and Janet B.L. Chan, *Representing Order: Crime, Law, and Justice in the News Media* (Toronto: University of Toronto Press 1991), 351

8 P.H. Weaver, 'Newspaper News and Television News,' in D. Cater and R. Adler, eds., *Television as Social Force: New Approaches to TV Criticism* (New York: Praeger 1975), 84

9 R.T. Bower, *The Changing Television Audience in America* (New York: Columbia University Press 1985). This finding is echoed, as one might expect, by Cana-

dian studies. In 1980, 73 per cent of respondents to a large survey conducted by Goldfarb Consultants indicated that they regularly used television as a news source: Canada, Department of External Affairs, *Perspectives on World Affairs and Foreign Policy Issues: A Research Report for External Affairs Canada* (Ottawa: Minister of Supply and Services 1980), 10. Likewise the Kent Commission reported that 52 per cent of Canadians believed that television kept them most up-to-date: Canada, Royal Commission on Newspapers, *Report* (Ottawa: Minister of Supply and Services 1981), 254.

10 D.C. Hallin, 'The American News Media: A Critical Theory Perspective,' in J. Forester, ed., *Critical Theory and Public Policy* (Cambridge, MA: MIT Press 1985), 135

11 The term 'authorized knower' is borrowed from Gaye Tuchman, *Making News: A Study in the Construction of Reality* (New York: Free Press 1978).

12 See M. Fishman, *Manufacturing the News* (Austin: University of Texas Press 1980).

13 The figure is taken from Edward Jay Epstein, *News from Nowhere* (New York: Vintage 1974), 4.

14 Herbert Gans, *Deciding What's News* (New York: Vintage 1979), 81

15 Postman, *Amusing Ourselves to Death*, ch. 1–2; Philip Schlesinger, *Putting 'Reality' Together: BBC News*, 2d ed. (London: Methuen 1987); Ericson, Baranek, and Chan, *Representing Order*, 345–6

16 For several U.S. examples, see Epstein, *News from Nowhere*, 13ff.; CBC, *The CBC: A Perspective*, Submission to the CRTC in Support of Applications for Renewal of Broadcast Licences (Ottawa, 1978), 374. In 1970, the Senate Special Committee report on the mass media was entitled *The Uncertain Mirror* (Ottawa: Queen's Printer 1970). The metaphor was presumed to be valid; only the performance was 'uncertain.'

17 Smith summarized the news of many media scholars in his remark that journalism was 'the art of structuring reality, rather than recording it': A. Smith, 'The Long Road to Objectivity and Back Again: The Kinds of Truth We Get in Journalism,' in George Boyce, James Curran, and Pauline Wingate, *Newspaper History from the Seventeenth Century to the Present Day History* (London: Constable 1978), 168.

18 See Richard V. Ericson, Patricia M. Baranek, and Janet B.L. Chan, *Visualizing Deviance: A Study of News Organization* (Toronto: University of Toronto Press 1987), 196.

19 Gans, *Deciding What's News*, 93ff. By contrast, see Stephen White, 'Why Journalism Schools?' *The Public Interest* 82 (1986), 39–57.

20 Richard V. Ericson, Patricia M. Baranek, and Janet B.L. Chan, *Negotiating Control: A Study of News Sources* (Toronto: University of Toronto Press 1989), 312

21 Ibid, 379
22 See Barry Cooper, 'Plato and the Media,' in Ethan Fishman, ed., *Political Theory and Public Policy* (New York: Greenwood Press 1991), 15–28.
23 Postman, *Amusing Ourselves to Death*, ch. 2
24 Ibid, 24
25 Ibid, 80. Postman's *obiter dictum* was suitably qualified by Ericson, Baranek, and Chan, *Representing Order*, ch. 2.
26 Postman, *Amusing Ourselves to Death*, 116–17, 124
27 Epstein, *News from Nowhere*, 42–3
28 Gans, *Deciding What's News*, 82–3, 279–81, and *passim*
29 Ericson, Baranek, and Chan, *Visualizing Deviance*, 4
30 Brooker-Gross, 'Nineteenth-Century News Definitions and Wire-Service Usage,' *Journalism Quarterly* 60 (1983), 24
31 Ericson, Baranek, and Chan, *Visualizing Deviance*, 4. For a more elaborate, but by no means contradictory, account of what counts as news, see Johan Galtang and Mari Ruge, 'Structuring and Selecting News,' in Stanley Cohen and Jock Young, eds., *The Manufacture of News: Deviance, Social Problems and the Mass Media* (London: Constable 1973), 62–73, and John Hartley, *Understanding News* (London: Methuen 1982), ch. 5.
32 Quoted in Epstein, *News from Nowhere*, 4–5
33 Ericson, Baranek, and Chan, *Negotiating Control*, 13
34 At this point in the argument, a branch called semiotics leads into its own conceptual labyrinth. See, for example, J. Fiske, *Television Culture* (London: Methuen 1987); Umberto Eco, 'Towards a Semiotic Inquiry into the TV Message,' in John Corner and Jeremy Hawthorn, eds., *Communication Studies: An Introductory Reader* (London: Arnold 1980), 131–49; Hartley, *Understanding News*, ch. 2. This is not the occasion to take issue with a semiotic approach or to undertake a discussion of narrative theory, reader/viewer–response theory, and the like. In this respect, political science remains, as Aristotle said, a practical science. Accordingly, for a common-sense understanding of TV news, it is perhaps sufficient to accept the proposition that, for viewers, the news is understood to be about the world of common experience, usually referred to as the real world. For semioticists, narrative theorists, and the like, such admissions are not shocking, though they may expose political science to good-natured or at least harmless ridicule.
35 Gans, *Deciding What's News*, 68
36 The term 'progress' is itself an ideological symbol referring to an imaginary reality created by identifiable deformations of consciousness. For details of the deformations involved, see Eric Voegelin, *From Enlightenment to Revolution*, ed., by John H. Hallowell (Durham, NC: Duke University Press 1975). In common-

sense language, progress is bunk, an imaginary object of belief for people whose souls are warped or lost – or, in contemporary language, progress is believed in by men and women with peculiar 'inner needs.'

37 Ericson, Baranek, and Chan, *Negotiating Control*, 398

38 Various 'cultural theories' of the media emphasize one or another aspect of this process. On the one hand, it is argued that reporting deviance encourages deviance – see G. Pearson, *Hooligan: A History of Respectable Fears* (London: Macmillan 1983); on the other hand, it is argued that reporting deviance turns into an element of social ritual the effect of which is to reinforce consensus – see J. Gusfield, *The Culture of Public Problems* (Chicago: University of Chicago Press 1981). At this point, 'cultural theories' often link up with semiotics and 'hegemony theory' in a complex intellectualized discourse that appeals chiefly to intellectuals with a taste for discursive complexities. See, for example, S. Hall, 'The Rediscovery of Ideology: The Return of the Re-pressed in Media Studies,' in Michael Gurevitch, Tony Bennett, James Curran, and Janet Woollacott, eds., *Culture, Society and Media* (London: Methuen 1982), 56–90.

39 S. Robert Lichter, Stanley Rothman, and Linda S. Lichter, *The Media Elite* (Bethesda, MD: Adler and Adler 1986), chs. 3–4

40 Interview with Fred Friendly, *TV Guide*, 1 Aug. 1981, 25

41 Gans, *Deciding What's News*, 231ff.

42 Lichter, Rothman, and Lichter, *The Media Elite*, 131

43 Ericson, Baranek, and Chan, *Visualizing Deviance*, 11–12

44 See Barry Cooper, *Michel Foucault: An Introduction to His Thought* (Lewiston, NY: Edwin Mellen 1981), ch. 12.

45 The issues involved are of great antiquity and cannot be analyzed here. See however, Barry Cooper, *The Restoration of Political Science and the Crisis of Modernity*, (Lewiston, NY: Edwin Mellen 1989), and Cooper, 'Plato and the Media.'

46 A. Smith, *Goodbye Gutenberg: The Newspaper Revolution of the 1980s* (Oxford: Oxford University Press 1980), 20

47 Jacques Ellul, *The Technological Society*, tr. by John Wilkinson (New York: Vintage 1964). See also Barry Cooper, *Action into Nature: An Essay on the Meaning of Technology* (Notre Dame, IN: University of Notre Dame Press 1991).

48 B. Phillips, 'Approaches to Objectivity: Journalistic versus Social Science Perspectives,' in P. Hirsch, P. Miller, and F. Kline, eds., *Strategies for Communications Research* (Beverly Hills, CA: Sage 1977), 65.

49 Lichter, Rothman, and Lichter, *The Media Elite*, 87

50 Ericson, Baranek, and Chan, *Visualizing Deviance*, 38

51 CBC, *Journalistic Policy* (Ottawa, 1982)

52 Ibid, 6

53 Ibid, 111, 6, 8

54 Gans, *Deciding What's News*, 173–5

55 Gaye Tuchman, 'Objectivity as Strategic Ritual: An Examination of Newsmen's Notions of Objectivity,' *American Journal of Sociology* 77 (1972), 660–70

56 Gans, *Deciding What's News*, 189

57 Ibid

58 See ibid, 41ff., for a discussion of these 'enduring values.' A little over a decade later, the 'values' of pastoralism and responsible capitalism, for example, seem quaint.

59 One may see the emptiness of the criteria of balance and fairness if, instead of exempting the 'socially and morally disorderly' individuals from its application, one considered the more contemporary category of the politically incorrect. Clearly it is *not* politically correct to treat the politically incorrect fairly.

60 Quoted in Epstein, *News from Nowhere*, 149

61 Gans, *Deciding What's News*, 234–5

62 CBC, *Journalistic Policy*, iv

63 Gans, *Deciding What's News*, 234–5; Epstein, *News from Nowhere*, 98–100

64 Ericson, Baranek, and Chan, *Visualizing Deviance*, 196

65 Epstein, *News from Nowhere*, 168–9

66 Ibid, 169

67 Ericson, Baranek, and Chan, *Negotiating Control*, 248

68 A thoroughly documented example is Renata Adler, *Reckless Disregard: Westmorland v. CBS et al., Sharon v. Time* (New York: Knopf 1986). A more general and less useful (but Canadian) example is Mary Anne Comber and Peter S. Mayue, *The Newsmongers: How the Media Distort the Political News* (Toronto: McClelland and Stewart 1986). For Britain, see James Curran and Jean Seaton, *Power without Responsibility* (London: Fontana 1981).

69 Ericson, Baranek, and Chan, *Visualizing Deviance*, 279ff.

70 Epstein, *News from Nowhere*, 144ff.

71 Ibid, 228. See also Tod Gitlin, *The Whole World Is Watching* (Berkeley and Los Angeles: University of California Press 1980), 146, and Hartley, *Understanding News*, ch. 5.

72 Ericson, Baranek, and Chan, *Visualizing Deviance*, ch. 5

73 Ericson, Baranek, and Chan, *Negotiating Control*, 361; *Visualizing Deviance*, 173ff.

74 Paul Lazarsfeld, Bernard Berelson, and Henry Gaudet, *The People's Choice* (New York: Columbia University Press 1944)

75 See, for example, William Glaser, 'Television and Voting Turnout,' *Public Opinion Quarterly* 29 (1965), 71–86; Jay Blumler and David McQuail, *Television in Politics* (Chicago: University of Chicago Press 1969); Kurt Lang and Gladys Lang, *Voting and Non Voting* (Waltham, MA: Blaisdell 1968).

76 V.O. Key, *Public Opinion and American Democracy* (New York: Knopf 1967), 372

77 T. Patterson and R. McClure, *The Unseeing Eye: The Myth of Television Power in National Elections* (New York: Putnam's 1976), 90

78 Paul Weaver, 'Is Television News Biased?' *Public Interest* 26 (1972), 57–74; Byron Shafer and Richard Larson, 'Did TV Create the Social Issue?' *Columbia Journalism Review* 11/5 (1972), 10–17

79 In fact, the thing, though not the word, was discussed as early as 1920 by Walter Lippmann in his *Liberty and the News* (New York: Harcourt, Brace and Howe 1920). See also M.E. McCombs, 'The Agenda-Setting Approach,' in D.D. Nimmo and K.R. Sanders, eds., *Handbook of Political Communication* (Beverly Hills, CA: Sage 1981).

80 B. Cohen, *The Press and Foreign Policy* (Princeton, NJ: Princeton University Press 1963), 13–16

81 M.E. McCombs and D.L. Shaw, 'The Agenda-Setting Function of the Mass Media,' *Public Opinion Quarterly* 36 (1972–3), 178

82 L. Erbring, E.N. Goldenberg, and A.H. Miller, 'Front Page News and Real World Clues: A New Look at Agenda-Setting by the Media,' *American Journal of Political Science* 24 (1980), 16–49

83 Michael J. Robinson, 'Public Affairs Television and the Growth of Political Malaise: The Case of "The Selling of the Pentagon,"' *The American Political Science Review* 70 (1976), 409–32

84 This work was first reported as Shanyo Iyengar, Mark Peters, and Donald Kinder, 'Experimental Demonstrations of the "Not-So-Minimal" Consequences of Television News Programs,' *The American Political Science Review* 76 (1982), 848–58; the definitive version is Iyengar and Kinder, *News That Matters: Television and American Opinion* (Chicago: University of Chicago Press 1987). Subsequent references are to this version.

85 Iyengar and Kinder, *News that Matters*, 211

86 Ibid, 33

87 Ibid

88 Ibid, 60

89 Mark R. Levy, 'The Audience Experience with Television News,' *Journalism Monographs* 55 (1978), 1–29; Epstein, *News from Nowhere*, 363ff; Gans, *Deciding What's News*, 220ff.

90 See M. MacKven, 'Exposure to Information, Belief Integration, and Individual Responsiveness to Agenda Change,' *The American Political Science Review* 78 (1984), 372–91

91 Iyengar and Kinder, *News That Matters*, 63

92 Ibid, 93–5; see also Harold D. Clarke, Jane Jenson, Lawrence Le Duc, and Jon

H. Pammett, *Absent Mandate: The Politics of Discontent in Canada* (Toronto: Gage 1984).

93 Joshua Meyrowitz, *No Sense of Place: The Impact of Electronic Media on Social Behavior* (New York: Oxford University Press 1985), *passim*.

94 Iyengar and Kinder, *News That Matters*, 117

95 Canada, Department of External Affairs, *Statements and Speeches* 83/10: *Foreign Policy and the Public Interest* (Ottawa: Minister of Supply and Services 1983), 2

96 See, for instance, Sean MacBridge, *Many Voices, One World: Communication and Society, Today and Tomorrow* (Paris: UNESCO, 1980); Thomas L. McPhail, *Electronic Colonialism* (Beverly Hills, CA: Sage 1981).

97 M. Rosenblum, *Coups and Earthquakes: Reporting the World for America* (New York: Harper & Row 1979)

98 McLuhan, *Understanding Media*, 203–4

99 Patricia Karl, 'Media Diplomacy,' American Academy of Political Science, *Proceedings* 24/4 (1982), 144

100 Edward W. Said, *Covering Islam: How the Media and the Experts Determine How We See the Rest of the World* (New York: Vintage 1981)

101 Ericson, Baranek, and Chan, *Negotiating Control*, 25; Meyrowitz, *No Sense of Place*, *passim*; Gans, *Deciding What's News*, 116

102 Ole Holsti, *Content Analysis for the Social Sciences and Humanities* (Reading, MA: Addison-Wesley 1969); Bernard Berelson, 'Content Analysis in Communication Research,' in Berelson and M. Janowitz, eds., *Reader in Public Opinion and Communication* (New York: Free Press 1966), 260–6

103 Holsti, *Content Analysis*, 95

104 For a discussion of this question, see David L. Altheide, 'Ethnographic Content Analysis,' *Qualitative Sociology* 10 (1987), 65–8.

105 Barry Cooper, *Coverage of Peace and Security Issues by Canadian Network Television* (Calgary: University of Calgary 1988). Copies of this report were submitted to the chief granting agencies, the Department of External Affairs, and the Canadian Institute for International Peace and Security.

106 The term was borrowed from William J. Starosta, 'Qualitative Content Analysis: A Burkean Perspective,' in William B. Gudykunst and Young Yun Kim, eds., *Methods for Intercultural Communication* (Beverly Hills, CA: Sage 1984), 185–94. See also Altheide, 'Ethnographic Content Analysis,' 65–77.

107 Michael Polanyi, *Personal Knowledge: Towards a Post-Critical Philosophy* (New York: Harper Torch Books 1958), 54

CHAPTER TWO

1 See *The New York Times*, 14 Mar. 1987, A6; 8 July 1988, A5.

234 Notes to pages 33–46

2 See ibid, 30 Jul. 1987, A5.
3 See ibid, 6 Apr. 1987, A1, 6; 26 Apr. 1987, A1, 12; 27 Apr. 1987, A8.
4 According to *The New York Times* account of the Tass report (9 Mar. 1988, A6), three, not two passengers were killed.
5 *The New York Times* (1 Mar., 1988, A7) reported that a woman and three of her sons, all jazz musicians, had hijacked the Soviet airliner by hiding weapons in their instrument cases. A graphic description of the assault on the aircraft was provided.
6 According to *The New York Times*, Lt.-Col. Mohammed Faris was a thirty-six-year-old pilot in the Syrian Air Force (23 Jul. 1987, A3) and a veteran of two wars with Israel (22 Jul. 1987, A20).
7 *The New York Times* (13 Nov. 1987, A12) said the printing of the Tass report in *Pravda* was 'the first of its kind in recent times,' and was done with Gorbachev's approval in order to help polish his image in the West. Another *Times* story (14 Nov. 1987, A16) called Yeltsin's ouster a 'purge' and 'stark evocation of the show-trial era, even down to the final confession and apology from the accused that was widely read by the public as a deliberate harkening to some of the party's darkest ritual' during the Stalinist 1930s.
8 For an alternative perspective on the significance of *glasnost*, see *Glasnost: How Open?* Perspectives on Freedom No. 8 (Lanham, MD: Freedom House 1987).
9 For details, see Dimitry Pospielovsky, *The Russian Church under the Soviet Regime, 1917–1982*, 2 vols. (New York: St Vladimir's Seminary Press 1984), vol. 1, ch. 4, 116–17; vol. 2, ch. 12, 387ff.
10 Ogorodnikov was, in fact, a famous 'dissident' from within the Orthodox church. He had a colourful past, having been arrested for preaching Christianity to Soviet hippies, and was a veteran of the Gulag. See Pospielovsky, *The Russian Church*, vol. 2, 333–5, and Jane Ellis, *The Russian Orthodox Church: A Contemporary History* (Bloomington: Indiana University Press 1986), 193, 382–6; 406–7, 417–19.
11 According to *The New York Times* (4 May 1987, A1), Goldfarb was diabetic. In a letter to the editor, published on 22 August 1987 (A26), he attributed his original obtaining of an exit visa to the 'intervention of an influential advocate,' in his case, Dr Armand Hammer. See also *The New York Times*, 13 Sep. 1987, A4.
12 In addition to the massive documentation of Solzhenitsyn, a simple reading of Articles 22–4 of the Soviet Criminal Code could lend itself to some very stark visualizations. See *Soviet Criminal Law and Procedure: The RSFSR Codes*, tr. by Harold J. Berman and James W. Spindler (Cambridge, MA: Harvard University Press 1966), 152–3. See also Amnesty International, *Prisoners of Conscience in the USSR: Their Treatment and Conditions* (London, 1975).

13 For details, see Boris M. Segal, *The Drunken Society: Alcohol Abuse and Alcoholism in the Soviet Union: A Comparative Study* (New York: Hippocrene Books 1990).

14 For details on the Crimean Tatars and their attempts to resettle in the Crimea after their rehabilitation in 1967, see Ann Sheehy, *The Crimean Tatars, Volga Germans and Meskhetians: Soviet Treatment of Some National Minorities* (London: Minority Rights Group 1971) or Alan Fisher, *The Crimean Tatars* (Stanford: Hoover Institution Press 1978), chs. 14 and 15. *The New York Times* report of the 27 July meeting (27 Jul. 1987, A3) was essentially the same as that of the CBC. (But see also *The New York Times*, 24 Jul. 1987, A9). The next day, however, *The New York Times* reported (28 Jul. 1987, A3) the Tatar leaders as saying 'there were no results' of the meeting with Gromyko, and Tass reported Gromyko as having informed the Tatars that 'any attempts to put pressure on the organs of state power can only complicate the work of the commission.' On 31 July, *The New York Times* reported (A3) that the Soviet government had accused the United States of inciting the Tatar protests, which 'signalled a hardening in the official attitude toward several hundred Crimean Tatars.'

15 Such information is available from standard sources such as the *Encyclopaedia Britannica* or the English translation of the *Great Soviet Encyclopedia*.

16 U.S. Information Agency, *Afghanistan Chronology, 1987* (Washington, DC, 1987), 24 April, 15. Another account of the longer-term Soviet–Afghan conflict is Martin Strmecki, 'Operation Avalanche and Soviet Capitulation,' *The American Spectator* 21 (Apr. 1988), 15–17.

17 *The New York Times*, 7 Jul. 1987, A6; *The Times* (London), 9 Jul. 1987, 9

18 *The Times*, 8 Jun. 1987, 10; 14 Jul. 1987, 10; *The New York Times*, 1 Jun. 1987, A1; 24 Jun. 1987, A8; 5 Aug. 1987, A5; 29 Sep. 1987, A8; 10 Oct. 1987, A6; 13 Dec. 1987, A24.

19 *The Times*, 30 Nov. 1987, 7

20 Ibid, 21 Dec. 1987, 7

21 Ibid, 24 Dec. 1987, 7; 28 Dec. 1987, 1; 2 Jan. 1988, 6; 20 Jan. 1988, 6; *The New York Times*, 20 Dec. 1987, A18; 25 Dec. 1987, A3; 29 Dec. 1987, A9; 31 Dec. 1987, A5; 1 Jan. 1988, A1; 20 Jan. 1988, A3

22 *The New York Times*, 24 Dec. 1987, A9. The AN-26 is a dual-use transport plane. It is frequently employed as a troop carrier and surveillance craft, as well as an airliner. Gerasimov did not say whether it had civilian or military markings. See *The Times*, 12 Jun. 1987, 20; *The New York Times*, 12 Jun. 1987, A8; 14 Aug. 1987, A7.

23 *The New York Times*, 1 Jan. 1988, A1, 4; 20 Jan. 1988, A3; *The Times*, 28 Dec. 1987, 1; 2 Jan. 1988, 6

24 See *Jane's Weapon Systems, 1984–85* (New York: Jane's Publishing Inc. 1985),

129. The British supplied Blowpipe missiles, less sophisticated than the Stingers, but designed for the same purpose and quite effective, to the mujahedeen.
25 *The New York Times*, 7 Jul. 1987, A6
26 Ibid, 7 Jul. 1987, A6; 14 Aug. 1987, A7; 17 Jan. 1988, D2; *The Wall Street Journal*, 16 Feb. 1988, 1
27 *The New York Times*, 7 Jul. 1987, A6; 29 Nov. 1987, A1. According to A.A. Khan, 'Soviet Strategy in Afghanistan: Success or Failure?' *Defence Journal* 14 (1988), 30, the USSR lost 512 aircraft between January and November 1987.
28 These talks began in August 1984. They were so named because the delegates from Pakistan and Afghanistan refused to meet face-to-face. They remained in close proximity, in different rooms of the Palais des Nations, and the personal representative of the U.N. secretary general acted as a messenger.
29 As early as November 1987 Gennady Gerasimov had indicated that Soviet troops would leave if the Americans stopped aiding the mujahedeen. *The New York Times*, 29 Nov. 1987, A9; see also 12 Jan. 1988, A6.
30 The conflict between the United States and the Soviet Union centred on whether the USSR could continue to supply the Afghanistan government with military equipment when the Americans cut off aid to the mujahedeen, or whether 'symmetrical' ending of military supplies to both sides was necessary. The Soviets took the former position, the Americans the latter.
31 For details on disinformation and propaganda during the Gorbachev era, see Ladislav Bittman, ed., *The New Image-Makers: Soviet Propaganda and Disinformation Today* (Washington, DC: Pergamon-Brassey 1988).
32 See *The New York Times*, 4 Mar. 1988, A11; 5 Mar. 1988, A1, 4; 11 Mar. 1988, A5; 25 Mar. 1988, A1, 10; 29 Mar. 1988, A6; 31 Mar. 1988, A1, 9; 1 Apr. 1988, A1, 6; 5 Apr. 1988, A1, 8; 6 Apr. 1988, A1, 12; 8 Apr. 1988, A1, 10, 11.
33 Gavin Bell described the devastation of a once-fertile countryside as being as if someone had dropped a bomb on the Garden of Eden: *The Times*, 21 Jul. 1987, 7. The documentation of Soviet atrocities is extensive, and begins in 1985. See *Rapport sur la situation des droits de l'homme en Afghanistan*, E/CN. 4/1985/21, (Human Rights Commission, Economic and Social Council, United Nations, 19 Feb. 1985); *Situation of Human Rights in Afghanistan*, A/40/843 (General Assembly, United Nations, 5 Nov. 1985); *Report on the Situation of Human Rights in Afghanistan*, E/CN. 4/1986/24 (Human Rights Commission, Economic and Social Council, United Nations, 17 Feb. 1986); *Situation of Human Rights in Afghanistan*, A/41/778 (General Assembly, United Nations, 9 Jan. 1987); *Report on the Situation of Human Rights in Afghanistan*, A/42/667 (General Assembly, United Nations, 23 Oct. 1987); Amnesty International, *Democratic Republic of Afghanistan: Background Briefing on Amnesty International's Concerns*, ASA/11/13/83 (London, Oct. 1983); Amnesty International, *Afghanistan: Torture of Political Prisoners*, ASA/11/04/86, (London, Nov. 1986); Amnesty Interna-

tional, *Afghanistan – Unlawful Killings and Torture*, ASA/11/02/88, (London, May 1988); Bernard Dupaigne, ed., *Les Droits de l'homme en Afghanistan* (Paris: AFRANE 1985); Michael Barry, Johan Lagerfelt, and Marie-Odile Terrenoire, 'International Humanitarian Enquiry Commission on Displaced Persons in Afghanistan,' *Central Asian Survey* 5/1 (1986), 65–99. There are, furthermore, several accounts by journalists of their adventures with the mujahedeen in the field. See, for example, Peregrine Hodson, *Under a Sickle Moon*, ed. by G. Fisketjan (New York: Atlantic Monthly Press 1987); Sandy Gall, *Behind Russian Lines: An Afghan Journal* (New York: St Martin's 1984); Mike Martin, *Afghanistan, Inside a Rebel Stronghold: Journeys with the Mujahedeen* (New York: Sterling 1984); Nigel Ryan, *A Little Hitch or Two in Afghanistan: A Journey Behind Russian Lines* (London: Weidenfeld and Nicolson 1983).

34 See, however, US *News and World Report*, 20 Jan. 1986, 30–1; *The New York Times*, 22 Jul. 1987, C22; *The Times*, 20 Jul. 1987, 8.

35 In Harrison's opinion, Americans had a 'romanticized' image of the mujahedeen. These 'Islamic fundamentalists,' he said, were not only divided among themselves, but pursued a goal that could never be accepted by the USSR, which 'has more at stake in adjacent Afghanistan than Washington does.' He published several op-ed pieces in *The New York Times* (4 Dec. 1987, A39; 29 Mar. 1988, A27; 20 May 1988, A31).

36 Harrison nevertheless thought a deployment of U.N. peacekeepers was desirable. See *The New York Times*, 29 Mar. 1988, A17.

CHAPTER THREE

1 For journalistic accounts of these problems, see, for example, Michael Ledeen, 'The Suave Gorbachev Wears No Clothes,' *The American Spectator* 22/2 (Feb. 1989), 16–17; Nick Eberstadt, 'The Latest Myths About the Soviet Union,' *Commentary*, May 1987, 17–27; Roger W. Robinson, 'Soviet Cash and Western Banks,' *National Interest* 3 (Summer 1986), 17–24.

2 See the summary of Peter Zwick, 'New Thinking and New Foreign Policy under Gorbachev,' PS: *Political Science and Politics*, 21/2 (June 1989), 215–24.

3 A thorough account of the INF and Euromissile questions can be found in Jeffry Herf, *War by Other Means: Soviet Power, West German Resistance, and the Battle of the Euromissiles* (New York: The Free Press 1991), and Jonathan Haslam, *The Soviet Union and the Politics of Nuclear Weapons in Europe, 1969–1987* (London: Macmillan 1989).

4 Compare the account in *The New York Times*, 1 Jul. 1987, A1.

5 See *The New York Times*, 17 Jul. 1987, A1, 5; 23 Jul. 1987, A1, 10.

6 Data on the strategic balances between NATO and the Warsaw Treaty Organization (WTO) are available in David Cox and Mary Taylor, eds., *A Guide to*

Canadian Policies on Arms Control, Disarmament, Defence and Conflict-Resolution: 1986–87 (Ottawa: The Canadian Institute for International Peace and Security [CIIPS] 1987), 267–70; Ron Purver and Roger Hill, eds., *A Guide to Canadian Policies on Arms Control, Disarmament, Defence and Conflict-Resolution: 1987–88* (Ottawa: CIIPS 1988), 326–7; International Institute for Strategic Studies (IISS), *The Military Balance: 1985–86* (London, 1986), 158–64; IISS, *The Military Balance: 1984–85* 130–5; IISS, *The Military Balance: 1983–84* (London, 1984), , 118–19; IISS, *The Military Balance: 1982–83* (London, 1983), 112–13; IISS, *The Military Balance: 1981–82* (London, 1982) , 104–5.

7 For data on conventional-force strength, see IISS, *The Military Balance: 1985–86*, 186–7, and the same source for other years, as in note 6 above.

8 In addition to being a Soviet specialist who has written several academic studies of the USSR and of Bukharin (an intellectual Bolshevik purged by Stalin in the 1930s), Cohen wrote a column, 'Sovieticus,' for the liberal U.S. magazine *The Nation*. Bertram was, for several years, director of the International Institute for Strategic Studies, London, after which he became political editor for the German daily *Die Zeit*; Simes was a senior associate at the Carnegie Endowment and an academic Soviet specialist.

9 Consider Vladimir Bukovsky, 'Will Gorbachev Reform the Soviet Union?' *Commentary*, September 1986, 19–24.

10 This elementary political science was evident even to Marxists, such as Merleau-Ponty. See *Signes* (Paris: Gallimard 1967), 366–85. More adequate treatment of the entire question can be found in Hannah Arendt, *The Origins of Totalitarianism* (New York: Harcourt, Brace and World 1966), 384–7 and ch. 13.

11 Ignatieff's more complete and rather more complex account of his grandfather's experience is *The Russian Album: A Family Saga of Revolution, Civil War and Exile* (Harmondsworth: Penguin 1987).

12 David Gilmour has written three novels, *Back on Tuesday* (Toronto: Coach House 1986), *How Boys See Girls* (New York: Random House 1991), and *An Affair with the Moon* (Toronto: Random House 1993); he is a regular contributor to CBC radio as well as to CBC TV. Terence McKenna is probably best known for his contribution to *The Valour and the Horror*, a highly inaccurate (and anti-war) film about Canadian troops in the Second World War.

13 See, however Eugene V. Rostow, 'Why the Soviets Want an Arms-Control Agreement and Why They Want It Now,' *Commentary*, Feb. 1987, 19–26; Kenneth W. Thompson, ed., *Unresolved Issues in Arms Control* (Lanham: University Press of America 1988); Stuart Croft, *The Impact of Strategic Defences on European-American Relations in the 1990s*, Adelphi Papers 138 (London: International Institute for Strategic Studies 1989).

14 Aleksandr I. Solzhenitsyn, *Letter to the Soviet Leaders*, tr. by H. Sternberg (New York: Harper & Row 1957), 62

15 The standard account – Robert Conquest, *The Great Terror: Stalin's Purge of the Thirties* – was published by Macmillan in 1968; a new edition, *The Great Terror: A Reassessment* (New York: Oxford 1990), was preceded by several articles on the topic.

16 Pantex is a large final-assembly site for nuclear weapons. The *production* of nuclear weapons is a complex operation that takes place at several sites of which Pantex is not the largest. For a summary of size, budget, personnel, and mission data, see Thomas B. Cochran, William M. Arkin, and Milton M. Hoenig, eds., *Nuclear Weapons Databook*, vol. 3: *U.S. Nuclear Warhead Facility Profiles* (Cambridge, MA: Ballinger 1987). A balanced account of life in Amarillo by an observer who recorded beliefs 'foreign to my own,' see A.G. Mjtabai *Blessèd Assurance: At Home with the Bomb in Amarillo, Texas* (Boston: Houghton Mifflin 1986).

17 Arkin was a director of the Arms Race and Nuclear Weapons Research Project at a liberal think-tank, the Institute for Policy Studies, and is co-author of *S.I.O.P.: The Secret U.S. Plan for Nuclear War* (New York: Norton 1983).

18 We met Gerasimov in chapter 2, where he was a spokesman for the Soviet foreign ministry complaining that the United States was supplying Stingers to the mujahedeen.

19 Sayre is the author of *Running Time: Films of the Cold War* (New York: Dial Press 1982). Among other things her work interpreted science-fiction movies as well as biblical extravaganzas in light of Manichean Cold War themes.

20 For a rather different appraisal of Kim Philby, see Andrew Sinclair, *The Red and the Blue: Intelligence, Treason and the Universities* (London: Weidenfeld and Nicolson 1986); Andrew Boyle, *The Climate of Treason: Five Who Spied for Russia* (London: Hutchinson 1979); B. Page, David Leitch, and Phillip Knightley, *Philby: The Spy Who Betrayed a Generation*, with an introduction by John le Carré (London: André Deutsch 1968).

21 Gouzenko still is a controversial topic. For a recent appraisal, see J.L. Granatstein and David Stafford, *Spy Wars: Espionage and Canada from Gouzenko to Glasnost* (Toronto: Key Porter 1990). See also John Sawatsky, *Gouzenko: The Untold Story* (Toronto: Doubleday 1982).

22 See Max Weber, 'Politics as a Vocation,' in Hans Gerth and C. Wright Mills tr. and ed., *From Max Weber: Essays in Sociology* (New York: Oxford University Press 1946), 120.

CHAPTER FOUR

1 See, however, Peter L. Berger and Bobby Godsell, 'Fantasies about South Africa,' *Commentary*, Jul. 1987, 35–40; Richard E. Bissell, *South Africa and the United States: The Erosion of an Influence Relationship* (New York: Praeger 1982).

Standard treatments of Ethiopian politics published in the late 1970s and early
1980s highlighted the strategic competition of the USSR and the United States
in the Horn of Africa. The focus of much of this work was on ideological as
well as strategic rivalries. See, for example, Tom J. Farer, *War Clouds on the Horn
of Africa: The Widening Storm* (New York: Carnegie Endowment for International Peace 1979); Bereket Habte Selassie, *Conflict and Intervention in the Horn
of Africa* (New York: Monthly Review Press 1980); Fred Halliday and Maxine
Molyneux, *The Ethiopian Revolution* (London: NLB 1981). The most thorough
treatment was completed after the Soviet disengagement: Robert G. Patman,
*The Soviet Union in the Horn of Africa: The Diplomacy of Intervention and Disen-
gagement* (Cambridge: Cambridge University Press 1990).

2 As early as 1985, the connection between the economic policy of the government of Ethiopia and the existence of famine was well known. See, for example,
the remarks of Nick Eberstadt ('Famine, Development and Foreign Aid,' *Commentary*, Mar. 1985, 27): 'Once again there is famine in Ethiopia. Though its
ultimate toll is yet to be determined, its causes are already apparent. After seiz-
ing power in 1974, Ethiopia's Marxist-Leninist *Dergue* (Armed Forces Coordi-
nating Committee) launched a campaign against "capitalism" in the
countryside, restricting and ultimately prohibiting the private sale and market-
ing of farm produce and agricultural implements. At the same time, a newly
formed secret police executed thousands of students and skilled workers in this
predominantly illiterate nation, imprisoned tens of thousands more, and caused
even greater numbers to flee their homeland. With the encouragement of
Soviet and Cuban advisers, the government used its foreign aid to underwrite
military build-up and war. In a country like Ethiopia, which has always been
subject to drought, such policies insured that widespread famine would be only
a matter of time.'

See also Independent Commisson on International Humanitarian Issues,
Famine: A Man-Made Disaster? (New York: Vintage 1985). A scholarly analysis
written a few years later that confirmed the active role of the Ethiopian govern-
ment in prolonging and exacerbating the famine is Steven L. Varius, *Reluctant
Aid or Aiding the Reluctant? U.S. Food and Policy and Ethiopian Famine Relief* (New
Brunswick, NJ: Transaction Publishers, 1990). See also Christopher Clapham,
Transformation and Continuity in Revolutionary Ethiopia (Cambridge: Cambridge
University Press 1988), 188–9. A discussion of the civil war in Eritrea and
Tigre can be found in Minority Rights Group, *Eritrea and Tigray*, Report No. 5
(London: MRG 1983).

3 Dawit Giorgis is the author of *Red Tears: War, Famine and Revolution in Ethiopia*
(Trenton: Red Sea Press 1989). When Emperor Haile Selassie was removed
from office, he was deputy chief of the Relief and Rehabilitation Commission;

he later served as deputy foreign minister and was a member of the Central Committee of the Workers Party of Ethiopia and its chief representative in Eritrea.

4 See, however, George Alfred Mudge, 'Starvation as a Means of Warfare,' *International Lawyer* 4/2 (1970), 228–68.

5 Data are taken from OECD, *Geographical Distribution of Financial Flows to Developing Countries (1971–77)* (Paris, 1978), and *Geographical Distribution of Financial Flows to Developing Countries, 1979–82* (Paris,1984). See also Peter Schwab, *Ethiopia: Politics, Economics and Society* (London: Francis Pinter 1985), ch. 3.

6 See Eberstadt, 'Famine, Development and Foreign Aid,' 27.

7 See Schwab, *Ethiopia*, 117–18, for a brief biography. The entry in *Who's Who* (London: Black 1987), 342, indicates only his current position, Chairman of the Provisional Military Administrative Council and Chairman of the Council of Ministries, his previous position, and his address.

8 See Clapham, *Transformation and Continuity in Revolutionary Ethiopia*, 109–13; *International Herald Tribune*, 5 Sep. 1977, 1; Patman, *The Soviet Union in the Horn of Africa*, 219.

9 See Arch Puddington, 'Ethiopia: The Communist Use of Famine,' *Commentary*, Apr. 1986, 30–8; Puddington's interpretation has recently been confirmed by political scientist Edmon J. Keller in 'Drought, War and the Politics of Famine in Ethiopia,' *The Journal of Modern African Studies* 30 (1992), 609–24; Jason W. Clay, 'Refugees Flee Ethiopian Collectivization,' *Cultural Survival Quarterly* 10/2 (1986), 80–5; Claude Malhuret, *Mass Deportations in Ethiopia* (Paris: Médecins sans Frontières 1985).

10 See, however, Amnesty International, *Human Rights Violations in Ethiopia*, AFR/ 25/10/87 (London, 1987).

11 See Puddington, 'Ethiopia: The Communist Use of Famine,' 31–2.

12 See Bogdan Szajkowski, 'Ethiopia: A Weakening Soviet Connection?' *The World Today*, Aug.–Sept. 1989, 45, 48–9.

13 Alternative interpretations of foreign aid and 'development' are abundant. The work of P.T. Baur is, perhaps, the most cogently argued. See, for example, *Equality, the Third World and Economic Delusion* (Cambridge, MA: Harvard University Press 1982); *Reality and Rhetoric: Studies in the Economics of Development* (Cambridge, MA: Harvard University Press 1984); Bauer and B.S. Yamay, 'Foreign Aid: Rewarding Impoverishment?' *Commentary*, Sept. 1985, 38–40; Nick Eberstadt, 'The Perversions of Foreign Aid,' *Commentary*, Jun. 1985, 19–33.

14 Alternative accounts, suitable for visualization were, of course, available. See, for example, James A. Phillips and Richard D. Fisher, Jr., *A Plan for Rescuing Starving Ethiopians*, Heritage Foundation Backgrounder No. 400 (Washington, DC: Heritage Foundation 1984); William Pascoe, *Time for Action against*

Mengistu's Ethiopia, Heritage Foundation Backgrounder, No. 568 (Washington, DC: Heritage Foundation 1987).

15 For an alternative appraisal of the significance of sanctions, see Fleur de Villiers, 'The Scandal of Sanctions: Progressive America Brings New Misery to the Black Workers of South Africa,' *The American Spectator* 21 (Mar. 1988), 12–13.

16 The following description of a necklace execution is taken from *Race Relations Survey* (Johannesburg: South African Institute for Race Relations 1988), 516: 'Step 1. The victim is grabbed by the executioner and to prevent a struggle his hands are either chopped off or tied with barbed wire. Step 2. The tyre is hung around the victim's shoulders and filled with petrol or diesel oil. Diesel oil is preferred as it clings to the skin. Step 3. The fuel is lit with a match. (This display of a matchbox is used by intimidators to frighten the inhabitants of black towns. Often the victim is forced to light his own 'necklace.') Step 4. The burning tyre releases thick clouds of smoke, mainly from carbon and hydrogen, which can reach a temperature of 300 degrees Celsius. Inhalation of the fumes destroys the tissue in the throat and lungs. Step 5. The burning tyre melts and drips down the neck and the upper part of the body. It gradually burns deeper into the flesh and tissue. Once this has happened, the tyre cannot be removed and the fire cannot be extinguished. Step 6. It can take up to 20 minutes before the victim dies. While he suffers the culprits laugh at him. The victim's relatives are often encouraged to try and help him – which is impossible due to the tyre's enormous heat. The melted rubber is like boiling tar and cannot be removed from the scorched tissue.'

17 In the 1974, he had been jailed for eleven months; in 1976, for six months.

18 See however, *Race Relations Survey, 1987–88* (Johannesburg: South African Institute of Race Relations 1988), 611–13.

19 Ibid, 626–7

20 Ibid, 678–84

21 'Matamela Cyril Ramaphosa,' in Gastrow Shelagh, ed., *Who's Who in South African Politics* (New York: Hans Zell 1990), 291

22 *Race Relations Survey, 1986*, Part II (Johannesburg: South African Institute of Race Relations 1988), 798–9; *Race Relations Survey, 1987–88*, 316–18

23 See *Race Relations Survey, 1987–88*, 727–37, 840–1.

24 See, however, the account of the ECC in ibid, 514–15.

25 For details, see ibid, 530–1, 586–9. In the gradations of repression in South Africa, one might say that the February action was to *curb* rather than to *ban* several organizations. 'Banning' is more severe than 'curbing.'

26 The evidence regarding the alliance of the ANC with the SACP is not secret and, given the conditions of ideological politics in the 'Third World,' the fact of the alliance can hardly be surprising. For evidence, see, for example, David Roberts, 'The ANC in Its Own Words,' *Commentary*, Jul. 1988, 31–7; for an analysis

of its origin, see David Everatt, 'Alliance Politics of a Special Type: The Roots of the ANC/SACP Alliance, 1950–54,' *Journal of Southern African Studies* 18/1 (1991), 19–39.

27 See J.P. Hayes, 'Divided Opinions on Sanctions against South Africa,' *World Economy* 11/2 (1988), 267–80; Paul Johnson, 'The Race for South Africa,' *Commentary*, Sep. 1985, 27–32.

28 A recent example of journalism that at least attempts to describe a miserable situation before judging it is William Finnegan, *A Complicated War: The Harrowing of Mozambique* (Berkley and Los Angeles: University of California Press 1992). Parts of Finnegan's account appeared in *The New Yorker* in 1989. Barbara Amiel's 'Postscript: A Tale of Two Countries,' in the 1991 edition of *Confessions* (Toronto: Totem Books 1991), 242–60, is a refreshing change from most of the reports on 'the consolidation of state power' in Mozambique.

29 Much of the discussion of the conflict between Renamo and Frelimo has appeared since the CBC aired 'The Siege of Mozambique.' Even so, there were some reliable accounts and interpretations available. See, for example, Paul Fauvet, 'Roots of Counter-Revolution: The Mozambique National Resistance,' *Review of African Political Economy* 29 (Jul. 1984), 108–21; Colin Legum, 'The MNR,' in Center for Strategic and International Studies, *Africa Notes* 16 (1963), 1–10; P. Moorcraft, 'Mozambique's Long Civil War: RENAMO – Puppets or Patriots?' *International Defence Review* 10 (1987), 313–16. For more recent accounts see Margaret Hall, 'The Mozambican National Resistance Movement (Renamo): A Study in the Destruction of a Country,' *Africa* 60 (1990), 39–68; Glenda Morgan, 'Violence in Mozambique: Towards an Understanding of Renamo,' *The Journal of Modern African Studies* 28 (1990), 603–19; Alex Vines, *Renamo: Terrorism in Mozambique* (Bloomington and Indianapolis: Indiana University Press 1991).

30 David Martin is a journalist who has published several *engagé* books in praise of 'Afro-Marxist' regimes. See, for example, Martin and Phyllis Johnson, *The Struggle for Zimbabwe: The Chimurenga War* (New York: Monthly Review Press 1981); Martin and Johnson, eds., *Frontline Southern Africa: Destructive Engagement* (New York: Four Walls, Eight Windows 1988).

31 See *International Yearbook and Statesmen's Who's Who*, 1988.

32 See *The New York Times*, 28 Jan. 1987, A3; 19 Feb. 1987, A18.

33 *The New York Times*, 4 Nov. 1986, A5; *The Times*, 24 Oct. 1986, 7, 4 Nov. 1986, 8

34 *The New York Times*, 3 Sept. 1987, A4; 23 Sept. 1987, A8

35 Certainly the circumstances of his death were unusual. He died in a plane crash on 20 October 1986, just over the border in South Africa. Early reports indicated that a sharp noise was heard just before the plane hit the ground; then South Africa was accused of luring Machel's plane to its destruction with a

mysterious 'decoy' navigational beacon. President Kaunda of Zambia said that unnamed 'circumstantial evidence' indicated South African involvement, and the Soviet Union agreed that sabotage was involved. The South African government claimed that two of the Soviet crew had alcohol in their blood. An international commission, which included a British Supreme Court judge and a U.S. astronaut, concluded that human error caused the crash. For details see *The New York Times*, 21 Oct. 1986, A1, 7; 22 Oct. 1986, A16; 28 Oct. 1986, A5; 31 Oct. 1986, A5; 26 Nov. 1986, A16; 22 Jan. 1987, A3; 27 Jan. 1987, A6; 10 Jul. 1987, A10; *The Times*, 21 Oct. 1986, 1, 24; 22 Oct. 1986, 7; 23 Oct. 1986, 8; 29 Oct. 1986, 9; 3 Nov. 1986, 9; 13 Nov. 1986, 11; 21 Jan. 1987, 7; 23 Jan. 1987, 16; 22 May 1987, 7; 10 Jul. 1987, 8; 22 Jul. 1987, 10.

CHAPTER FIVE

1 This focus on the CBC is not meant to exonerate CTV or U.S. or British television. I would expect that a similar study of other productions of TV news would produce similar conclusions.
2 S. Hall, 'Culture, the Media, and the "Ideological Effect"' in James Curran, Michael Gurevitch, Janet Woollcott, John Marriott, and Carrie Roberts, eds., *Mass Communications and Society* (Beverly Hills, CA: Sage 1979), 325
3 Richard V. Ericson, Patricia M. Baranek, and Janet B.L. Chan, *Representing Order: Crime, Law, and Justice in the News Media* (Toronto: University of Toronto Press 1991), 357–8
4 Harvey Mansfield, Jr., *America's Constitutional Soul* (Baltimore, MD: Johns Hopkins University Press 1991), 163. Mansfield's remarks have been very helpful in accounting for the political significance of TV both in the United States and in Canada.
5 I have discussed this topic at some length in my *Action into Nature: An Essay on the Meaning of Technology* (Notre Dame, IN: Notre Dame University Press 1991).
6 See Barry Cooper, 'What Is Post-Modernity?' *Canadian Journal of Social and Political Thought* 9 (1985), 77–89; Cooper, 'Modernity, Postmodernity and Culture,' in Evan Alderson, Robin Blaser, and Harold Coward, eds., *Reflections on Cultural Policy: Past, Present and Future* (Waterloo: Wilfrid Laurier University Press 1993), 163–71; Thomas L. Pangle, *The Ennobling of Democracy: The Challenge of the Postmodern Age* (Baltimore, MD: Johns Hopkins University Press 1992), Part I.
7 See Eric Voegelin, *The New Science of Politics: An Introduction* (Chicago: University of Chicago Press 1952), ch. 6, for an elaboration of these themes.

Index

actors, 143, 157; political, 26; reporters as, 15; socially and morally disorderly, 20

Adamov, Joe, 103–4

Adams, Claude, 67–8

Adelman, Kenneth, 89

Afghanistan, 32, 36, 45, 54–5, 62–81, 83, 85, 110, 129–32, 156, 158, 161, 174, 214, 219, 236–7*n*

Africa, 30, 175–217 *passim*; news coverage, 175, 219–20

African National Congress. *See* ANC

agenda setting, 22–8 *passim*, 83, 143, 173, 205, 219, 224

Agnew, Spiro, 10

alcohol, 47–9, 54, 85, 235*n*

ambivalence, 15–16, 94, 97, 109

American Comprehensive Anti-Apartheid Act, 207

American Federal Communications Commission, 19

ANC, 195–6, 199–203, 215; and Communist party, 204–6, 242*n*; violence, 205–6

Angola, 85, 163, 196, 202

anti-communism. *See* communism

Antipov, Yevgeny, 37, 44

Apartheid, 184–5, 191–8, 201–2, 204–6, 217, 219, 221; effects on Mozambique, 211

Arkin, William, 127, 239*n*

Armenia, 32, 55–60, 62, 83

Armenian Christians, 59

arms control, 94, 96, 107, 117, 132–3, 149, 165; adverse effects, 95, 112; breakthrough, 103; conventional, 90; Gorbachev offer, 88–9; talks, 91; treaties, 127

artefact, news as, 10

artificial: contact, 221; innocence, 20

audience: credibility, 24; research, 17; size, 24; studies, 24–5; surveys, 21; unseen, 9

authorized knowers, 6, 15, 61, 70, 78–9, 94, 103–6, 136, 140, 162, 168, 223, 228*n*

Azerbaijan, 55–60, 62, 83

Baker, Howard, 66

balance, xi, 28, 128, 138, 180, 198, 205, 219, 231*n*; CBC style, 157; conventional arms, 90; fairness and, 18–22; moral equivalency and, 130; NATO/WTO, 122; nuclear, 93; occasion for,

225; inconvenient, 207; mere, 100,
145; misconstrued, 183; omissions,
59, 174, 182; plausible interpretation, 170; relevant, 19; reliability,
226; stubborn, 171, 225; well-known,
32
fairness. *See* balance
fakes. *See* visuals
Federenko, Igor, 33
feedback, 21
Fenga, Anders, 77
Foucault, Michel, 18
Frank, Reuven, 14, 18, 20
freedom, Reagan's talk of, 157–8

Gandhi, Rajiv, 209
Gans, Herbert, 10–11, 13–14, 17, 20,
228–9*n*, 231*n*
Garthoff, Raymond, 140–1
Garvey, Bruce, 94
Gearing, Julian, 79
Geldof, Bob, 216
Geneva accord, 68, 75
Geneva arms talks, 89
Gerasimov, Gennady, 62, 131–2, 236*n*,
239*n*
Gilmour, David, 106, 238*n*
Giorgis, Dawit, 179, 182, 240*n*
glasnost, 32, 36, 41, 43, 45–6, 49, 51,
54–5, 60–1, 83, 85, 89, 101–3, 116,
125, 145–6, 156, 158, 167, 234*n*
Goldfarb, David, 43–4, 234*n*
Gorbachev, Mikhail: Afghanistan, 63–
4, 69, 80; and American foot drag-
ging, 169; American protest rally
and, 111; Azerbaijan, statements on,
57; church/state relations, 40–2; data
issue and, 171; domestic difficulties,
49, 83; and *glasnost*, 36, 45, 51, 55,
61, 102–4; increased trade with

United States, 168; as initiator, 88,
120; as Kremlin commissar, 166; liberalism, 86; new thinking, 128; opposition, 104; as peacemaker, 100, 120,
161; and *perestroika*, 26, 51, 83, 104,
106, 108; Philby and, 146; and
progress, 220; and Raisa, 107;
Reagan's Berlin Wall challenge and,
84, 87; Reagan's visit and, 149–50,
152–3, 155–7, 164–5, 167; as
reformer, 41, 54, 83, 98, 100–1, 110,
119, 151, 160; responsible journalism
and, 173; sexism, 106; Soviet TV and,
91; traditional Soviet policy, 97, 99;
Washington visit, 116, 118–20, 122–
3, 125, 130, 132–3, 138–9, 141, 159;
as Western, 114–15; and Yeltsin, 35,
107
Gorbachev, Raisa, 50, 107, 114, 118,
123–4, 131, 138, 158, 172
Gouzenko, Igor, 143, 147, 239*n*
Gregorian, Sergei, 151
Gromyko, Andrei, 55
Gulag, 45

Halperin, Jonathan, 136–7
Hare Krishna, 118
Harrison, Selig, 69–71, 237*n*
Heckmatyar, Gulbaddin, 79
high-tech, 168; and American paranoia,
169
homeless children, 49, 51
Hough, Jerry, 168–9
Howe, Geoffrey, Sir, 206–8
human rights, 43, 114, 117, 130–1, 133,
141, 149, 151, 158–9, 164–5, 167,
169, 173–4
Hyman, Anthony, 78–80

Ignatieff, Michael, 105, 238*n*

Machel, Samora, 213–14
Mandela, Nelson, 195–6, 198, 202, 223; rock concert, 201
Mandela, Winnie, 198
Mariam, Mengistu, 179
Marshall, Peter, 78–80
Martin, David, 211–12, 215, 243n
Marxism, 128, 169; Gorbachev's contribution, 120; Leninism, 120; Mozambique, 214
Marxist-Leninist theory, 108
mask, 39
May Day parade, 1988, 36
Mbeki, Govan, 195–6
media: content (stimulus), 3; as epistemology, 12; experts, 130; intellectuals, 225; model, 8–9; studies, 3, 7, 24; technologies, 10; world, 225
The Media Elite, 15, 17
medium, 8, 12–13; influence on message, 4; literary, 26
merchants of death, 112
method of journalism, 13–14, 28–31; visualization as, 13–14
Meyrowitz, Joshua, 27, 233n
Milanov, Sergei, 78
mirror theory, 10–11, 13
misguided patriotism, 112
MNR, 11, 212–13, 215–16
modernity, 221
momentum, 120–1, 123–4, 130, 133
moral equality, 87
moral equivalence, 64, 104, 130, 161, 163, 174, 219; *see also* equivalent coverage
Moscow State University, Reagan lecture, 157–8
Mozambique, 202, 209–17 *passim*, 219; Communist government, 213; economic strangulation, 211; food

shortage, 216; massacres, 210; news coverage, 219; popular resistance, 216; relief, Canadian, 210; right-wing rebels, 210, 216; terrorist wars, 215; tin-cup diplomacy, 215; violence, 211
Mozambique National Resistance. *See* MNR
Mugabe, Robert, 208
mujahedeen, 62–3, 65–6, 69, 71–6, 78–81, 110, 236–7n; U.S. support, 219
Mulroney, Brian, 205, 208–9
Murrow, Edward R., 17
myths, 15; of a dangerous United States, 173; of a progressive USSR, 173

Nagorno–Karabakhskaya, 57–8, 61
Najibullah, President, 62, 65, 69–70, 74, 77–9, 81
name-calling, 6, 151
Namibia, 196
narcissism. *See* journalists
National Party (South Africa), 207
national self-determination, 86
National Union of Mineworkers, 190
nationalities question, 86
NATO, 29, 88, 91–100, 113, 116, 174
NATO/WTO balance, 122
necklacing, 185–6, 194
needs for achievement and intimacy, 15–16; *see also* journalists
Neumann, Robert, 66
neutrality, 19
new thinking, 87, 107, 120, 128
New World Information and Communication Order. *See* NWICO
news: creation, 10, 18; formatting, 22; leaks, 27

United Nations, 64, 77
United States, 32, 34, 43; and Afghanistan, 63–9, 71, 129; aid to Mozambique, 214; arms control, 88–9, 90, 93, 96, 100; – opposition, 121; comparison with USSR, 141; as deviant, 116, 125–6, 220; European faith in, 98; meddling, 142; nuclear weapons production, 126; paranoid competition, 137; relationship with Soviet Union, 132, 162; Soviet inventions and, 168; summit, 93, 110–11, 115–16, 120–4, 171; as teacher of morals, 131; Third World and, 163
USSR, 30–1, 32–82 *passim*, 103–5, 128; Afghanistan, 110; American opposition, 112, 128; American suspicion, 129, 164; autocratic heritage, 85; change, 106, 161; church, 36, 39–43, 54; computer technology, 85; disarmament, 94, 97, 100, 169, 171; disintegration, 174; distorted view of, 138; domestic life, 32, 47; dynamic image, 124, 130; economy, 85; emigration policies, 33; and Ethiopia, 183; evil empire, 166; *glasnost*, 102–3; health and safety, 85; human rights, 114, 117, 149; in the 1930s, 147; inventions, 168; media coverage, 116, 135; – CBC, 81, 172, 220; moral equivalence, 141, 161, 174, 219; negative image, 118; new era, 123; opposition to arms control, 121; paranoid competition, 137; progress, 173, 220, 223; Reagan and, 153; reforms, 98, 151, 152; refuseniks, 167; relationship with United States, 132–3, 150; secret police, 33; strategic imbalance, 90; Third World and, 162–3; U.S. technological superiority, 125; violent beginning, 106; vote condemning, 214

validity of information. *See* information
Velikov, Yevgenyi, 169–72
Venture, 51
verification, 22
visuals, 5–6, 73, 136, 212; fakes, 7, 15, 143; file, 7; stock, 22
Vladimir, Father, 39

Walker, Martin, 158–9
Wall. *See* Berlin Wall
war criminal, 33
war machine, 126
Warnke, Paul, 132–5
Weaver, P.H., 6, 227n
Weber, Max, 173, 239n
Weiler, John, 180
Western Alliance, 97, 99
Western foot-dragging, 168
Western nations, 32
Western security interests, 168
White minority government, 185–6, 200
White Russian Church, 38–9
words: electronic transformation, 7; as performances, 7; as things, 7, 218
writing, 9, 12, 218; corrections, 7
written communication, 9
WTO/NATO relations, 92

Yeltsin, Boris, 35–6, 102–4, 107, 123, 159, 167, 234n

Zambia, 202
zek, 46
zero option, 116
zero-zero option, 88
Zimbabwe, 202